Webster's Shape Up Your English

Published 2019 by Geddes & Grosset, an imprint of
The Gresham Publishing Company Ltd,
Academy Park, Building 4000,
Gower Street, Glasgow, G51 1PR, Scotland.

First published 2017. Reprinted 2019.

www.geddesandgrosset.com
info@geddesandgrosset.co.uk
facebook/pages/geddesandgrosset

Copyright © 2017 The Gresham Publishing Company Ltd.

Contributors: Betty Kirkpatrick, Sue Moody and Eleanor Abraham.

Editor: Eleanor Abraham.

Illustrations, courtesy of Shutterstock,
Copyright © CartoonResource.

All rights reserved. No part of this publication may be reproduced, stored in a retrieval system or transmitted in any form or by any means, electronic, mechanical, photocopying, recording or otherwise, without the prior permission of the copyright holder.

Conditions of Sale:
This book is sold with the condition that it will not, by way of trade or otherwise, be resold, hired out, lent, or otherwise distributed or circulated in any form or style of binding or cover other than that in which it is published and without the same conditions being imposed on the subsequent purchaser.

ISBN 978 1 910965 38 2

Printed and bound in India.

Readers may find it useful to explore https://www.britishcouncil.org/english

CONTENTS

INTRODUCTION	**5**
EXPANDING YOUR SKILLS	**7**
Practice	7
Spoken English	8
Listening skills	9
Grammar and usage	10
Idioms	10
Punctuation	11
Writing and reading English	12
SPOKEN ENGLISH	**13**
Turn-taking	13
Non-verbal communication	16
Telephone conversations	18
Beginnings and endings	21
Vocabulary	32
PRONUNCIATION	**34**
IPA	35
Syllables and stresses	37
Vowels	37
Consonants	38
Sounds particular to English	39
Silent letters	42
IDIOMS	**50**
Origins	51
Common idioms	51
Proverbs	69
CLICHÉS	**72**
A bit of colour	72
Clichés from idioms	73
Clichés from over-used phrases	76
Archaic clichés	80
Clichés as 'fillers'	83
EVERYDAY EXPRESSIONS	**85**
Interjections	86
SENTENCES	**113**
Minor sentences	114
Simple sentences	115
Compound sentences	117
Complex sentences	118
Types of sentence-statements	119
Answers	127
Clauses	129
Phrases	131
NOUNS AND PRONOUNS	**133**
Uncountable nouns	134
Plural forms of noun	134
Pronouns	138
Personal pronouns and sexist language	141
ADJECTIVES	**143**
Gradable and non-gradable adjectives	144
Position	146
Predicative adjectives	147
Colour adjectives	148
Emphatic adjectives	148
Interrogative adjectives	151
Compound adjectives	151
Adjectives used as nouns	151
Adjective or adverb?	152
Comparative forms of adjectives	152
Superlative forms	153
DETERMINERS	**155**
Referring and quantifying	155
Definite and indefinite articles	156
Demonstrative determiners	159
Possessive determiners	159
Indefinite determiners	160
Number determiners	161
Determiners and nouns	161

ADVERBS	**163**	**PUNCTUATING PROPERLY**	**317**
Modifying	163	Preserving meaning	317
Types of adverb	165	Apostrophe	318
Gradable and non-gradable	169	Brackets	323
		Capital letters	324
CONJUNCTIONS	**171**	Colon	326
Coordinating conjunctions	171	Semicolon	326
Subordinating conjunctions	173	Comma	327
VERBS	**176**	Dash	334
'Doing' and 'being' words	176	Exclamation mark	334
Infinitive	177	Full stop	335
Tenses	177	Hyphen	337
Participles	181	Question mark	339
Gerund	184	Quotation marks	339
Mood	185	Three-dot ellipsis	340
Voice	186	**WRITING**	**341**
Auxiliary verbs	190	Plain English	341
Modal auxiliary verbs	191	Editing your writing	348
Regular verbs	193	Writing a non-fiction composition	351
Irregular verbs	196	Essays	357
Verb agreement	198	Letters, emails and texting	363
Irregular verb list	201	**READING COMPREHENSION**	**366**
PHRASAL VERBS	**207**	Approaching a reading interpretation	366
What's the problem?	207	What kind of questions?	367
Position of the object	209	Preparing for a book report	368
Figurative or literal meaning?	212	A writer's style	369
Complex phrasal verbs	215	What are the themes involved?	369
PREPOSITIONS	**220**	Narrative	369
Simple prepositions	220	Close reading	370
Complex prepositions	221	Literary terms	370
Common errors	221	**MAKING A SPEECH**	**374**
Word pairs	223	Both worlds	374
CONFUSABLE WORDS	**261**	Your audience	375
Problems	261	Mind map	375
Homophones	262	The speech	376
Homographs	273	Making the speech	378
Homonyms	275	**INDEX**	**380**
Which word?	278		

INTRODUCTION

THERE is more to flying than just flapping your arms as fast as you can. There is also more to speaking a language fluently than just learning the rules of grammar.

In order to present yourself in a professional way, it is important to have a competent grasp of 'good English'. BUT sometimes it is as important to know when you can break the rules as it is to know the rules. Language is constantly changing and evolving, so, while it is essential to have a good understanding of grammar and usage, it is also vital that your English usage should sound contemporary and natural. Fluent speakers pay attention to modern conventions without lapsing into the common mistakes that many people make.

INTRODUCTION

This book presents information on spoken English, English usage, English grammar and strategies to improve your written English. We list many of the common errors of grammar and usage that are often made, but we also look at modern usages that are now accepted as standard, that, just a few years ago, might have been labelled as 'wrong'.

One of the main purposes, and pleasures, of learning a language is to be able to communicate with a broad variety of people in a wide range of situations in a fluent and natural way. Being familiar with English idioms is one of the ways to help you achieve this.

Idioms are phrases where the obvious meaning of the words involved can be far removed from the actual meaning of the phrase. In this book there is substantial material on English idioms in all their different forms. It is important to understand this side of language, beyond the obvious literal meaning of the words, if you are to be truly fluent. We look at these with the emphasis on how they keep the conversation flowing in spoken English.

We aim to help you, as a competent reader and speaker of English, to take your understanding of written and spoken English a few steps further – to speak idiomatic English fluently and comfortably and take your written English to the next level.

GRAMMAR BITES

It is easiest to learn when you do so in bite-sized chunks. We recommend spending ten to fifteen minutes a day concentrating on just one topic in each section – till you know it thoroughly – before carrying on to the next part.

EXPANDING YOUR SKILLS

Good morning, Madam. I'd like to take advantage of this awkward social situation to practise my English.

IN ORDER to become fluent in English you need to use every opportunity that presents itself to practise your English, be that conversational, reading, writing or listening practice.

PRACTICE

As a learner of English you need to be confident in order to gain fluency in spoken English. You need to have quite a lot of courage to try and understand what someone is saying and to make a reply. Inevitably, you will make mistakes, but you must not let that prevent you from

EXPANDING YOUR SKILLS

trying. Do not be afraid that people will laugh at your errors or make fun of you. People will admire you for trying. Because English is so widely spoken, most native speakers of the language do not even try to learn another language. They rely on speakers of other languages to learn English and they will be pleased to help you to do so.

In order to become fluent in spoken English you need to practise as much as possible. It is very useful to spend some time in an English-speaking country so that you are forced to communicate in English in order to survive from day to day. However, that is not always possible.

Those who cannot do so need not despair. You can spend time with English speakers who are in your area – they don't need to be native speakers – and practise your English in that way. And, of course, if you have a good teacher that will help enormously.

SPOKEN ENGLISH

Spoken English refers to the words used in conversations and verbal communication between people – and it can take various forms. In this book we will touch on the typical structure of conversation (pages 13–33) and also look at the common phrases, filler phrases, idioms, and clichés used in spoken English (pages 50–112).

Dialogue is a conversation between two or more people. Such conversations can cover a vast variety of topics, take place in a wide range of situations and vary greatly in levels of formality.

Most dialogue is spontaneous, meaning there is little or no possibility for planning it. There are some exceptions to this. If the dialogue is quite formal and the topic has been pre-arranged, then you may be able to give some thought to what you are going to say and how you are going to say it. An example of this is a job interview. However, you can attempt to memorize phrases and sentences for future use but there is no guarantee they will fit your conversation. You have to respond immediately to whatever the other person involved in the interview is saying. You may anticipate some of the areas of discussion, but you cannot be totally sure what the questions will be or how they will be put. All dialogue is a form of social interaction.

Much dialogue is completely informal. It may be a conversation between close friends or family members. It may be an exchange of greetings between strangers. It may involve buying something in a shop. Everyday life is full of such informal dialogue.

To become fluent in the language and engage in such everyday dialogues, learners of English need to be aware that informal language also has some conventions attached to it.

Conversations do not always take place when people are face to face. They often take place by telephone. There are different conventions relating to this type of dialogue where you cannot share visual clues about the progress of your conversation. We will discuss this in more detail on pages 16–21 and 29–31. The invention of the mobile phone has greatly increased the amount of time people spend engaged in informal communication. Never before has there been so much informal dialogue.

It is important to remember that there are significant differences between spoken and written English. The differences are most obvious when everyday informal dialogue is involved. This form of spoken English is often disjointed, with sentence fragments used in preference to complete sentences. More formal forms of spoken English, such as formal speeches (pages 374–9), are closer to written English than informal dialogue is.

LISTENING SKILLS

If you want to become a fluent English speaker you need to improve your listening skills as well as your speaking skills. By listening to others, and by listening to the radio and television, you will learn a great deal about spoken English and how it works. Listening often requires a great deal of concentration.

English is an important global language and there are many

versions of it spoken around the world, such as British English, American English, Australian English, Indian English, South African English, and so on. These different versions of English often differ from each other in significant ways, and this is particularly true of pronunciation. You may well have difficulty in understanding what someone from another country is saying, even although you can both speak English.

Your listening skills will also prove valuable in other aspects of dialogue. These include understanding the significance of tone and volume of voice which can vary according to the situations in which the conversation is taking place. For example, someone who is angry or excited is likely to speak quickly and in a much louder voice than usual. Someone who wants to keep what they are saying private or secret will speak in a soft voice, or a whisper, and might speak slower as a consequence.

GRAMMAR AND USAGE

Spoken English of the more informal kind is much simpler in form than written English. The structure is simpler, the grammar is simpler and the vocabulary is simpler. Does this mean that spoken English is much easier to learn than written English? Can you forget all about grammar, structure and learning new words?

Absolutely not. In fact, fluent spoken English can be much more difficult to master. Although spoken English does not always follow the rules of grammar, this does not mean that you can neglect these or forget about them. In many ways you have to know what the rules are in order to deviate from them with confidence.

IDIOMS AND EVERYDAY EXPRESSIONS

English can be hard to *get your head around*. It can have you *tearing your hair out*. Don't let idioms be *your Achilles heel*. Our sections on idioms, proverbs, similes and clichés – including those 'filler phrases' that add no real meaning to the conversation but keep it flowing – give a great grounding on the kind of language that can *trip you up* and that can also regularly *crop up* in conversational English (pages 50–112).

PUNCTUATION

Our chapter on punctuation (pages 317–40) talks about the common mistakes that often occur when we are writing. Good punctuation is something people feel passionately about, so making an error can potentially be an embarrassing thing.

PARDON IMPOSSIBLE, TO BE SENT TO SIBERIA

Misplaced punctuation can cause great irritation, and putting punctuation in the wrong place or missing it out can sometimes drastically change the meaning of a sentence.

There's a famous story, which may or may not be true. Russian Czarina Maria Fyodorovna (1847–1928) is said to have saved a man's life by moving a comma in a warrant written by her husband Alexander III (1845–94). The warrant is reported to have initially read:

> Pardon impossible, to be sent to Siberia.

The story is that the man was set free after the Czarina sneakily moved a comma so the document read:

> Pardon, impossible to be sent to Siberia.

The story is unlikely to be true, but it's a useful example. Here's one that could make dinner time awkward:

> Do you know a nice place to eat, Grandad?
> Do you know a nice place to eat Grandad?

And a potentially sexist one:

> A woman without her man is nothing.
> A woman: without her, man is nothing.

EXPANDING YOUR SKILLS

WRITING AND READING ENGLISH

In day-to-day life we may be required to write formal or informal letters or emails, a composition in class, job applications or a CV or résumé, or a report at work. There are various sections in this book that give you specific tips on good, clear writing for all types of situations.

Throughout the learning process you will most likely be presented with passages of text to interpret, in order to test your understanding of written language. Our chapter on reading comprehension and interpretation discusses written classwork of this type and of various levels of difficulty.

We also explain how to combine the skills of composition writing with those of speaking in English in our chapter on making a speech – showing you how to research and give a formal speech, lecture or presentation in public.

Angela still hadn't got the hang of summarising her reports.

SPOKEN ENGLISH

So that Derek can get a word in edgeways, today he's waving the 'may I speak?' sign.

HOW DO you know whose turn it is to say something? Conversation is an extremely important part of social interaction and most of us take part in many different kinds of conversations in the course of the average day. The content and style of conversation can vary a lot according to the situation but there are some conventions which are common to most.

TURN-TAKING

In English, as in other languages, conversation, whether this is formal or informal, is based on a system of **turn-taking**.

Basically, turn-taking involves one person making a remark, another person responding to this in some way, then the first person making a further comment, and so on. Obviously, the number of turns taken will vary with the situation and the subject and length of the conversation.

So, how *do* you know whose turn it is to say something? When the conversation takes the form of **questions** and **answers** it is easy to know whose turn it is to speak. The answer is a direct response to the question. In other circumstances, it is often obvious from the flow of the conversation when you are expected to speak. In many conversational situations people know intuitively when it is their turn to say something. When you are face-to-face with the other person involved in the conversation, you can sometimes judge from their **facial expressions**, from their **gestures**, or from their **body language**, when it is your turn to say something.

However, conversation does not always flow smoothly. Sometimes one of the participants feels the need to say something before the other person has finished speaking and makes an **interruption**. Sometimes the person who is speaking interrupts *themselves* because something occurs to them while they are talking. The short piece of **informal dialogue** below illustrates these two possibilities, with interruptions highlighted in blue italic:

> **Helen**: Sue, I've made a list of who's doing what at the conference. I'm going to be greeting delegates as they arrive, Jane's in charge of welcome packs, you're distributing the agenda, Amy's organizing …
>
> **Sue**: *Wait a minute, Helen!* I can't. I'll be at the trade show in London.
>
> **Helen**: What? You might have told me earlier. I could have …
>
> **Sue**: *But I did tell you earlier.* We talked about it weeks ago.
>
> **Helen**: Did we? When?
>
> **Sue**: We had a meeting last month about all the trade shows. I've got … *oh wait …* you weren't in that meeting, you were on holiday.
>
> **Helen**: Well, I need to find somebody else to help then.

In the following example Sam interrupts himself and then he and Ben interrupt each other. It doesn't disrupt the conversation too much though. It is an informal chat between friends and such *overlaps* are normal and not considered rude:

> **Ben**: Have you seen Jim recently?
> **Sam**: No, I haven't seen him since Christmas … *hang on* … I *have* seen him. We were on the same train about a month ago.
> **Ben**: How was he? Is he …?
> **Sam**: *Well again?* Mmm … he seemed a bit …
> **Ben**: *… Because I met him last week and he wasn't himself.* I must call him.
> **Sam**: Good idea. I should too.

The *turn-taking* in a *formal conversation* is much more structured, as in the following short piece of dialogue – an extract from an *interview for a job*. The person who is being interviewed is likely to know the kind of questions that will be asked and to have mentally prepared what she considers to be relevant answers.

> **Mr Brown**: Good morning. Please have a seat.
> **Ms Jones**: Good morning. Thank you.
> **Mr Brown**: Tell me, where did you hear about the vacancy in our firm?
> **Ms Jones**: I saw an ad in the newspaper and I also heard about it from my friend Mary Kemp. She works here.
> **Mr Brown**: Ah, yes – Mary. And what do you know about our company and what we do?
> **Ms Jones**: I know that it is a long-established company publishing non-fiction books, particularly biographies and autobiographies.

The flow of the conversation is led both by the conventions of polite conversation and by the person who is conducting the interview – this person asks the questions, the interviewee answers.

TELEPHONE ETIQUETTE

In addition to linguistic challenges, speaking on the telephone can present a few challenges of etiquette. Here are some tips to avoid common phone call pitfalls:

Identify yourself at the beginning of a call so that the recipient does not have to ask the question: *Who is this, please?*

Do not answer a call by saying *Yes*. It sounds abrupt.

Be polite and confident in tone. It will make you easier to understand.

Plan what you want to say before you make the call. Make a few notes if it helps. This is especially useful if you need to leave a message. You want the message to be short but to give more useful information than *Call me, please*.

To save time, especially if you are phoning on business, try to find out exactly which department you need to ask for and the relevant person's name.

Avoid side conversations with other people around you. It's rude and it is potentially harder for the person to whom you are talking on the phone to understand what is going on.

Avoid typing on your computer keyboard as you talk.

If you must take calls in the car while you are driving (it's quite noisy, after all), get a hands-free kit. In some countries it is illegal to take calls while driving.

NON-VERBAL COMMUNICATION

It must be remembered that people can convey a lot without actually saying anything at all. Such non-verbal communication can be conveyed by facial expression and requires observational, rather than speaking or listening, skills. You do not have to hear someone saying angry words to know that they are annoyed because their mood will probably be obvious from their angry expression. This is true of other moods such as sadness and happiness. Other methods of non-verbal communication include common gestures. These include nodding the head to indicate *yes* or agreement, shaking the head to indicate *no* or disagreement, shrugging the shoulders to indicate lack of knowledge or understanding and so on. Some of these gestures are fairly international, some not.

There are non-verbal cues that a person makes when they want to interrupt. They may make eye contact with you or lean towards you, open their mouth slightly, raise a finger, or smile. These gestures may be accompanied by a short interjection, such as:

'Well ...', 'Hmm,' 'But ...', 'OK,', 'Oh'.

WHO IS IT?

Someone may call you without first stating their name. It's important to politely (and quite formally) ask who they are, rather than just say *Who is it?* especially if you need to take a message for a work colleague:

May I ask who's calling, please?
Can I ask who I'm speaking to, please?
To whom am I speaking?

And more informal:
Who's calling, please?
Who's speaking?
Who is this, please?

Yeah. What do you want?

SPOKEN ENGLISH

When someone is **winding down** what they are saying, i.e. finding a way to end the conversation, they may lean back slightly, the intonation of their voice may lower. If hands are gesturing while they talk, the hands will become still and be retracted towards the body.

This is not a book about reading body language, but using and interpreting non-verbal cues can be very important in the to-and-fro of polite conversation.

When we come to discuss instances where we are not able to use or interpret visual indicators, such as when talking on the telephone, knowing the rules of how to end a conversation, or interrupt politely, and the typical structure of such dialogue is very important.

TELEPHONE CONVERSATIONS

The convention of **turn-taking** is also followed in conversations conducted on the **telephone**. However, it is more difficult to judge whose turn it is to speak when you are conducting a conversation on the phone. You do not have the advantage of being able to interpret **facial expressions** or **gestures**.

It is sometimes quite difficult to know when the other person has finished speaking and when you are expected to speak. The result is that the gaps between remarks made by the participants in a phone conversation may be longer than those that occur in face-to-face conversation. This can result in a rather stilted, if perfectly comprehensible, conversation.

Sometimes **interruptions** may occur or you may both start speaking at once and cause **overlaps**. When you are taking part in an informal chat with an old friend on the phone it does not matter so much whether one of you interrupts the other or whether you both start speaking at once, as in the following piece of dialogue:

Anne: Hello?
Mary: Hi Anne. It's Mary.
Anne: Hi. How are you?
Mary: Good. I'm just calling quickly …
Anne: Oh right …
Mary: … are you still coming to see the film this evening?
Anne: Sure. I'll meet you there at 6.
Mary: 6? Didn't we …?
Anne: *… is that not right?* No, sorry we said 8.
Mary: No, actually we …
Anne: *… I've just remembered we said 7!* Sorry … my memory is …
Mary: *… OK, see you at …*
Anne: *… Wait a minute.* I might be a few minutes late. I'm taking the kids to my parents' house. You see, they are treating them to …
Mary: *Sorry … sorry to interrupt.* Tell me later. I need to take the dog out. I need to go. No problem if you're a bit late, I'll wait for you outside the cinema. Must go though.
Anne: Oh … OK then. See you later, Mary.
Mary: Bye.

There were quite a few overlaps and interruptions in that last dialogue. In a formal conversation such interruptions are best avoided because they make what is being said less clear.

If you are aware of an interruption or overlap you can put this right by using expressions like those in the blue box below.

WAYS TO APOLOGIZE/REPAIR

I'm sorry …
I interrupted you …
Please do go on …
My apologies …

Carry on …
You were saying …?
Pardon me …
Excuse me …

WAYS TO INTERRUPT IN A CONVERSATION

The beginnings in this column can be used in combination with ...	... the endings in this column.
Can I ...?	... say something
Can I just ...?	... butt in for a second
Do you mind if I ...?	... mention something
Before you move on, I'd like to ...	... stop you there
Before you go on, I'd like to ...	... make a point
Just a moment, I'd like to ...	... ask you to repeat that
If I could just ...	... come in here
Before we move on to the next point, can I ...?	... add something
	... clarify something
I'm sorry to interrupt, but can I ...?	... jump in here
I don't mean to intrude but can I ...?	
Excuse me for ...	... interrupting but ...
Sorry for ...	... butting in but ...
	... intruding but ...

This is known as a **repair**. The words in blue italic in the dialogue below are the repairs:

> **Chris**: We can come to you for a meeting next Friday morning before lunch. Before that my team will ...
> **Barbara**: *Did you say Friday?* I won't be in the office on Friday. Could you make it Thursday?
> **Chris**: We could, but it would have ...
> **Barbara**: *Sorry ... I forgot.* I *will* be in on Friday after all. *Sorry. Please carry on.*

Chris: I was just going to check times on Thursday, but if Friday's OK …
Barbara: It is. That's fine. *I'm sorry, I got mixed up.*
Chris: Not a problem. We all get mixed up sometimes! *As I was going to say …* on Tuesday my team will email you a summary of what we want to discuss.
Barbara: That's great, thank you.
Chris: Have a nice day, Barbara.
Barbara: And you. Bye.

Conducting telephone conversations, especially rather formal conversations, makes some people nervous, and one of the reasons is that you do not get the visual interaction that you do face-to-face. If the conversation is in a foreign language it is understandable that this might be even more nerve-racking. As well as deciding on what you are going to say you have to learn to listen carefully to what the other person is saying. It might be something of great importance. When you are nervous, this can be very difficult to do. However, like other aspects of learning a language, participating in phone conversations improves greatly with practice.

BEGINNINGS AND ENDINGS

In any conversation there has to be someone who starts it off and someone who ends it, although this may be the same person. Obviously conversations start for all sorts of reasons.

Greetings

Many conversations may start off as a form of greeting and greetings tend to involve the use of certain words. These include such informal words as *hi*, *hiya*, more neutral words such as *hello*, and more formal expressions such as *good morning*, *good afternoon*, or *good evening*. The expressions *good morning*, *good*

SPOKEN ENGLISH

afternoon, and *good evening* are often shortened by omitting the word *good*. See these fragments of **informal** opening dialogue below. Greetings are shown in blue italic:

Sally: *Hi*, Joe. *Nice to see you*.
Joe: Sally! *Nice to see you too*. Haven't seen you in ages. *How are you?*
Sally: I've been very well, thank you. And you?
Joe: I've been good too!

Pat: *Hiya*, Liz. You off to college?
Liz: *Hey there*, Pat! Yeah, but just for the morning. I'm going swimming this afternoon. Come with me!

Amy: *Hello*. I wasn't expecting to see you here. What a nice surprise!
Sue: I nearly never made it. My car broke down. *How's it going?*
Amy: Oh no! Glad you made it. I'm fine, thanks.

WAYS TO SAY 'HELLO!'

All right? [Informal]

G'day! [Informal]

Good morning!
Good afternoon!
Good evening!
[Formal. More informal versions of these are *Morning!*, *Afternoon!*, and *Evening!*]

Greetings! [Formal or humorous]

Hey! [Informal]

Hi!

Hiya! [Informal]

How are you doing?

How are you?

How have you been?

How's it going? [Informal]

How's tricks? [Informal]

Long time no see! [Informal; said to someone you've not seen for a while]

Look what the cat dragged in! [Humorous, informal]

Nice to see you!

Pleased to meet you. [Formal; said when first meetiing someone]

What's going on? [Informal]

What's happening? [Informal]

What's new? [Informal]

What's up? [Informal]

Yo! [Informal]

The following dialogue is between neighbours who are meeting for the first time. It's still informal even though it is between strangers:

> **Ben**: *Hello*, I'm Ben. I just moved in next door.
> **Geoff**: *Pleased to meet you*, Ben. I'm Geoff.
> **Ben**: *Nice to meet you too.* Is it a nice neighbourhood?

The previous dialogue is not as formal as the following. What follows are some possible ways to greet people in a work situation. The greetings are in blue italic as before:

> **Boss**: *Good afternoon everyone. I'd like to welcome you all here today*, and thank you for visiting our new offices. I'd also like to introduce you to our new Human Resources manager, Roger Swan. Roger ... over to you.
> **Roger**: *Hello everyone.* I'm so glad to have joined the firm and I'm looking forward to meeting you all individually.
>
> **Receptionist**: *Good morning, sir, how may I help you?*
> **Businessman**: *Good morning.* Could you direct me to Roger Swan's office. He's expecting me.
> **Receptionist**: Certainly, sir. I'll show you the way myself.

In business (and other social situations, of course), you may have to introduce yourself to people you have never met before, and these may be people whose identity you do not yet know, for example, in a networking situation. You don't want to be too formal even though it is business related, or your conversation will sound awkward. But it can't be too informal either or you risk offence. The key is to be respectful. To break the ice, a simple informal greeting and introduction can be made, followed with a few general questions (rather than talking about yourself) to open up the conversation. Ask questions that require more than *yes* or *no* as an answer (*see* pages 121–6):

SPOKEN ENGLISH

> **Joe**: Hi. Excuse me, am I in the right room for the meet and greet?
> **Jim**: You are indeed.
> **Joe**: Thanks. I'm Joe, from Gold and Sons. [Extends hand.]
> **Jim**: I'm Jim, from Diamond Services, good to meet you.
> **Joe**: Good to meet you, Jim. Do you have much planned for this week?

Asking for information, directions, etc

When you wish someone to supply you with some information, direct you to somewhere, or otherwise give you some assistance, it is usual to open the conversation with a polite expression such as *Excuse me* or *Sorry to bother you*. See the short pieces of dialogue below:

> **Visitor**: *Excuse me. I wonder if you can help me?* I'm looking for the library.
> **Sam**: You're almost there. It's one block further down on this street. You can see it from here. It's that big white building on the corner.
> **Visitor**: Thanks very much!

> **Visitor**: *Sorry to bother you. Could you possibly help me?* I need to get to the bus station.
> **Sue**: The bus station? Let me think. I think it's over there. Yes, that's right. Cross this road and go straight along that street over there. Then turn right. Got that?
> **Visitor**: Yes, thanks for your help.

More questions

There is more on types of questions, and how these questions might be answered, on pages 121–7. On those pages we discuss the grammar of questions as sentence-statements and also touch on how they occur in spoken English.

Beginnings and endings

The beginning of a telephone conversation

If the person you want to speak to actually answers the phone (i.e. you don't have to ask someone to get them), then opening a phone conversation can be similar to the way you open a face-to-face conversation as in:

Molly: Hello – Price Pencils – Molly speaking.
Wendy: Hi Molly. It's Wendy from Campbell's Packaging.
Molly: Hi Wendy. It's been a while since we heard from you. How are you?
Wendy: It has, hasn't it. I'm fine – thanks for asking – and you?
Molly: I'm great, thank you.
Wendy: That's good to hear. Well – I'm calling to ask if I can come to your office sometime and chat to you all about our new products.
Molly: Em ... I'll just have to check with Robert but I think that will be OK.

In some phone conversations you may have to ask someone else to connect you to the person you want to talk to. These are often more formal conversations, as in the short piece of dialogue that follows:

Secretary: Good morning. Strong, Hamble and Richards – Barbara speaking – how can I help you?
Mrs Smith: Hello. My name's Susan Smith. Could I speak to Mr Strong, please?
Secretary: May I ask what it is in connection with?
Mrs Smith: I've been charged with a driving offence. I need to speak to Mr Strong urgently. He's my lawyer.
Secretary: Mr Strong's very busy this morning but I'll see if he can speak to you. I'll just put you on hold ...
Mrs Smith: Thanks.
Secretary: Hello, Mrs Smith. Mr Strong will speak to you now.

SPOKEN ENGLISH

Mrs Smith: Thanks.
Mr Strong: Good morning, Mrs Smith. How can I help?

Sometimes – for example, when you phone a call centre – you will not be asking for a particular person, or even a department, and may just launch into your question or request without a socially formal conversation opening:

Call Centre: Good morning. Tech Support. This is Roger. How can I help you?
Mrs Smith: Hi, Roger. My computer is randomly shutting down – it's driving me insane. Can you help me?

Closing a conversation

There are conventions for *closing a conversation*. At the end you will close with a *goodbye* – and there are lots of ways of doing this – but you don't simply say what you were going to say then add *goodbye* and walk off. That would seem abrupt and odd.

Conversations must gradually come to a close, and this happens via a *winding down* process. One speaker usually starts this process by starting to hint that they must go soon, or making a general statement about the conversation, and this might start with an interjection such as *well* or *listen*. Also, listen out for phrases that describe how nice it has been to talk to or to see the person:

Well, what a nice surprise to see you.
Well, it has been so lovely chatting today.

Then a person may say that they have to be going or that they should be doing something else.

This has been lovely but I must try to catch that bus.
I must let you go, you're so busy.

Beginnings and endings

Sometimes there is a suggestion that the two participants in the conversation should meet again.

> Let's catch up soon. I'll call you.
> Listen, I don't have much time today, but it would be good to catch up another time.

See the following short piece of closing dialogue. Harry and Tom have been talking for a little while. Tom needs to go and is going to start winding down first as you will see in the blue italic text:

> **Harry**: I haven't seen you around lately. Been away, have you?
> **Tom**: Yes. I was working in London for a month.
> **Harry**: Oh right, why was that?
> **Tom**: My company's got two offices. The London one deals with legal stuff so I was learning about that.
> **Harry**: Was that interesting?
> **Tom**: Surprisingly, yes it was. It will be useful too. *Listen ... great bumping into you, but I really must go. I've got a doctor's appointment in about 15 minutes.*
> **Harry**: Of course. *Good to see you too. Fancy a catch up sometime?*
> **Tom**: *Absolutely. Next weekend suit you?*
> **Harry:** *Weekend after is better. Give me a ring and we'll arrange it properly.*
> **Tom:** *Great.*
> **Harry:** *Good luck at the doc's. See you later.*

In the following short piece of dialogue, Jenny and Alice have just bumped into each other on the train. Alice wants to wind the conversation down almost as soon as it has started because she wants to get to her seat:

SPOKEN ENGLISH

Jenny: Hi, Alice.
Alice: Oh hi, Jenny. Didn't see you there. How are you?
Jenny: Good. Off to London too?
Alice: No. Peterborough. Visiting a cousin there.
Jenny: How's everyone?
Alice: We're all fine, thanks. And you and the family?
Jenny: Great, thanks.
Alice: *It's great to see you. Listen, my seat's in the next carriage. It's so busy, I'd better get going in case someone tries to take it.*
Jenny: Yes of course. I hate when you've reserved a seat and someone takes it. *Good to see you.*
Alice: *I'll get settled and pop back later on the way to the snack bar.*
Jenny: *Great. Catch you later then.*
Alice: *Bye.*

WAYS TO SAY 'GOODBYE!'

Be seeing you! [Informal, old-fashioned]

Bye for now! [Informal]

Bye bye! [Informal]

Bye! [Informal]

Catch you later! [Informal]

Cheerio! [Informal, old-fashioned]

Farewell! [Formal, old-fashioned, humorous; also *A fond farewell!*]

Good day. [Formal]

Good afternoon. [Formal]

Good night. [Formal. Informal versions are *Night!*, or *Night, night!*, or *Nighty night*]

Have a good day!

Have a good one! [Informal]

Have a nice day!

I must be going. [Formal]

I'm off [Informal]

I'm out of here! [Informal]

Later! [Informal]

Peace out! [Informal]

See you later. [Informal]

See you later, alligator [Informal, humorous]

So long! [Informal]

Ta ta! [Old-fashioned]

Take care! [Informal]

Take it easy! [Informal]

Talk to you later!

Toodle-oo! [Humorous]

Closing a telephone conversation

It can be more difficult to bring a telephone conversation to an end because of the absence of facial expressions or gestures, but, in order to be polite, there has to be some dialogue that leads up to the ending of the conversation.

As with a face-to-face conversation, one of the participants may say that they have to be going or that they should be doing something else. Sometimes one of the participants may suggest that the two participants should speak again. See the dialogue that follows:

> **Ken**: Thanks for getting in touch, Bill. It was really good to talk over old times, but I'd better dash. I'm meeting my wife in town. She hates it when I'm late.
> **Bill**: Of course. It was good to talk to you, Ken. We shouldn't leave it so long again. Give me a call soon.
> **Ken**: I'll do that, Bill. When is a good time for you?
> **Bill**: Evenings are always good. We should meet for a drink soon.
> **Ken**: Sounds good. Let's do that. See you later.
> **Bill**: Cheers now.
> **Ken**: Bye.

Below is an example of a more formal conversation in a call centre. In this instance, the call centre assistant is initiating the *winding down* of the conversation, and though the customer interrupts that slightly, the assistant repeats the relevant information and then continues to follow the process of winding down. They have a formal procedure to follow and so repeating a whole sentence word for word – which might normally be seen as an aggressive thing to do – is actually normal and helpful here. The assistant uses the word *implement* too, which you wouldn't tend to use in an informal conversation:

> **Call centre assistant**: ... So, I will implement the new changes to your account, Mrs Jones.
> **Mrs Jones**: OK, but please can you assure me it will happen this time? Because this is the third time I've phoned about this.

SPOKEN ENGLISH

Assistant: I'm sorry for your trouble, Mrs Jones. I think, looking at the notes here, that there was a problem with an incorrect sort code last time. I'm making the changes now. I can confirm that the previous direct debit is still cancelled and the new details are input. It will take 24 hours to be processed. Is there anything else I can do for you today?
Mrs Jones: Just assure me I don't have to phone again about this.
Assistant: I can confirm that, Mrs Jones, but it will take 24 hours to be processed. Is there anything else I can do for you today?
Mrs Jones: No, that's fine. Thanks for helping.
Assistant: It has been no trouble, Mrs Jones. Enjoy your day.
Mrs Jones: Thanks. Bye.
Assistant: Goodbye.

Mrs Jones, to reassure herself that her problem is being sorted, **interrupts** the **winding down** process so that the assistant has to repeat what he has already told her. Also notice how the assistant uses the **passive voice** (*see* pages 186–8) to politely avoid saying that the fault might be the customer's: *there was a problem with an incorrect sort code last time*.

Sometimes, with particularly chatty people, you can go through the **winding down** stage several times, as you can see with this example which is the end of a phone conversation between friends:

Lesley: It was such a lovely surprise to hear from you! It's been too long. We must meet up soon. Listen, I have to go and bath the baby and try to get him to sleep now, but let's speak next week and arrange a night out.
Karen: Oh, yes. Definitely.
Lesley: Lovely. You take care now. Speak soon.
Karen: Yes, speak to you next week. Is Thursday good?

Oh and we must meet up with Jane too. Did you know she's got a new job?
Lesley: No …
Karen: Well, it's a long story, but she got a job in her husband's office and there have been all sorts of problems because of it. She's very unhappy.
Lesley: Poor Jane. Yes, we must see her too. We've got a lot of catching up to do!
Karen: We certainly do.
Lesley: Well, you take care, and yes, let's speak on Thursday. Thursday is a quiet day for me. Tell Jane I'd love to see her.
Karen: I will. She's always asking after you. She really enjoyed the play you were in last month. She said you were a star!
Lesley: She saw that? How funny! I was trying to keep that quiet.
Karen: There's no hiding talent, my dear!
Lesley: Ha ha! Oh dear! How embarrassing. Well, enough about my terrible acting, I really must go. Peter needs me to help with the baby.
Karen: OK. It's been great to talk. I can't wait to see you. Shall we go out for dinner?
Lesley: Well … I'm on this mad diet right now … can we just have drinks?
Karen: Wine instead of food. I can cope with that.
Lesley: I'm not even allowed wine. Mineral water for me.
Karen: Oh dear. Poor show!
Lesley: I know, I know. Listen, I must dash, Peter's changing a nappy and it's all going wrong.
Karen: Oh dear, we can't have that. I'll talk to you on Thursday.
Lesley: Talk to you then. Have a great week.
Karen: You too.
Lesley: Bye, honey.
Karen: Bye, Lesley … oh, I just remembered …
(Lesley has hung up.)

SPOKEN ENGLISH

VOCABULARY

In some forms of conversational English – particularly in everyday, short conversations – fewer words and simpler words are used than is usually the case with written English.

However, more formal forms of spoken communication may well involve longer sentences and complex vocabulary.

For example, you may be taking part in a job interview, seeking travel information, trying to find accommodation, dealing with a banking problem, making a formal spoken complaint about something, or talking to a lawyer about a legal issue, and so on. All of these, and other similar situations, require quite particular vocabulary.

You can acquire such vocabulary from actual conversational practice, but it will help you a lot if you familiarize yourself with

NICE

In conversation or in writing, you might want to avoid using the word *nice* too often. Nice is not a very descriptive word, but it is regularly used to describe many different things. So to find other words similar to *nice* you would consult a **thesaurus**. When you look up *nice* in any thesaurus you will see that it lists quite a few alternatives, for use in different contexts.

- If you are saying that someone is *a nice person*, you might consider using *pleasant*, *friendly*, *kind*, *agreeable* or *charming* instead of *nice*.
- If you are talking about how nice the weather is and saying that it is *a nice day*, you might consider using *fine*, *sunny* or *lovely* instead of *nice*.
- If you want to say that you had *a nice time* at an event of some kind, you might consider using *pleasant*, *enjoyable* or *delightful* instead of *nice*.

certain word lists, in preparation for conversations about specific subjects. For example, the world of business uses phrases and jargon that you might not hear anywhere else, and when you first hear them you might find them very confusing. If you are interested in improving your business vocabulary you should purchase an up-to-date business dictionary that explains all the latest terms. We recommend that you regularly refer to **phrasebooks**, **dictionaries** and **thesauruses** – make it a daily routine to learn a new word or two.

A thesaurus is much like a dictionary of synonyms – a synonym is a word that has a similar meaning to another word. Knowing several synonyms for a word will help keep your English vocabulary varied and more interesting to listen to. Consult your English dictionary and thesaurus every day and you will be amazed at how quickly you can increase your vocabulary power.

That's a really bad way to increase your word power.

PRONUNCIATION

PHONEMIC ORTHOGRAPHY describes a pronunciation system where one **phoneme** (a sound) corresponds directly to one **grapheme** (a letter). Putting it a simpler way, the spelling of words corresponds directly to the way they are pronounced. The Serbian language is almost perfect in terms of phonemic orthography. The English language, however, is very irregular in this respect. The spellings of many English words bear little resemblance to how they are pronounced. This can confuse many learners of English (and many native speakers too). In addition, some English words may vary in pronunciation in different parts of the UK, or the world, due to differences in **accents**.

WHY IS ENGLISH SPELLING SO IRREGULAR?

English does not have, and has never had, an authoritative body – like the French *Académie Française* – regulating spelling, grammar and vocabulary.

English has borrowed words from many other languages and retained the spellings but not necessarily the pronunciation.

For hundreds of years French and Latin had priority as the languages of court and official papers, not English.

Some spelling still reflects a pronunciation that existed several centuries ago. English spelling was standardized during the 15th and 16th centuries with the invention of printing; however, pronunciation went through a process of change (the language developed long vowels) between 1400 and the mid-twentieth century, known as the Great Vowel Shift.

On the pages that follow, we're going to look at the ways in which there can be differences between pronunciation and spelling in English and see if there are any patterns that help to predict either of these.

IPA

The International Phonetic Alphabet (IPA) is a system of written symbols designed to enable the speech sounds of any language to be consistently represented. Some of the symbols are the ordinary letters of the Roman alphabet but some have been specially invented. The International Phonetic Alphabet was first published in 1889. There are over 150 different characters used in the IPA. What follows is a selection of the characters that are commonly used to represent British English:

PRONUNCIATION

Vowel sounds

- æ   h**a**t, s**a**ddle, b**a**ggy
- ɑ   **a**jar, al**a**rm, ap**a**rt
- əɪ   b**i**le, b**i**ke, al**igh**t
- aɪ   h**igh**, h**i**ve, str**i**ve
- aʊ   sh**ou**t, b**ough**, c**ou**ch
- ɛ   fr**e**t, v**e**t, s**ay**s, s**ai**d
- eɪ   w**ay**, h**ey**, c**a**ge, n**eigh**
- ɪ   h**i**t, s**ie**ve, k**i**tty, b**ui**ld, w**o**men
- iː   h**ea**ve, j**ee**p, s**ie**ge
- ɒ   h**o**t, g**o**t, all**o**tment, b**o**ther
- ɔː   th**ough**t, fr**augh**t, th**aw**
- oː   n**o**te, fl**oa**t, t**o**te, b**oa**t
- ɔɪ   b**oy**, av**oi**d, empl**oy**
- ʊ   w**o**man, w**oo**d, c**oul**d
- ɐ   tr**u**mp, fr**o**nt, fl**oo**d
- uː   tr**ue**, br**ew**, y**ou**, sh**oe**
- ə   th**e**, hard**er**, doct**or**, brew**er**

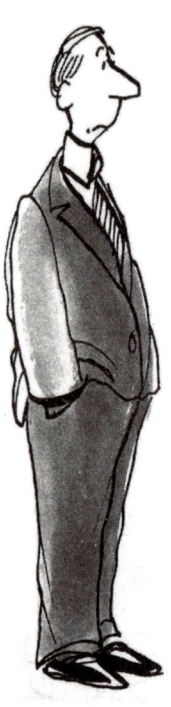

English has silent letters, like 'e' or 'b', but what it really needs is a silent 'I' so people can't talk about themselves as much.

Consonant sounds

In IPA, the following consonant symbols sound the way you would expect the letter to sound: b, d, f, h, k, l, m, n, p, r, s, t, v, w, z. The symbols below have different sounds:

- g   **gh**ost, e**x**ample [ɪgˈzæmpl], **g**ive
- j   **y**es, sen**i**or [siːnjə], on**i**on [ɐnjən], f**u**ture [fjuːtʃə]
- ʃ   **sh**ould, ma**ch**ine, **s**ugar
- ʒ   lei**s**ure, a**z**ure, inva**s**ion
- tʃ   ha**tch**, cap**t**ure, **ch**ew
- dʒ   **j**am, he**dge** [hɛdʒ], sol**di**er [səʊldʒə]
- θ   **th**in, brea**th**, **th**oughts
- ð   **th**ere, **th**en, **th**e, brea**the**
- ŋ   si**ng**, li**ng**er [lɪŋgə], amazi**ng**
- f   cou**gh**, enou**gh**, **f**an
- k   bo**x** [bɒks], **c**art, hi**k**e
- x   lo**ch** [the Scots **voiceless velar fricative**, *see* pages 48–9]

SYLLABLES AND STRESSES

Words are made up of syllables. These are the different blocks of sound within the word. Each word has a stressed syllable. The word apologize has four syllables and the stressed one is the sound pol. The word gymnasium has four syllables too, and the syllable that is stressed is the sound nay:

apologize /əˈpɒləˌdʒaɪz/, /a-**pol**-o-jize/
gymnasium /dʒɪmˈneɪziəm/, /jim-**nay**-zee-um/

In this chapter we have 'spelled out' some of the pronunciations. This means we have used similar English spellings to describe the sound. Spelled-out pronunciations follow the IPA examples. In spelled-out examples, stressed syllables are marked in bold, and in IPA they have a ˈ symbol in front of them. In IPA, secondary stresses (weaker but important stress) are shown by the symbol ˌ .

VOWELS

A vowel is a sound produced by the passage of air through the larynx, virtually unobstructed, with no part of the mouth being closed and none of the vocal organs being so close together that the sound of air can be heard passing between them.

The term is also applied to a letter of the alphabet sounded in this way. We're taught in school that the vowels in the alphabet are a, e, i, o and u. There is also another letter that creates a vowel sound that is usually considered a consonant; and that is y. It can have a short sound [/ɪ/, /ih/], or a long sound [/aɪ/, /eye/].

In English pronunciation, the sound of the consonant r is elided (missed out) when it follows a vowel sound [e.g., soldier /ˈsəʊldʒə/ /**sole**-jeh/]. Some IPA symbols for vowel sounds are on page 36.

Long and short vowels

The vowel sound in win [/wɪn/, /win/] is short and the vowel sound in wine [/waɪn/, /wine/] is long. The vowel sound in fat [/fæt/, /fat/] is short and the vowel sound in fate [/feɪt/, /fayt/] is long. The vowel sound in tram [/træm/, /tram/] is short and the vowel sound in train [/treɪn/, /trayn/] is long.

PRONUNCIATION

To help remember the difference you could think of the names of the vowel letters as you probably learned them at school: the capitals A, E, I, O, U are pronounced [/eɪ/, /ay/], [/iː/, /ee/], [/aɪ/, /eye/], [/oː/, /oh/], [/juː/, /yoo/], and have long vowel sounds. The lower-case vowels, a, e, i, o, u as you were taught them, were probably described as [/æ/, /ah/], [/ɛ/, /eh/], [/ɪ/, /ih/], [/ɒ/, /aw/], [/ɐ/, /uh/], and these sounds are short vowels.

Short vowels

short a	/ah/	æ	cat, paddle, saggy
short e	/eh/	ɛ	pet, friend, head, many
short i	/ih/	ɪ	pit, give, tyranny, women
short o	/aw/	ɒ	hot, got, allotment, bother
short u	/uh/	ɐ	trump, front, flood
shwa	/uh, ih, eh/	ə	the, harder, doctor, brewer

You might not have heard of **shwa**, ə, before. It is an unstressed sound that sometimes occurs at the end of a word when the word ends in a **vowel** and a consonant like **r** (*see* the blue box on page 40 for more on **silent r** and the pronunciation of **r**).

Long vowels

ɑ	ajar, alarm, apart		ɔː	thought, fraught, thaw
əɪ	bile, bike, alight		oː	note, float, tote, boat
aɪ	high, hive, strive		ɔɪ	boy, avoid, employ
aʊ	shout, bough, couch		ʊ	woman, wood, could
eɪ	way, hey, cage, neigh		uː	true, brew, you, shoe
iː	heave, jeep, siege			

CONSONANTS

A consonant is a speech sound that is produced by a closing movement, either partial or total, involving the vocal organs, such as the lips, teeth, tongue or the throat, which forms such a narrow constriction that the sound of air can be heard passing through. The term also applies to a letter of the alphabet sounded in this way. *See* **vowels**, pages 37–8. The IPA symbols of some consonant sounds are on page 36.

SOUNDS PARTICULAR TO ENGLISH
One sound, one letter

Single letters often represent one sound. Let's take a simple one-syllable word such as pot. The sound of the letter p is made by the lips and by a burst of outward breath, /p/. This is known as a plosive sound. The letter o sound in this instance is a short vowel [/ɒ/, /aw/], a voiceless sound (a sound that is spoken without using the vocal cords) between rounded lips. The sound made by the letter t is made with a voiceless breath and the placing of the tip of the tongue near the teeth.

One letter, successive sounds

In the case of the letter x, one letter can represent two sounds, ks:
box [/bɒks/, /boks/]
axel [/ˈæksəl/, /**ak**-sel/]

Two letters, one sound

Two letters can represent one sound:
gh f: as in laugh [/lɑf/, /laf/], or rough [/rʌf/, /ruf/]
ph f: as in pharmacy [/ˈfɑməsi/, /**fah**-mu-see/] (but not shepherd!)
th θ or ð: as in bath [/bɑθ/, /bahth/]; or bathe [/beɪð/, /baythe/]
sh ʃ: as in shop [/ʃɒp/, /shop/]
ch tʃ: as in chop [/tʃɒp/, /chop/]

Two letters, three sound

Two letters can represent three sounds within one syllable:
ni nyu: as in senior [/ˈsinjə/, /**seen**-yu/]
fu fyoo: as in future [/ˈfjuːtʃə/, /**fyoo**-chu/]

Doubled consonants

Doubled consonants sometimes mean that the preceding vowel is a short one. Compare:
    latter and later   hatter and hater   tapper and taper

Letters that change sounds

Some letters vary their pronunciation depending on what other letters are next to them:

PRONUNCIATION

SILENT R, RHOTIC R, LINKING R AND INTRUSIVE R

In English received pronunciation (page 49) many rs are silent. That goes for Australian and New Zealand pronunciation too. However, in certain accents of English – Scottish, Irish, West Country, Canadian, and most accents of American English – they are are not silent, they are rhotic.

In English received pronunciation you only pronounce the r when it appears before a vowel sound.

row   borrow
remember   random
hurrah   trap

You don't pronounce the r when it appears before a consonant or at the end of a word. The r then lengthens the vowel.

tar   car
torte   quark
hard   third

When er, or, or ir is at the end of a word it becomes an unstressed sound known as schwa. The IPA symbol is ə.

bender   tender
wander   horror
never   remember

There is such a thing as an intrusive r sound which occurs between two words, to make them easier to say.

law and order   law-ren-aw-deh
an idea of mine   an-eye-deer-ov-mine

There is also the phenomenon of the linking r, when a previously unpronounced r sound is audible when followed by a word that begins with a vowel.

mother and father   mu-thuh-ran-fah-tha
whether or not   weth-eh-raw-not

tot /tɒt/ when an e follows the t, becomes *tote* /toːt/, /toat/
bat /bæt/ with the addition of i after a, becomes *bait* /beɪt/, /bayt/
bat /bæt/ with the addition of h after t, becomes *bath* /bɒθ/, /bath/
sin /sɪn/ with the addition of g, becomes *sign* /saɪn/, /sine/
mat /mæt/ when an e follows the t, becomes *mate* /meɪt/, mayt/
met /mɛt/ when an a follows the e, becomes *meat* /miːt/, /meet/

The letters gh

in *laugh*; **gh** has an **f** sound – /læf/, /laff/
in *rough*; **gh** has an **f** sound – /rɐf/, /ruff/
in *bough*; **gh** has a **w** sound   – /baʊ/, /bow/ [NOT /bɐf/, /buf/]
(*also see* 'ough' words *below*)

in the word *Edinburgh*;
  gh has an **uh** sound   – /ˈɛdɪnˌbɐɾɐ/, /**ed**-in-bu-ruh/
[NOT /ˈɛdɪnˌbɐɾɡ/, /**ed**-in-burg/ or
/ˈɛdɪnˌbɐɾf/, /**ed**-in-burf/]

in the word *Pittsburgh*;
  gh has a hard **g** sound – /ˈpɪtsˌbɐɾɡ/, /**pitts**-burg/
[NOT /ˈpɪtsˌbɐɾɐ/, /**pitts**-bur-uh/]

in *ghost*; **gh** is a hard **g** sound – /ɡoːst/, /gost/

'Augh' words

in *naughty*; **augh** is a long **aw** sound [/ɔː/, /aw/], [/ˈnɔːti/, /**naw**-tee/]
in *daughter*; **augh** is a long **aw** sound [/ɔː/, /aw/], [/ˈdɔːtə/, /**daw**-tah/]
in *draught*; **augh** is a short **aff** sound [/æf/, /af/], [/ˈdræft/, /draft/]
in *laughter*; **augh** is a short **aff** sound [/æf/, /af], [/ˈlæftə/, /**laf**-tuh/]

'Ough' words

in *though* and *dough*; **ough** is a long **o** sound [/oː/, /oh/]
in *tough*, *rough* and *enough*; **ough** is a short **uff** sound [/ɐf/, /uf/]
in *cough*, *trough*; **ough** is a short **off** sound [/ɒf/, /off/]
in *plough*, *bough*, *drought*; **ough** is a long **ow** sound [/aʊ/, /ow/]
in *through*; **ough** is a long **oo** sound [/uː/, /oo/]
in *nought*, *ought*, *sought* and *thought*; **ough** is a long **aw** sound [/ɔː/, /aw/]
in *lough* and *hough*; **ough** is like the Scottish **och** in *loch* [/ɒx/, /och/]
in *borough* and *thorough*; **ough** is a short **uh** sound [/ɐ/, /uh/]

PRONUNCIATION

SILENT LETTERS

A

In some adverbs ending in -ally the a sound is elided to lee [/li/, /lee/]. You *could* pronounce the a, and it wouldn't be *wrong* but it might sound odd.

academically
acoustically
actually
biographically
casually
classically
comically
drastically
energetically
logically
romantically
stoically

Words where the a of -ally is always sounded:

abdominally
abysmally
agriculturally
anecdotally
antisocially
brutally
congenially
eternally

When a comes before e, we only hear the e sound [/i/, /ee/]. The ae spelling is not used in American English, e is preferred on its own. This spelling is optional and is becoming less and less common in British English:

aegis
aeon
palaeontology
encyclopaedia

Hi my name is Tom ... spelled T, as in tzar; O, as in Oedipal; M, as in mnemonic.

Silent letters

B

The letter b is not usually pronounced before t when it appears at the end of a word.

debt
doubt
subtle

B is not pronounced after m at the end of a word.

aplomb
bomb
catacomb
climb
comb
crumb
dumb
entomb
jamb
lamb
limb
numb
plumb
plumber
succumb
thumb
tomb
womb

C

The letter c is often not pronounced when it appears after s.

abscess
ascend
ascent
conscience
conscious
corpuscle
crescent
descend
descent
discipline
discern
fascinate
fluorescent
incandescent
isosceles
luminescent
miscellaneous
muscle
obscene
omniscience
resuscitate
scenario
scene
scent
science
scientology
scissors
susceptible

Exceptions

There are *many* exceptions, of which these are just a few, where the c has a /k/ sound.

confiscate
couscous
mollusc
minuscule
muscular

When c appears before q or k it is not usually pronounced distinctly from the other letter:

acquaint
acquaintance
acknowledge
acquiesce
acquit
acquire
attack
bicker
bannock
block
brick
buck
chick
cricket
fickle

PRONUNCIATION

K WITHOUT C

K is usually accompanied by c at the end of a word, but not when another consonant comes before it:

milk   silk
talk   blink
walk   park
work

K also appears without c after a long vowel:

took   crook
hook   bleak
meek   weak
take   broke

kick
mimicked
neck
nickle
sack
sick
track
tick
hijack

D

The letter d is not pronounced when paired with g to make the soft consonant sound j [/dʒ/, /j/]. It may be silent, however, it serves a purpose: it indicates that the immediately preceding vowel is **short**.

abridge
acknowledge
badge
bludgeon
budgie
dodge
edge
fridge
hedge
nudge
partridge
pledge
ridge
sledge
wedge

In addition, there are other words where the sound d is **elided** (missed out).

Wednesday
handsome
handkerchief

E

The letter e is not pronounced at the end of words, but instead lengthens the sound of the vowel before it.

bite
cage
drive
gave
grave
hope
write
site
role
rude
nude
slate
mate

Exceptions

Some words ending in e do not have a long vowel.

some
have
castle
rustle

Silent letters

minute (time measurement)
Anything ending in –ette or –elle

G
The letter g is often silent when it comes before n. In addition, the letters gn lengthen the sound of the vowel before them.

align
assign
campaign
champagne
cologne
design
foreigner
gnarl
gnash
gnaw
gnome
reign
resign
sign
sovereign

Exceptions
cognitive
igneous
magnet
signature

GH
Following a vowel, gh is silent.

borough
daughter
drought
fight
light
might
sigh
slaughter
thorough
thought
through
weigh

Exceptions
Sometimes gh is pronounced like f.

enough
cough
laugh
rough
tough
draught

H
The letter h is silent after w.

what
which
why
whether
white
while
where
whip

H is silent at the beginning of a word.

herb (in US English this is sometimes pronounced /ɜːrb/, /erb/)
heir
honest
honour
hour

[In some accents of English (such as Cockney) the h sound is dropped at the beginning of a word.]

Often h is not pronounced when it comes after c, g or r.

aghast
choir
chorus
echo
ghastly
ghost
ghoul
rhinoceros
rhythm

PRONUNCIATION

I
In the word bus**i**ness, the **i** sound is silent.

K
When it comes before **n** at the beginning of a word, **K** is not pronounced.

knack
knee
knew
knife
knight
knitting
knob
knock
knot
know
knuckle

L
Following the vowels **a**, **o** and **u**, **l** is silent.

a**l**mond
ba**l**m
ca**l**f
ca**l**m
ca**l**ve
cha**l**k
cou**l**d
fo**l**k
ha**l**f
ha**l**ve
pa**l**m
sa**l**mon
shou**l**d
ta**l**k
wa**l**k
wou**l**d
yo**l**k

Exceptions
bu**l**k
fo**l**d
ha**l**o
ho**l**d
mou**l**d
su**l**k
so**l**d

M
The letter **m** is silent in **m**nemonic.

N
After **m** at the end of a word, **n** is silent.

autum**n**
colum**n**
dam**n**
hym**n**
solem**n**

O
The combination **oe**, pronounced **ee**, is spelled with just an **e** in American English, and increasingly often in British English.

am**oe**ba
hom**oe**opathy
ph**oe**nix
oedipal

In the following words the **o** sound is elided (missed out):

col**o**nel [/ˈkɜːnəl/, /**ker**-nel/]
opossum
soph**o**more

P
P is not pronounced at the beginning of many words using the combinations **ps**, **pt** and **pn**.

pneumonia
pneumatic
pseudo
pseudonym
psychiatrist
psychologist
psychology
psychotherapy
psychotic
pterodactyl

S

The letter s is not pronounced before i in the following words:

aisle
island
isle
islet

T

The letter t is not pronounced in these words:

ballet
bustle
butcher
castle
Christmas
fasten
gourmet
hasten
listen
mortgage
often
rapport
scratch
thistle
tsunami
tzar
watch
whistle
witch

U

The letter u is not pronounced when it comes after g and before a vowel.

beguile
guard
guess
guest
guidance
guild
guilty
guitar
rogue
tongue
vogue

U is sometimes not pronounced in the combination ui.

build
building
biscuit

U almost always follows q but the sound that follows is the w sound.

quit
quiet
acquit
question
quench

W

The letter w is not pronounced at the beginning of a word when it is before the letter r.

wrap
wreck
wrestle
wrestling
wriggle
wring
wrinkle
wrist
write
writing
wrote
wrong

W is not pronounced in the following words:

answer
sword
two
who
whose
whom
whole
whoever

PRONUNCIATION

SOUND TERMS

accent a regional, national or individual way of pronouncing words, as in 'a French accent', 'a Cockney accent'. The accent that the words in this book are transcribed into is an accent of Standard English known as **RP, received pronunciation**.

alveolar describing a sound made by placing the tongue on the ridge behind the teeth (known as the alveolar ridge). Includes consonants such as *t* and *s*.

coronal referring to a consonant sound made by the front parts of the tongue.

consonant *see* pages 36 and 38.

dental describing a sound produced by the tip of the tongue positioned near the front teeth, as in *d*.

digraph a group of two letters representing one sound, as in *ey* in *key*, *oy* in *boy*, *ph* in *phone* and *th* in *thin*.

diphthong describing a vowel sound that changes its quality within the same single syllable. The sound begins as for one vowel and moves on as for another. It is sometimes called a **gliding vowel**. For example *rain*, *either*, *voice*, *height*, *soul*, *pure*, *during*, *here* and *weird*. *See also* **triphthong**

disyllabic describing a word with two **syllables**.

elision the omission of a sound.

fricative describing a sound produced by forcing air through a partly closed air passage, as in the pronunciation of *th*.

gliding vowel same as **diphthong**.

grapheme another word for a letter.

inflection a varying of tone or pitch.

IPA *see* page 35–6

labial describing a sound formed by closing, or partially closing, the lips, as in the pronunciation of the letter *m*.

labiodental describing a sound produced by the lips and

teeth together, as in the pronunciation of the letter v.

length mark a mark used in phonetics in relation to a vowel to indicate that it is long *see* pages 37–8. This can take the form of a macron, a small horizontal stroke placed above a grapheme (¯), or a symbol resembling a colon (:) placed after a vowel phoneme in the IPA pronunciation system.

macron *see* **length mark**.

monosyllabic referring to a word with only one syllable.

phoneme the smallest unit of speech sound, e.g., ɐ, uː, ə, g.

phonetics the scientific study of speech sounds.

plosive a sound that is like a burst of air, such as is produced when pronouncing the letter p.

received pronunciation (RP) is the accepted standard accent of British English, based on that of an educated person of southern England.

rhotic an accent that pronounces r sounds in, at, or near the end of words, *see* page 40.

sibilant describing a sound suggestive of a hissing noise, as that which is produced when pronouncing the letter s.

syllable a syllable is a unit of sound, *see* page 37.

transcribe to write out sounds using IPA symbols. Such a translation is known as a phonemic transcription.

triphthong a triphthong is like one vowel sound that has three tones to it. In RP, words such as *hour, shower, liar* and *employer* contain a triphthong, *see also* diphthong.

velar a sound that is produced by the back of the tongue on the soft palate, as in the pronunciation of g in *grand*.

voiced a sound that is spoken using the vocal cords, as in the pronunciation of the letter b.

voiceless a sound that is spoken without using the vocal cords, as in the pronunciation of the letter p.

vowel *see* pages 36–8.

IDIOMS

He's always been quiet but I think the cat really has got his tongue this time.

AN IDIOM is a phrase whose meaning cannot easily be understood just from the definitions of the individual words that make up the phrase. Idioms are often metaphorical (page 372), symbolic or use imagery. And so, knowing what all the words mean in an idiom will not necessarily help you to work out what it means. This can make them hard to learn.

Speakers of English use idioms on a regular basis. Learners of English have to learn how to use them correctly if they are to become truly fluent in the language. Take, for example, the common idiom *cat got your tongue*. Most learners will know all the words in this phrase, but they do not literally mean that a cat has made off with someone's tongue. This phrase is said when someone is being unusually shy or silent: *You're very quiet tonight. Cat got your tongue?*

ORIGINS

Many idioms have rather unusual origins. In the pages that follow we've highlighted these origins where they are known. It is useful to know the history of a particular idiom because it can help to remember it. *Cat got your tongue* probably has an interesting source. However it has been lost in the mists of time!

However, we know the origin of another cat-based phrase: *let the cat out of the bag*. It is thought to refer to a very old former fairground trick of selling someone a cat in a bag when the buyer thought it was a piglet. It was not until the buyer opened the bag and discovered a cat instead of a pig that he realized he had been tricked.

Similarly, if you use the phrase *jump the gun* you are not suggesting that someone has leapt over a firearm. The gun referred to here is the gun that is fired as the starting signal for a race. If an athlete jumps the gun they start running before the signal to start is given. Idiomatically, the phrase is used to refer to someone who does something too early or before conditions are right.

COMMON IDIOMS

We include here a selection of common idioms, together with an explanation of the meaning, the origin of the idiom where appropriate (where it is known), and a short piece of dialogue showing how the idiom is used.

Achilles' heel

This idiom indicates that someone has a weak spot of some kind.

Achilles, a hero famous in Greek legend, is said to have been dipped by his mother in the River Styx in order to make him invulnerable, but his heel was left vulnerable because she was holding him by it. He was killed by an arrow shot through his heel.

IDIOMS

Bill: I'm surprised you decided to fire Lucy.
Tony: I was sorry to have to do it. She's very talented but her *Achilles' heel* is her bad temper.

the acid test

This idiom refers to a test that will prove or disprove something so that there is no doubt.

> *Nitric acid was once used as a test for gold. If the metal tested was not gold, it decomposed because of the acid.*

Sally: The new range of cosmetics looks wonderful.
Alice: It does – many people have admired it. *The acid test* will be how well it sells.

have an axe to grind

This idiom means to have a personal or selfish reason to be involved in something.

> *This idiom originates from a story told by the American politician Benjamin Franklin about an incident in his boyhood when a man asked him to show him how well his grandfather's grindstone worked. The man gave Franklin his own axe to demonstrate on and so got it sharpened for nothing.*

Liz: Jenny wants me to look critically at Bill's project.
Pat: Oh, be careful, she has *an axe to grind*.
Liz: What do you mean?
Pat: She wants funding for her own project.

the back of beyond

This idiom refers to a remote place that is difficult to get to and probably has very few people living there.

Sam: You've obviously lived in the city a long time. Were you brought up here?
Ken: No, I came to university here and just stayed on. I was

brought up on a farm in the north of the country in *the back of beyond*. I couldn't wait to get away.

beat about the bush/beat around the bush

This idiom, *beat about the bush* in British English, *beat around the bush* in American English, means to approach a subject in an indirect way, rather than getting straight to the point.

When hunters are shooting game birds, people are employed to beat the bushes, heather, etc to make the birds fly up.

Jane: The new assistant I hired is no good. I'm going to have to let her go. I don't know how to tell her.
Sue: There's no point in *beating around the bush*. You're just going to have to tell her straight.

have a bee in your bonnet

This idiom means that you are unable to stop thinking or talking about something so that it becomes an obsession.

The imagery behind this idiom is that a bee trapped under a hat cannot escape and goes buzzing around under it.

Kate: Ben has just spent half-an-hour criticizing me for buying a car.
Pat: Ben *has a bee in his bonnet* about cars. He thinks everyone should use public transport and save the environment.

a big fish/frog in a small pond

This idiom refers to an important or influential person whose importance is restricted to a small group, organization, area, etc. The fish idiom is found in both American and British English, but the frog idiom is restricted to American English.

Jim: Do you think Pete's wise to take the new job?
Ben: No, I don't. I'm not sure he'll cope with it.

IDIOMS

Jim: But he has a very senior job in his present company.
Ben: It's a small firm and Pete's *a big fish in a small pond*. The firm that's offered him the job is a multinational.

burn your boats

This idiom means to carry out an action that results in you being unable to return to your original position or situation.

> *If you burn your boat after reaching land you have no means of getting back across the sea to where you came from.*

Sam: Did Ben really shout at the boss?
John: Yes, he did and he was very rude to him.
Sam: Do you think the boss will forgive him?
John: Absolutely not. Ben's really *burnt his boats* this time. The boss fired him and won't give him a reference.

the buck stops here

This idiom is used to indicate who the person who is finally responsible for something that has to be dealt with.

> *The expression refers to a card game such as poker, the buck being a marker passed around to indicate who the dealer is. Harry S Truman, US President (1945–53), had a sign on his desk with this inscription.*

Will: Why are you going to resign? The mistake wasn't your fault.
Jim: I know it wasn't, but it was the fault of someone in my department and I'm in charge. *The buck stops here*.

carry the can

This idiom means to take the blame or responsibility for something that has gone wrong, even though someone else may be at least partly responsible.

Anne: I can't believe that Joe's been fired.
Jane: Neither can I, but some people are saying that he

just *carried the can* for everyone else's mistakes in that department.

catch someone red-handed

This idiom means to find someone in the actual act of doing something wrong.

This is reference to the blood that would be on the hands of someone who had just murdered someone.

Pat: Do you think Joe really broke into the Brown's house? He seems such a nice quiet boy.
Jenny: There's no doubt about it. Police *caught him red-handed* when he was trying to sell stolen jewellery.

catch someone with their hand in the till

This idiom means to discover someone in the act of stealing or doing something dishonest.

Paul: I hear the company accountant's been fired.
Will: Yes. He's been *caught with his hand in the till*. The auditors have found out that he's been embezzling money.

chalk and cheese

This idiom is used to emphasize how completely different two things are.

Amy and Lily are sisters, but they're *chalk and cheese*. They don't look the least alike and they have completely different personalities.

cross that bridge when you come to it

This idiom means to worry about a problem or try to cope with it only when it actually affects you, rather than worrying, perhaps unnecessarily, before it happens.

Mary: It's a lovely house and we can just about afford the rent, but what if the landlord puts the rent up?

IDIOMS

Alice: We'll *cross that bridge when we come to it*. Let's go and tell the landlord we'll take it before someone else takes it.

be at daggers drawn

This idiom means that two people are being extremely hostile towards each other.

> *This is a reference to people pulling out their daggers when they were ready to fight.*

Amy: I didn't know that Dave was Tom's brother. They never seem to speak each other.
Pam: They don't. They've been *at daggers drawn* since their father died more than ten years ago.

a diamond in the rough/a rough diamond

This idiom, *a diamond in the rough* in American English, *a rough diamond* in British English, refers to a person who behaves in rather a rough manner, but who has some very good qualities.

Ken: What do you think of Sue's new boyfriend?
Alice: The first time I met him he seemed a bit boorish, but he's really *a rough diamond*. He's very kind and sweet.

dog eat dog

This idiom is used to refer to a situation in which rivals or opponents are prepared to do anything at all to get what they want.

Dave: My son's just graduated and he's job-hunting.
Bob: It's a difficult time to be looking for a job.
Dave: Yes, it is. There's a lot of competition. It's *dog eat dog* out there.

Dutch courage

This idiom refers to a confidence (or at least a lack of nervousness) that has been brought about by consuming alcohol.

This is perhaps a reference to a former Dutch custom of drinking alcohol before going into battle.

Sam: It's a bit early for you to be drinking.
Mark: I need a bit of *Dutch courage*. I'm going on a date with Sally and I'm really nervous.

be at the end of your tether

This idiom means that you are no longer able to tolerate or put up with something.

A tether is a rope used to tie up an animal, extending a certain distance to let the animal move around or graze.

Jane: You look very tired, Molly.
Molly: I am and I'm *at the end of my tether*. I'm not getting much sleep because of my upstairs neighbours.
Jane: Why's that?
Molly: They play loud music all night. I'm going to call the police if it happens again.

flog a dead horse

This idiom means to go on trying to rouse interest or enthusiasm in something when this is no longer of interest, making your efforts likely to be unsuccessful.

Diane: Jack keeps trying to get Jenny to forgive him for cheating on her, but he's *flogging a dead horse*.
Mary: He certainly is. Jenny has no intention of forgiving him.

IDIOMS

with flying colours
With great success.

> *This is a reference to a ship leaving a place of battle with its colours or flag still flying, rather than being lowered in surrender.*

Frank: My son's just got his exam results. He's passed *with flying colours*!
Ben: That's great! You must be delighted for him.

go by the board
This idiom is used to indicate that something is being abandoned or is no longer likely to be possible or successful.

> *This is a nautical reference. The expression originally meant literally, to go overboard and vanish.*

Jill: Are you still thinking of going back to work full time?
Wendy: No, my work plans have *gone by the board*. I'm having another baby.

have green thumbs/green fingers
This idiom means to be very skilful at growing plants.

Molly: I'm looking after my mother's house plants and I'm scared they're going to die. My mother has *green fingers*, but I'm hopeless with plants.
Lily: Remember to water them, but don't water them too much. They should be OK.

hit the ground running
This idiom means to begin some kind of new activity immediately and energetically.

> *A reference to soldiers running swiftly into battle immediately after leaving a helicopter or being dropped by parachute.*

> **Lucy**: I must say our Spring fashion range looks very good.
> **Amy**: It does, but there's a lot of competition around. We really need to find some exciting ways to promote our range and *hit the ground running* when we launch it.

hit the sack/hit the hay

Hit the sack is common in American English but also found in British English, **hit the hay**, more common in British English, means to go to bed.

> **Ben**: Mark and I are going clubbing later. Want to come?
> **Dan**: No thanks. I've got a busy day tomorrow. I'm going to *hit the sack*.

the jewel in the crown

This idiom refers to the most valuable or successful thing associated with someone or something.

> **Mary**: What a wonderful painting.
> **Jane**: Yes, it is, isn't it? The gallery has a marvellous collection, but this is definitely *the jewel in their crown*.

jump on the bandwagon

This idiom means to become involved in something because it is fashionable or because it will be profitable, although you may not be really interested in it.

> *A reference to the brightly coloured vehicle, carrying a musical band at the head of a procession which often encourages people to follow on.*

> **Tom**: I hear George has gone into property development. I didn't know he was interested in property.
> **Jim**: He's not the least bit interested in it. The property market's doing quite well in his area and he's just *jumping on the bandwagon*.

IDIOMS

kill two birds with one stone

This idiom means to carry out two aims by means of one action.

Sue: What are you planning to do in the city today?
Jane: I'm going to *kill two birds with one stone*. I have an appointment with my dentist and I need to collect some books I ordered from the central library.

be left holding the baby

This idiom means to be left to cope with a situation on your own when often this was really the responsibility of other people.

Joe: What's wrong with you? You look really mad.
Mark: I'm furious. My boss is responsible for organizing the sales conference, but he's suddenly decided to go on holiday. I've been left *holding the baby*.

let off steam/blow off steam

This idiom means to do something active that helps you get rid of your strong feelings, excess energy, etc about something.

This is a reference to steam being released from a steam engine in order to reduce pressure.

Harry: Dad is really stomping about upstairs.
Bob: Don't worry. He's just *letting off steam*. He was so annoyed when the new TV wouldn't work.

lock, stock and barrel

This idiom is used to emphasize how complete something is, with everything included.

This is a reference to the main parts of a gun.

Tim: Ben will have to buy furniture now.
Joe: No, he won't. He bought the house and contents *lock, stock and barrel*.

make a mountain out of a molehill

This idiom means to exaggerate the extent of a difficult situation or problem.

> **Lucy**: What did Tony say to Jim? He's really annoyed.
> **Jill**: He was just teasing him. He apologized, but Jim wouldn't listen.
> **Lucy**: Jim's always *making mountains out of molehills*.

the moment of truth

This idiom refers to a crucial time when you find out whether something has proved to be successful, will work, etc.

> *This is a translation of the Spanish expression* el momento de la verdad, *which refers to the moment in a bullfight when the matador is about to kill the bull.*

> **Jill**: Your brother's spent ages working on that old car.
> **Pat**: He's taking it for a test drive tomorrow. That'll be *the moment of truth*.

the nail in someone's coffin

This idiom refers to something, often the latest in a series of events, which helps to bring about someone's ruin or destruction.

> This morning Mike was very rude again to one of our best customers. That was the final *nail in his coffin*. The boss told him to leave immediately.

once in a blue moon

This idiom means almost never, very rarely.

> **Joan**: Do you go to the movies much these days?
> **Alice**: *Once in a blue moon*. It's not easy to get someone to look after the children.

be over the moon

This idiom means to be extremely happy or joyful.

IDIOMS

Lucy: Amy seems in a very good mood today.
Anne: She's *over the moon*. She's just got engaged.

be par for the course

This idiom refers to what usually happens or what might be expected to happen, and is often used with reference to something undesirable or bad.

> *This is a golfing reference to the number of strokes that would be made by a good player playing reasonably well.*

Jack: Dan's closed down his computer business already. He only opened it last year.
Will: That's *par for the course* for small businesses these days, I'm afraid.

paint the town red

This idiom means to go out and celebrate something, usually in a lively, extravagant way.

We're all going to *paint the town red*. We're celebrating our daughter's graduation.

pass the buck

This idiom means to try to shift the blame or responsibility for something on to someone else instead of accepting it yourself.

> *The expression refers to a card game such as poker, the buck being a marker passed around to indicate who the dealer is.*

Pete: Kevin broke the vase, Mum.
Mum: Stop trying to *pass the buck*. You were both larking about.

pie in the sky

This idiom refers to an idea, hope or plan, relating to something good, that is unlikely to happen.

This is a reference to lines by American poet Joe Hill written in 1911 from a parody poem called The Preacher and the Slave.

Phil really wanted to be a doctor and he worked really hard at school, but it was *pie in the sky*. He's not at all academic.

the rat race

This idiom refers to a way of life in which people compete aggressively for success in business, etc.

Steve's given up his job and gone to live in the country. He was making a lot of money as a stockbroker, but he got tired of *the rat race*.

a red herring

This idiom refers to a piece of information, sometimes a false clue laid deliberately, which misleads someone.

A reference to a strong-smelling fish whose scent could mislead hunting dogs and distract them from their prey.

The burglars trashed the house, but I think that was done as *a red herring*. I think that someone went to Frank's place intending to break the safe.

rest on your laurels

This idiom refers to the fact that you are not trying very hard for further success because you are relying on the good reputation brought about by past successes.

This is a reference to the ancient Greek practice of crowning successful poets and winners with laurel wreaths.

Bob used to be the best player by far but there are now quite a few good young players in the team. He really can't afford *to rest on his laurels*.

IDIOMS

score an own goal

This idiom means to do something that is harmful or disadvantageous to your own interests.

> This is a reference to kicking a ball between the goalposts on your own team's side of the field and so giving a point to the opposing team.

Mike: Did Kate get the job?
Sam: No, she didn't. She *scored an own goal* at her interview. She criticized her old company.

shoot yourself in the foot

This idiom means to do something which is disadvantageous or harmful to yourself or to your situation.

Mark: I'm not doing any more work for Smith & Sons.
Tom: I've stopped too, they never pay in a decent time.
Mark: They're *shooting themselves in the foot* and losing some reliable suppliers.

smell a rat

This idiom means to suspect that something is not right or normal.

> This is a reference to a dog hunting rats by scent.

Amy: How did Alice find out her husband was planning a surprise party?
Lily: She *smelled a rat* when he said she had to keep the weekend of the 12th free, and not go away with her cousin to York. He said he needed her help for some urgent DIY!
Amy: He never does DIY. No wonder she guessed!

stab someone in the back

This idiom means to behave treacherously towards someone, often a friend or colleague; to betray someone.

I thought Pete was my friend, but he *stabbed me in the back*. I told him in confidence that I owed a lot of money and he told everyone.

stick to your guns

This idiom means to refuse to change your decision or opinion about something, no matter what happens.

This is reference to a soldier who keeps firing at the enemy.

Liz: Is Pat still thinking of emigrating?
Jane: I think so, but some of her family are trying to persuade her not to.
Liz: I hope she *sticks to her guns*. You need to follow your dreams.

a storm in a teacup

This idiom means a great fuss over something that is not at all important.

Lucy: Was Alice hurt? Somebody said she'd been bitten by a dog.
Molly: No. The whole thing was *a storm in a teacup*. The dog just jumped up on her, but it was a large dog and Alice was a bit scared and made a big fuss.

throw a spanner in the works

This idiom means to stop, to prevent, or to delay a plan, project, etc from going ahead.

Sam: Your holidays start next week, right?
Harry: Not any more. My boss has *thrown a spanner in the works*. He wants me to go on a management course.

tighten your belt

This idiom means to reduce the amount of money that you spend regularly.

IDIOMS

> *If you spend less money on food, and get thinner from hunger, you will have to tighten your belt to make your clothes fit.*

Jane: Prices seem to keep going up and up. We're finding it difficult to manage.
Jenny: So are we. We're really having to *tighten our belts*.

too big for your boots

This idiom means that you have become very proud and conceited and think that you are superior to others.

Sue: Are you still friendly with Amy?
Sally: No. She doesn't see any of her old friends. She's got *too big for her boots* since she got famous.

turn over a new leaf

This idiom means to start to act in a better, more acceptable way.

We're very pleased with your work, Paul. You really seem to have *turned over a new leaf*.

twist someone's arm

This idiom means to try to persuade or force someone to do something that they really do not want to do, though not by physical means.

> *If you literally twist someone's arm you use physical force.*

I didn't want to go to Jill's party, but *she twisted my arm*. You know how determined she is!

be up in the air

This idiom means to be still undecided or uncertain.

> **Jill**: Where are you and Jim going on holiday this year?
> **Pat**: Our plans are still *up in the air*. It is proving difficult to get time off.

be up in arms

This idiom means to protest in a very angry way.

Arms in this sense means weapons.

> Apparently they're planning to extend the airport. They're thinking of adding another runway. The people who live near the airport are *up in arms*. They're organizing an official protest.

wash your hands of someone/something

To indicate that you are no longer going to be responsible for, or involved with, someone or something.

From a reference in the Bible to such an action by Pontius Pilate after the crucifixion of Jesus.

> **Wendy**: Jill's teaching young Tom to play the piano, isn't she?
> **Liz**: She was, but not any more. She says that Tom has a lot of talent, but he just refuses to practise. She's *washed her hands of him*.

IDIOMS

SIMILES

A simile is a figure of speech in which a thing or person is, for the sake of comparison, said to be *like* another. The word *simile* is derived from *similis*, the Latin word for *like*. The words *like* or *as* usually appear in the simile, as in: *'She was as pretty as a picture'*. For the most part, similes are self evident, rather than metaphorical like most idioms.

agile as a monkey
alike as (like) two peas in a pod
blind as a bat
bold as brass
brave as a lion
brown as a berry
cheerful as the day is long
clear as daylight
clear as mud (not at all clear)
common as muck
cool as a cucumber
cunning as a fox
dead as a doornail
deaf as a post
drunk as a lord
dry as a bone
easy as pie
fit as a fiddle
flat as a pancake
good as gold
hard as nails
hot as hell
keen as mustard
light as a feather
mad as a hatter
neat as a pin
old as the hills
playful as a kitten
pleased as Punch
poor as a church mouse
pretty as a picture
proud as a peacock
quick as a flash
quiet as a mouse
rare as hen's teeth
safe as houses
sharp as a razor
sick as a dog (ill)
sick as a parrot (disappointed)
silent as the grave
sly/wily as a fox
smooth as silk
sober as a judge
straight as a die
stubborn as a mule
swift as an arrow
tall as a steeple
thick as thieves (friendly)
thick as two short planks (stupid)
tough as old boots
uncertain as the weather

PROVERBS

A proverb is a traditional saying that offers advice, wisdom, a truth, or a moral comment. Some of them have been in the English language for centuries. Some of them might be quite difficult to understand without a little historical context or explanation of unusual or archaic words, some are metaphorical like idioms, while others are more obvious. Some are overused and have become clichés (*see* pages 72–84). Sometimes the proverbs are so well known that people only need to repeat part of the proverb: 'When in Rome ...', 'Don't count your chickens ...', 'Every cloud ...'.

Absence makes the heart grow fonder
When the things and people that you love are not there you love them even more.

An apple a day keeps the doctor away
Eating healthily keeps you well.

The early bird catches the worm
Being the first/earliest person to do something can bring you the most benefits.

A bird in the hand is worth two in the bush
An opportunity that is actually within your grasp is much more valuable than several that you are merely dreaming of.

Don't bite the hand that feeds you
Don't be ungrateful to the person who looks after you or who is paying your wages.

Once bitten, twice shy
Having made a mistake once, you'll be more careful the next time.

You can't judge a book by its cover
What is on the outside might not relate to what is on the inside.

You cannot have your cake and eat it
You've consumed your cake, it's gone, you can't eat it again. Another way of saying 'you can't have it both ways'.

Curiosity killed the cat
Nosing into others' affairs will get you into trouble.

IDIOMS

When the cat's away the mice will play
    Without supervision we're all going to have a little fun!
Don't count your chickens until they are hatched
    Don't assume something to be true or possible until you have proof that it is so.
Every cloud has a silver lining
    Good and happy things can come from bad situations.
You can't teach an old dog new tricks
    It is nearly impossible to unlearn old habits and learn new ones.
Let sleeping dogs lie
    Don't instigate trouble when it can be avoided easily.
Fools rush in where angels fear to tread
    The inexperienced will tackle things that more experienced people will know to be fearful of.
A friend in need is a friend indeed
    Someone who is there for you in times of trouble is a true friend.
Never look a gift horse in the mouth
    Don't be critical of things that are given to you for free.
The darkest hour is that before the dawn
    Things often seem bleakest during the night when one cannot sleep.
Better late than never
    Better to do something eventually than not at all.
The leopard cannot change its spots
    What is intrinsic to a person cannot be changed.
Live and let live
    Don't judge people or interfere in their lives.
Look before you leap
    Don't act or make decisions till you know all the facts.
Love is blind
    When you are in love with someone you don't see their flaws.
Practise what you preach
    Behave in the way in which you would advise other people to behave.
When in Rome, do as the Romans do
    When abroad, or in unfamiliar surroundings, follow the local customs.

Proverbs

When the cat's away, the mice will play.

Better safe than sorry
 It is better to prepare in advance, or to double check something to prevent something going wrong, than to regret it later.

Slow and steady wins the race
 Slow but determined and careful progress can get you far (from Aesop's fable *The Tortoise and the Hare*).

A stitch in time saves nine
 If you stitch a tear when it happens you'll stop it getting worse and save yourself a lot of work. In other words, don't procrastinate!

Too many cooks spoil the broth
 Decisions made by big groups often have too many conflicting ideas and lack the vision of work achieved by just a few people.

One good turn deserves another
 If you do someone a favour then you deserve a favour in return.

Variety is the spice of life
 Change is what keeps life interesting.

CLICHÉS

That would be the last time they called Gerald a loose cannon.

CLICHÉS are expressions that have become so over-used, and so part of our everyday language, that people tend to use them without thinking. Some people feel that their use should be restricted as they regard them as making the language rather dull and predictable.

A BIT OF COLOUR

Clichés should be avoided in formal written English, however, they are a very common feature of spoken English and, indeed, an essential part of it. They can add interest and colour to what has been said, but they can be difficult for learners to become familiar with. Like other aspects of language learning, spoken and listening practice will aid in the learning of such phrases.

CLICHÉS FROM IDIOMS

A lot of clichés are idiomatic phrases. The previous chapter on idioms contains a lot of common clichés. The clichés which follow are also idiomatic:

between a rock and a hard place

Faced with two equally unpleasant or unacceptable choices.

> **John**: I'm going to stay with my parents at the end of the week but I can't decide whether to go by train or plane. I'm *between a rock and hard place*. The plane is quicker but it's very expensive while the train is much slower but it's much cheaper.
> **Sam**: I suppose it depends whether time or money matters most to you.

fall on your sword

Historically it meant to commit suicide in this way, but the modern cliché means to resign from a position of power or importance, often because you have been found committing some kind of crime or wrongdoing which would have resulted in your being fired anyway.

> **Bill**: Did you hear about Frank's father?
> **Sam**: Yes. He's been accused of tax fraud.
> **Bill**: He's a fairly senior politician. Will he be fired?
> **Sam**: I think he'll *fall on his sword*. Politicians usually do when something like that happens.

flavour of the month

A person or thing that is particularly popular at a particular time, although this is likely to last only for a short time.

> **Pat**: This toy was *flavour of the month* at Christmas and it was almost impossible to find it. Now none of the kids will play with it.
> **Rose**: I know. They've all moved on to something else.

CLICHÉS

the jury's still out
No decision has yet been reached or some issue has not been resolved.

>**Harry**: Has your family decided where to go on holiday yet?
>**Pete**: Every year we each vote on where we prefer – and *the jury's still out*. If the kids and I can't agree my wife gets to choose.

keep the wolf from the door
To earn just enough money to cover your basic needs, such as food. The "wolf" is a metaphor for poverty, illness or starvation. This phrase is often used in an exaggerated way for humorous effect. Also, you *wolf your food* when you are hungry!

>I earn just enough money to *keep the wolf from the door*. I certainly can't afford any luxuries.

>I grow vegetables and fruit in my small allotment, but there is barely enough food to *keep the wolf from the door*.

leave no stone unturned
To try by every means possible to find or do something.

>**Mary**: The police haven't found the missing paintings yet, have they?
>**Jane**: No, but the report in the local paper says that they're *leaving no stone unturned* in an effort to find them.
>**Mary**: They've certainly asked all the museum staff for information, but they've not made much progress.

a level playing field
A situation which is completely fair to everyone involved because none of the people taking part has any advantage over the others.

> **Ben**: Some people say that the college gives preference to wealthier students.
> **Sally**: The college authorities have denied that. They say that entrance to the college is *a level playing field*.

a loose cannon

A person who is apt to behave in a unpredictable or reckless fashion and cannot be relied upon not to cause trouble or do something embarrassing.

> **Sally**: Should we ask Sue to come clubbing with us?
> **Alice**: I don't think so. She can be such *a loose cannon*. Last time she had a bit too much to drink and started shouting at people.
> **Sally**: I'd forgotten about that. We'll definitely not ask her.

move the goalposts

To change the aims, conditions, rules, etc relating to a project after it is under way.

> **Jack**: Have you not started building the extension to your house yet?
> **Harry**: No. We haven't got planning permission yet. The officials keep *moving the goalposts*.
> **Jack**: That must be very annoying.

open the floodgates

To remove some form of control or restriction so that it makes it possible for a huge number of people or things to do something.

> **Ben**: The tennis club is getting a bit short of members. Do you think we should drop the minimum age qualification?
> **Joe**: The trouble is that might *open the floodgates*. We don't want a whole lot of young children joining.
> **Ben**: Well, we could keep the age restriction, but lower it.
> **Joe**: I suppose the committee could discuss that.

CLICHÉS

CLICHÉS FROM OVER-USED PHRASES

Not all clichés are idioms. Many of them are simply phrases that have become over-used. As with other clichés, in your written English these should be avoided, but in spoken English they can help to keep the conversation flowing. They can sum things up in a neat and quick way.

Some people do find clichés irritating to listen to in conversational English, so bear this in mind when using them. But you should at least be able to recognize them when you hear them and understand how they are used in the right context.

an accident waiting to happen

A situation which has always had the potential to be dangerous and which might have resulted in injury or tragedy at any time.

> **Will**: That old burnt-out house is *an accident waiting to happen*. It's falling to bits. They should pull it down.
> **Sam**: They certainly should. The local kids are all playing there.

the end of an era

When used correctly, the word era suggests something relatively important, or a considerable length of time. It is used of an important period of history or period of time that is characterized by a particular feature, event, person, etc like the Victorian era in Britain. As a modern cliché, **the end of an era** is often used to refer to a fairly unimportant event or one which lasted a relatively short time.

> **June**: It's the *end of an era*. Our next-door neighbours are moving house and we've lived next door to each other for six years.
> **Lucy**: You'll miss them.
> **June**: I certainly will.

a hidden agenda

A secret motive or reason behind some plan, action, etc.

Jim: I'm surprised that Mark is in favour of the new office block. We're all protesting against it.
Frank: Ah, but Mark has *a hidden agenda*. His father-in-law is the property developer behind the office scheme.
Jim: Well, that explains it.

it goes with the territory

This is said when a particular kind of problem or difficulty occurs in connection with a directly related situation.

Amy: Jim is so much more stressed since he got promoted at work.
Rose: A lot of senior managers suffer from stress. *It goes with the territory*.

it's the thought that counts

A comment or response made on the giving of a gift that has not cost very much. Sometimes the comment is made ironically to refer to a low-cost gift when a higher-priced gift would have been more appropriate.

Jenny: What did your son give you for your birthday?
Meg: He gave me this little book of poems.
Jenny: It certainly is very small.
Meg: But it's by my favourite poet and he spent ages looking for a copy. Besides, *it's the thought that counts*.

Amy: My brother had obviously forgotten all about my birthday. He arrived late last night with a bunch of flowers that he must have bought from the local garage. Still, *it's the thought that counts!*
Diane: You're lucky. My brother never remembers my birthday at all.

CLICHÉS

last but not least
Used when giving a list of names or items when there is no order of merit.

> **Jane**: I am so pleased to have won the championship. I want to thank my parents, my sister and brother, my cousin Tom and, *last but not least*, my friends Sue and Lucy for their continuing support.

a merciful release
Used to say that you think a person's death was a good thing for that person because it put an end to the suffering caused by a long, painful illness.

> **Mary**: My grandfather died last night.
> **Alice**: I'm sorry to hear that. You must be very sad.
> **Mary**: I am, but actually it was *a merciful release*. He had terminal cancer and was in terrible pain.

needs no introduction
Used by someone who is introducing a person to a group of people. In spite of saying this, they often go on to give an introduction, sometimes a long one!

> Our final speaker, Sally Brown, *needs no introduction*. She is one of our most talented actresses and many of you will recognize her from her TV appearances. However, she is particularly well known for her charitable work and she spends a great deal of her time helping to raise money for children's charities.

one hundred and ten per cent
Used to emphasize the great amount of effort used to do something. The maximum mathematical percentage is, in fact, one hundred per cent.

> **Bill**: What qualifications are you looking for in your new assistant?

Jack: I want someone with the right academic qualifications and with business experience. Most of all, I want someone who will give the job *one hundred and ten per cent*. I don't want someone who complains about having to work late or come in early.

only time will tell

A cliché suggesting that the outcome of something will not be known for quite a long time.

Sally: I hear Joe's still in hospital, but he's going to be all right, isn't he?
Meg: *Only time will tell*. He suffered severe head injuries in the accident.
Sally: We'll just have to hope for the best.

a race against time

Used to describe an extremely urgent situation.

Mike: The mine has collapsed and some of the miners are trapped underground. It's going to be *a race against time* to get them out.
Bob: And it's not going to be easy. There's a lot of rubble on top of the men.

and the rest is history

Used to indicate that no more need be said about a subject because the details are already well-known to the listeners.

Anne: Jack seems to give a great deal of money to local charities. Was he born in this area?
Mary: Yes, Jack was born of very poor parents in a slum down by the dock. He started work at a very young age doing just about anything. Then he set up his own clothing company and *the rest is history*.
Anne: Yes, and he's now a millionaire several times over and a very generous man.

CLICHÉS

these things happen
Used to remind someone who may have experienced some kind of misfortune that bad things happen to people all the time.

> **Dave**: Sam's been laid off. The firm he works for is closing down.
> **Bill**: That's a pity he's lost his job, but *these things happen*. And we *are* in the middle of a recession.

too numerous to mention
Used in more formal spoken contexts supposedly to mean that there are too many people or things involved to mention them all by name. In fact, the phrase is often used as an introduction to a list of the names.

> **Jack**: I would also like to thank the volunteers who helped to make the event such a great success. They are *too numerous to mention*, but many thanks to Sue, Amy, Anne, Diane, Lucy, Pat, Jim, Ben, Joe, John, Mark and Steve.

the usual suspects
Used to describe the people who are usually involved in something.

> 'Round up the usual suspects,' Casablanca, Warner Bros, 1942.

> **Jane**: Were there many people at Sally's barbecue?
> **Anne**: Not really. It was mostly just *the usual suspects*.

ARCHAIC CLICHÉS
Some of the phrases used as clichés have been in use for a long time and some of them are more formal, or even more archaic, than you would expect to find in the context in which they are being used. These include:

Archaic clichés

bow to the inevitable

To have to tolerate or accept a situation, however unpleasant, because you cannot avoid it.

Sue: It's dreadful that the landlord's not renewing our lease.
Sally: It is, but he's not going to change his mind. We'll just have to *bow to the inevitable*.
Sue: You're right. We'd better start looking for somewhere else to live.

by the same token

In the same way or for the same, or a similar, reason.

Ben: The students are furious that they're not allowed to leave the school at lunch time any more.
Jim: I'm sure they are, but, *by the same token*, the parents are mostly very pleased. It means the kids can't buy junk food at lunch time and they can't get into any trouble.

a daunting prospect

Something very difficult or alarming that you have to face or deal with.

Emma: We love the house and we'd like to buy it, but it needs a lot of work done. We'd have to do it ourselves. That's *a daunting prospect*.
Sally: It certainly is. Neither of you has ever done any of that kind of work before.

dulcet tones

Sweet or musical tones. This cliché is mostly used ironically.

Ken: We knew we were home when we heard our neighbour's *dulcet tones* shouting at her poor husband.
Pete: I bet you wanted to go away again immediately.

CLICHÉS

a moot point

Something that is not at all certain, but is doubtful or debatable. A moot court is a simulated legal case participated in by law students for practice.

> **Lily**: We're going for a meal to The Gourmet Scene tonight. We'd better make a reservation. It's still the best restaurant in town.
> **Rose**: That's *a moot point*. There are one or two others that are just as good now.

pale into insignificance

Used to indicate that something which seems very bad, or unfortunate does not seem quite so bad, etc when compared with something which is worse, etc.

> **Anne**: I was feeling very depressed yesterday. But my problems *paled into insignificance* compared with Sue's.
> **Sally**: What's wrong with Sue?
> **Anne**: She's just lost her job.

speculation is rife

A cliché indicating that a lot of people are forming opinions about something and spreading these around without knowing the facts of the situation.

> *Speculation is rife* that police have arrested a member of the murder victim's family. Up till now the police have neither confirmed nor denied that.

CLICHÉS AS 'FILLERS'

Some clichés add very little meaning to what is being said. They can be described as **fillers**, phrases which fill up space, rather than adding significantly to the meaning. You might notice that some people have certain expressions that they use on a very regular basis. Fillers give you thinking time in a conversation. Although such clichés can be annoying, they help to allow a conversation to flow along. Without them, conversation would be more stilted. Such phrases include:

at this moment in time

One of today's most overused clichés which really just means now or just now.

> **Mr Brown**: *At this moment in time* we have no plans to get rid of any staff.
> **Jim**: What about in the future?
> **Mr Brown**: We can't really say. It depends on the financial situation.

at the end of the day

Another of today's most irritating and overused clichés, used in much the same way as **when all is said and done** (*see* page 84) and often used almost meaninglessly.

> **Kim**: My sister can say what she likes, but *at the end of the day* it's my decision whether I go out with Tim or not.
> **Anne**: I think you are quite right.

if you ask me

In my opinion.

> **Joan**: *If you ask me*, Harry's thinking of leaving.
> **Lily**: What makes you think that?
> **Joan**: Well, he's always saying how bored he is and he's been looking at job vacancies in the local paper.

CLICHÉS

in all honesty

To be frank, to be honest.

> **Sue**: Shall we go for a drink after work?
> **Pat**: I'm too tired. *In all honesty*, I just want to go home to bed.

in point of fact

A rather meaningless phrase, rather like *in fact*.

> **Ken**: I wouldn't know John if I met him in the street. *In point of fact*, I've never met him.
> **Sam**: I must introduce you sometime.

mark my words

Pay attention to what I'm going to say.

> **Anne**: Sally and Tom have just got engaged.
> **Mary**: *Mark my words.* It won't last. Tom's been engaged at least three times before, but he's never been married.

the thing is

A filler used to pre-empt an explanation that you are about to make.

> **Amy**: I'm not sure whether I'll be able to play tennis with you tomorrow. *The thing is*, my parents are away and I have to walk their dog.
> **Rose**: Let's leave it till next week, then.

when all is said and done

This phrase is sometimes used to refer to the most important point of a situation, but it is often used almost meaninglessly.

> Hopefully, my son will realize that he needs to spend more time studying if he's to pass the exams. We're doing all we can to encourage him, but *when all is said and done* he is the only one that can do anything about it.

EVERYDAY EXPRESSIONS

THERE ARE many expressions that are used in everyday communication that are an essential part of spoken English. Some of these are **interjections**, short phrases often used to express some kind of emotion or reaction, such as excitement, surprise, annoyance, disgust, joy, pain, etc. They often end with an exclamation mark. Sometimes they consist of single words, sometimes they consist of short phrases or very short sentences, and sometimes they consist of just a sound.

In many cases they provide the links that help conversation to move along smoothly. A speaker simply cannot be considered fluent without having the ability to use these. Yet it can be difficult to acquire information about this feature of English. Dictionaries, especially the smaller ones, do not provide such information; and if the larger ones do include it, they do not necessarily do so in enough detail to be useful.

INTERJECTIONS

about time too!

You use this rather rude expression to indicate that someone has arrived late or has taken a long time to do something.

> **Locksmith**: That's all the locks on your doors and windows changed.
> **Mrs Smith**: *About time too!* I didn't think it would take that long.
> **Locksmith**: I worked as fast as I could. There are a lot of windows in this house.

ah!

You use this interjection in various ways. It can be used to express a variety of emotions such as pleasure, surprise or disagreement.

> **Bill**: *Ah!* Now I get the joke!
> **Sue**: That took you a while.

alas

This expression can be used to show that you are sad or sorry about something, but it is sometimes used ironically or humorously.

> **Bob**: I was going to offer to pay half the restaurant bill, but, *alas*, my brother paid it before I had a chance to offer.
> **Ken**: That's fair enough, isn't it? He's a wealthy lawyer and you're still a student.

ahem!

A sound like a short cough made by someone who is trying to attract attention, sometimes in a difficult or embarrassing situation.

Interjections

Ahem ... you call this dinner?

Jill: Let's ask John to organize the meeting. He's not working at the moment and has plenty of free time.
John: *Ahem!* I heard that and it's not true. I'm working freelance and I've got plenty to do.
Jill: Sorry, John! I didn't see you there.

all right (*see also* page 281)

You use this expression when you wish to say yes to something that someone has asked you.

Sue: I'm going shopping. Do you want to come?
Sally: *All right.* I need a new dress, anyway.

as a matter of fact

You can use this expression in two ways. You can use it to add a piece of interesting or surprising information to what has just been said.

Jack: I think that our sales figures are down.

EVERYDAY EXPRESSIONS

>**Will**: You're right, they are. *As a matter of fact*, I'm organizing a meeting for tomorrow to discuss a new marketing strategy.

You can also use this expression when you want to indicate that the truth about a situation is the opposite of what has just been stated.

>**Amy**: The air fare must have been very expensive.
>**Jill**: No. *As a matter of fact*, it was surprisingly cheap. I booked very early and got a very good deal.

believe it or not

You use this expression when you are mentioning something that is true, although very unlikely or surprising.

>**John**: Have you found a flat yet?
>**Mike**: Yes. *Believe it or not*, we've found quite a cheap one in the city centre. The owner's abroad and just wants someone to take care of it.
>**John**: That was lucky.

believe you me

You use this expression in order to stress the truth of what you are going to say or have said.

>**Jane**: *Believe you me*, Joe will regret not going to university.
>**Mark**: I think you're right, but he's really keen on this job he's been offered.
>**Jane**: That's just because it's quite well paid and he wants to get some money fast. It doesn't offer very good promotion prospects though.

Interjections

by all means

You use this expression when you are telling someone that you are happy for them to do something.

> **Sue**: Could I possibly leave work a bit earlier today? It's my father's sixtieth birthday and we're having a surprise party for him.
> **Boss**: *By all means*, go as early as you need to. Give your father my best wishes.

by the way

You use this expression when you mention something which is connected in some way, if sometimes indirectly, with what has just been said.

> **Jack**: I visited Sam yesterday. *By the way*, he's moving to a new flat.
> **Harry**: Can you give me his new address?
> **Jack**: I forgot to ask him for it. He'll probably let us know soon.

come on!

You say this expression to someone when you want them to hurry or to do something.

> **Joe**: *Come on*, Tom! We'll miss the plane!
> **Tom**: I'll be there in a minute. We've plenty of time to get to the airport.
> **Joe**: No we haven't. It's the rush hour!

come to think of it

You use this expression when you have just thought of or remembered something.

> **Joe**: Apparently, Ben's not very well. He's going to the hospital for some tests.

EVERYDAY EXPRESSIONS

> **George**: I'm sorry to hear that. *Come to think of it*, he's not been going to the gym recently, but I just thought he was busy. I didn't know he was ill.

don't bank on it

You use this expression when you want to advise someone not to rely on something happening.

> **Mary**: Sue said that she'd help me look after my sister's baby tomorrow. I was feeling a bit nervous about it.
> **Lily**: *Don't bank on it.* Sue doesn't always keep her promises.

don't say that!

You use this expression when someone says something that you do not wish to be true.

> **Pete**: I've had a quick look at your car and I think it might need a new engine.
> **John**: *Don't say that!* That'll cost a fortune!
> **Dan**: I could be wrong, but you'd better get a mechanic to look at it right away.

dream on!

You use this expression in an informal context to indicate to someone that something is not at all likely to happen.

> **Sue**: I'd love to have a flat overlooking the park.
> **Mark**: *Dream on!* The monthly rent would be more than your annual salary.

for goodness' sake

You use this expression when you are very annoyed or surprised.

> **Mother**: *For goodness' sake*, Alice, get up and get dressed. We've got guests coming to lunch.

Interjections

Alice: OK, I'm just getting up. There's plenty of time. It's not nearly lunch time yet.
Mother: But I need you to help me tidy the house.

good!

You use this expression to show that you approve of something or are pleased about something.

Sam: The builder said the work on the house is nearly finished. We can move in next week.
Jill: *Good!* I'm tired of living in this small flat.

good grief!

You use this expression to show great surprise or shock.

Sally: *Good grief!* It's been snowing! I've never known it to snow here before.
Meg: And look how deep it is too.

good heavens!

You use this expression when you are surprised about something. You can also use **Heavens!** In the same way.

Jane: *Good heavens!* There's our neighbour over there.
Jim: So it is. Imagine coming halfway across the world and meeting someone we know.

good question!

You use this expression in reply to a question to which it is difficult to find an answer.

Jack: I hear you're going to Jim's wedding in New Zealand next year. How're you going to afford it?
Sam: *Good question!* I'm hoping to get an evening job to earn some extra money. If not, I might get a loan.

EVERYDAY EXPRESSIONS

great!

You use this expression to indicate that you are very pleased about something.

> **Jim**: I've found us a flat near the town centre.
> **Sue**: *Great!* When do we move in? I can't wait to get out of here.

You can also use the expression ironically to indicate that you are not at all pleased about something, but are disappointed, upset, etc.

> **Harry**: The landlord's putting the rent up.
> **Joe**: *Great!* Where am I going to find the extra money? I've just taken out a loan on a car.

hang on!

You use this expression when you want to ask someone to wait for you.

> **Meg**: I'm just going to the library. I'll see you later.
> **Rose**: *Hang on!* I'll come with you. I've got some books to return.

You can also use it to ask someone to stop what they are doing or thinking.

> **Ben**: It must have been Jack who set fire to my garage. He wanted revenge. I'm going to call the police.
> **John**: *Hang on*, Ben. You've no proof it was Jack.

hardly!

You use this expression when something seems very unlikely in your opinion.

> **Kate**: Is Tom taking you to that new French restaurant?
> **Liz**: *Hardly!* He couldn't possibly afford it. It's very expensive.

having said that

You use this expression before you add something that makes what you have said less strong.

> **Bob**: Dave doesn't seem to treat his wife very well. *Having said that*, I don't think she's an easy person to get along with.
> **Mike**: No, she isn't. I think they deserve each other.

heaven knows!

You use this expression to emphasize that you do not know something or that it is difficult to find an answer to something.

> **Jill**: The landlord's told us to go.
> **Mary**: Where will you live?
> **Jill**: *Heaven knows!* Houses are difficult to find around here.

how's it going?

You use this expression informally when you ask someone how they are. It's another way of saying 'hello', *see* page 22.

> **Ken**: Hi, Jack *how's it going?*
> **Jack**: I'm OK. I'm a bit tired because I've been working very hard.

I can't tell you

You use this expression when you wish to emphasize what strong feelings you have about something.

> **Diane**: *I can't tell you* how much I appreciate your help. I simply couldn't have coped without it.
> **Jane**: I'm just glad I was able to help.

I can't think why

You use this expression to emphasize that you do not understand something at all.

EVERYDAY EXPRESSIONS

> **Ben**: Jim's decided to leave his job.
> **Joe**: Yes, I heard that, but *I can't think why*. It's well paid and it sounds interesting.
> **Ben**: He says he can't stand his new boss.

I could do without

You use this expression when you want to emphasize that you do not want to do something or have someone or something.

> **Sue**: *I could do without* working late tonight. I have guests coming for dinner.
> **Lucy**: I've got to work too and my parents are coming round to see the kids. They won't be pleased.

I dare say

You use this expression when you want to say that something is probable or likely.

> **Alice**: *I dare say* Jenny thinks that she's doing the right thing moving in with her parents, but I think she'll regret it. She doesn't get on with them very well.
> **Diane**: She doesn't think she's got a choice. Both her parents have got health problems.

If you don't mind my saying so

You use this expression when you are going to say something that criticizes someone in some way or is likely to annoy or upset them. It is also very common to hear the grammatically non-standard *If you don't mind me saying so* ... see **possessive case gerunds** page 184.

> **Mrs Smith**: *If you don't mind my saying so*, that child should be in bed by now.
> **Mrs Brown**: She usually goes to bed much earlier than this. She's fine though, thank you for your concern.

Interjections

I'm afraid

This expression does not, in this instance mean that you are feeling fear. You use it when you are apologizing or when you are politely telling someone something that may upset or annoy them.

Sam: Do you have two single rooms for one night?
Hotel receptionist: *I'm afraid* we don't have any vacancies. It's peak tourist season.

I hate to think

You use this expression when you want to stress how bad you consider a situation is or might be.

Ken: My wife wants us to go on a world cruise when I retire next year.
Bill: That'll be nice.
Ken: *I hate to think* what it will cost though.

I must say

You use this expression when you want to emphasize how you feel about something or what you think about something.

Jane: *I must say* that meal was absolutely delicious.
Bob: Yes, it was. And it wasn't expensive.

I suppose so

You use this expression when you say that you agree with someone, but rather reluctantly.

Ben: It's getting late and we're tired. I think we should leave the rest of this job until tomorrow.
Tom: *I suppose so*, though I wish we could have finished it tonight.
Ben: It's just taking longer than we thought.

EVERYDAY EXPRESSIONS

I thought as much

You use this expression when you find out that something that you suspected, turns out to be so.

> **Dan**: It's the cat next door that's been digging up our plants. I've just seen it doing it.
> **Anne**: *I thought as much*, but when I mentioned it to the owner she said the cat was never out at the front of the house.

I thought I'd

You use this expression when you want to tell someone what you are planning to do.

> **Rose**: What are you going to do on your day off?
> **Wendy**: *I thought I'd* go and look for a present for Jane.
> **Rose**: That's a good idea. I've got to find something as well.

I told you so

You use this expression when you are reminding someone that you had warned them that something bad or unfortunate would happen before it did.

> **Jim**: I wish I hadn't bought this cheap TV. The quality of the picture's terrible.
> **Mark**: *I told you so*. I said that you get what you pay for. You should've bought a better quality one.

it's beyond me

You use this expression when you want to stress that you do not understand something.

> **Will**: My daughter's on the phone again – and to her best friend. *It's beyond me* what they find to say to each other. They're at school together all day.
> **Ron**: My daughter's just the same. She's always on her mobile phone, either talking or texting.

it's just that

You use this expression when you are giving a reason or explanation for something.

> **Lucy**: It's a pity you can't go on holiday with us.
> **Amy**: Yes, I'm sorry, but it can't be helped. *It's just that* I can't get away from the office at that time of year. It's our busiest time.

it's no big deal

You use this expression to indicate that something is not at all important.

> **Jill**: Thanks very much for offering to help me move all these books.
> **Bob**: *It's no big deal!* I wasn't doing anything else anyway and it shouldn't take long.

I've no idea

You use this expression to emphasize that you do not know anything about something.

> **Diane**: We've run out of petrol. How far is it to the next town?
> **Jill**: *I've no idea*, but I'm pretty sure it's too far to walk, especially in these shoes.
> **Diane**: We'll just have to hope that someone comes along to help.
> **Jill**: And this looks like quite a quiet road.

I was wondering if/whether…?

You use this expression as a polite way of asking somebody something.

> **Sally**: *I was wondering if* I could borrow your laptop this evening for a couple of hours? My computer's being repaired.
> **Diane**: Sure! It's on the desk in my study.

EVERYDAY EXPRESSIONS

let me see

You use this expression when you are thinking about something. You can also say **let's see**.

> **Tourist**: Excuse me, do you know of a good seafood restaurant in this area?
> **Peter**: *Let me see*. There are two or three, but the one I like best is the one down on the shore. It's called the Crab Shell. It's very good.
> **Tourist**: Thanks very much.

listen

You often use this interjection when you want someone to pay attention or if you want to interrupt someone. It's usually not meant rudely and is often followed by **sorry**.

> **Salesman**: Hello, sir. Can I ask if you've ever thought about the doors and windows in your home and whether ...
> **Bill**: *Listen*. Sorry to stop you there. But I don't want to waste your time, I'm not interested in double glazing.

look!

You use this interjection when you want someone to pay attention to what you are going to say, often when you are annoyed.

> **Sam**: *Look!* I forgot I was supposed to be meeting you and I've said I'm sorry. What more do you expect me to do?
> **Amy**: You could say sorry as though you meant it.

look out!

You use this interjection to warn someone of possible danger.

> **George**: *Look out!* This road's very icy.
> **Lucy**: Thanks for the warning. I've already fallen on the ice today.

Interjections

me too

You use this expression when you wish to agree with someone or when you wish to be included in something.

Liz: I'm furious that they're pulling down that lovely building.
Anne: *Me too*. It's disgraceful. I'm thinking of organizing a protest.

never mind

You use this expression when you want to tell someone that something is not important.

Mary: I'm sorry I can't come to the meeting tonight. I promised to have dinner with my parents.
Jim: *Never mind*. I'll let you know what happens and you can come to the next one.

no chance!

You use this expression when you think that it is extremely unlikely that something will happen.

Jill: Do you think Tom and Sally will get back together?
Lucy: *No chance!* She said it's definitely over. She discovered he was cheating on her with her best friend.

no fear!

You use this expression in informal contexts to stress that you are definitely not going to do something or that something is not going to happen.

Mark: Will Jim really leave his job, do you think? He's always saying he will.
Will: *No fear!* He's far too well paid to do that.

EVERYDAY EXPRESSIONS

not on your life!

You use this expression when you want to stress that you are definitely not going to do something.

Bill: Are you going to help Bob move house tomorrow?
Sam: *Not on your life!* I'm exhausted after a week's hard work. I need a rest. And Bob never does anything to help other people.
Bill: That's true. I don't think I'll help him either.

not to worry/don't worry

You use this expression to show that you do not think that something is important.

Mary: I'm sorry I can't come to the cinema tonight. The boss's asked me to work late.
Jim: *Not to worry*. We can go some other time. I'll give you a ring.
Mary: Yes. Do that.

no way!

You use this expression to emphasize that you are not going to do something or that something is not likely to happen.

Sam: Are you going to apologize to Anne?
Will: *No way!* I didn't do anything wrong.

no wonder

You use this expression when you consider that something is not at all surprising or that it is to be expected.

Harry: Jack's really furious with me.
Will: *No wonder.* You borrowed his bike without asking him and then damaged it.

Interjections

oh dear!

You use this expression when you are disappointed, upset, worried, etc.

> **Kate**: *Oh dear!* We've just missed a bus. We'll have to wait an hour for the next one.
> **Lucy**: We might as well go and have some coffee. Where's the nearest café?

oops!

You use this expression when you drop something or nearly drop something, when you have made a mistake, or accidentally revealed a secret, etc.

> **Jane**: *Oops!* I've dropped a contact lens. Can anyone see it?
> **Jenny**: There it is, over there. I'll get it.

ouch!

You use this interjection when you feel a sudden pain.

> **Ben**: *Ouch!* I've been stung by a wasp.
> **Diane**: I'm going inside. I hate wasps.

You might also use *ouch* if someone has hurt your feelings.

> **Janice**: That dress does nothing for you.
> **Jenny**: *Ouch!* At least you're honest, I suppose.

ow!

You also use this interjection when you feel a sudden pain.

> **Jane**: *Ow!* That hurt my arm. Don't throw the ball so hard.
> **Jack**: Sorry, but you were supposed to catch it.

EVERYDAY EXPRESSIONS

phew!

This interjection can be used in several situations. You can use it to indicate that you are feeling tired or hot.

> *Phew!* That climb was much higher than I thought. I'm exhausted.

> *Phew!* I find this heat unbearable. I'm going inside.

You can also use it to indicate that you are feeling very relieved because something did not happen.

> *Phew!* I'm glad the teacher didn't ask me any questions about the play. I haven't read it yet.

quite right too!

You use this expression to emphasize how much you agree with something.

> **Jill**: I'm thinking of moving to a bigger house.
> **Alice**: *Quite right too!* You need more space.

rather you than me!

You use this expression to stress that you would certainly not want to be involved in something that someone else is going to do.

> **Tom**: Are you really going to swim in the sea at this time of year. *Rather you than me!* It will be freezing.
> **Jack**: I know, but the others are going to do it. I don't want to look like a coward.

really?

You say **really?** in response to something that you hear that surprises you or interests you very much.

> **Jill**: I bumped into Wendy. She's just got married.
> **Mary**: *Really?* That's a nice surprise.

Interjections

right you are

This British-English expression is quite an old-fashioned one, used when you agree to do as someone has suggested.

Jack: I'm going to be a bit late. I won't have time to come for a drink before the meal. I'll meet you at the restaurant.
Mike: *Right you are*, Jack. See you there.

roll on…!

You use this expression when you want something that you will find pleasant to happen very soon.

Jim: I'm so tired. I've been working late every day this week.
Sam: So have I. *Roll on* the weekend so we can get a rest!

same here

You use this expression to indicate that you share someone else's opinion, feelings, etc or that you are in a similar situation to theirs.

Anne: It seems to be taking me longer to get to work these days.
Jenny: *Same here*. The traffic's got much worse in the morning for some reason.

search me!

You use this expression when you want to stress that you do not know the answer to a question.

Joe: Why's the boss looking so angry?
Ben: *Search me!* He's been in a terrible mood all morning. He's losing his temper over the least thing.

EVERYDAY EXPRESSIONS

shh!

You use this expression to ask someone to be quiet or make less noise.

> **Molly**: *Shh!* I've just got the baby to sleep.
> **Mark**: Sorry. I hope we didn't wake her.

shoo!

You use this interjection to tell an animal or someone who is annoying you to go away.

> **Jack**: There's that cat from next door again. I'm going to try and get rid of it. *Shoo!*
> **Bill**: It'll just come back again. It seems to like your garden.
> **Jack**: It's just a nuisance and it makes such a mess.

some hope!

You use this expression to emphasize that you think that there is very little, or no, chance of something happening.

> **Diane**: Do you think Karen will go out with Bob?
> **Mary**: *Some hope!* She told me she thinks he's a nice guy but a terrible bore.

so what?

This expression is rather rude. You use it when you think that something someone has said is not relevant or important.

> **Sally**: You were a bit late getting to the students' meeting.
> **Pam**: *So what?* These meetings are a complete waste of time. I wish I hadn't bothered to go at all.

so what's new?

You use this expression in an informal context to stress that you do not think that something is at all surprising or unexpected.

> **Will**: My computer's crashed again.
> **Ken**: *So what's new?* It's always breaking down. You need to get a new one. That one's ancient!

Interjections

speaking of

You use this expression when you want to say something more about a person or thing that has just been mentioned.

> **Jane**: Sue won't be at work this week. She's on holiday.
> **Anne**: *Speaking of* holidays, are you still thinking of going to Australia this year?
> **Jane**: Yes. I'm going to visit my sister.

suit yourself!

You use this expression, rather rudely, to tell someone that they can do what they want: usually when they refuse to follow your advice.

> **Helen**: Jill's having a party tonight. Do you want to come with me?
> **Sally**: Sorry, I can't. I've an English essay to finish.
> **Helen**: *Suit yourself!* I'll get Anne to come, but it would do you good to have some fun for a change.

sure!

You use this expression when you mean *yes* or *yes certainly*.

> **Mike**: Are you going to work by car today?
> **Sam**: Yes. I'm just about to leave.
> **Mike**: Could you possibly give me a lift? My car won't start.
> **Sam**: *Sure!* Come round right away.

talk about …!

You say **talk about …** when you want to emphasize something.

> **Jane**: *Talk about* stinginess! Joe's just asked me for the money for the coffee he bought me yesterday.
> **Lucy**: That's typical of him!

EVERYDAY EXPRESSIONS

that's all I need!

You use this expression when a problem or difficulty arises when you are already having several other problems or difficulties to cope with.

Mark: *That's all I need!*
Bill: What's wrong?
Mark: My car won't start and the boss has just rung to say he needs me in the office right away. Before that I spilled coffee on my shirt and had to change it and I slipped on the stairs and hurt my ankle.

that's fine by me

You use this expression when you are indicating that you agree to do something which has been suggested.

Mike: The film starts very early. We could go to the cinema first and eat later.
Alice: *That's fine by me*. I'm not very hungry, anyway.

that's news to me

You use this expression when you hear about something that you did not know, often when you feel that you should have known about it earlier.

Ben: Apparently they're renovating our office.
Tom: *That's news to me!* Who told you?
Ben: The office manager.
Tom: Well, she should have told me as well. I've got a lot of stuff to move.

that's OK with me

You use this expression when you are indicating that you agree to something which has been suggested.

Sue: We're going to have to go by train. My car's broken

Interjections

down and they can't repair it till tomorrow.
Kate: *That's OK with me*. I love going by train and I sometimes get sick in a car.

that's too bad

You use this expression when you want to say that something is unfortunate.

Mark: The picnic's been cancelled because of the rain.
Jenny: *That's too bad*. The kids will be upset. They were really looking forward to it.

there's no doubt about it

You use this expression to emphasize that something is definitely true or certain.

Frank: I can't believe that Bob would steal money from the company. He seems such a nice guy.
Mike: It's very shocking, but *there's no doubt about it*. The police have got proof and he's confessed.

there you go/are

You use this expression when you are giving something to someone or have done something for them.

Customer: A kilo of red apples please.
Shopkeeper: *There you go*. A kilo of my very best apples. Enjoy.
Customer: Thank you.

though

You use this word at the end of a sentence when you want to make the previous statement less strong or less important.

Ken: I've got to work on Saturday. It's annoying because I'd made plans. I've got an extra two days off next week, *though*.

EVERYDAY EXPRESSIONS

>**John**: That's not too bad. It's good to get some time off during the week sometimes.

too true!

You use this expression when you want to stress how true you consider a statement to be or how much you agree with it.

>**Jane**: It's so cold in this office. They should really put the heating on.
>**Mary**: *Too true!* My hands are freezing. I can scarcely work my keyboard.

tut!/tut, tut!

You use this sound to show that you disapprove of something. It is often used humorously.

>**Mrs Brown**: *Tut!* Look at what those children are doing. They're disturbing everyone. You'd think their parents would stop them.
>**Mrs Smith**: They're not paying any attention to them. Some parents just don't care.

>**Bill**: *Tut, tut!* What are you doing here, Jenny? Aren't you meant to be at work?
>**Jenny**: No. I took the day off to come to the fair. How about you, Bill?
>**Bill**: I've just come for an hour. It's my lunch break.

ugh!

You use this expression to show that you dislike something very much or that it disgusts you.

>**Anne**: *Ugh!* This sauce has mushrooms in it. I hate them!
>**Jenny**: I think it's delicious.

Interjections

uh-huh

You make this sound when you are agreeing with someone or saying *yes*.

> **Harry**: Are you going to Pam's party tonight?
> **Sue**: *Uh-huh*, but I might be a bit late.

what about?

You use this expression when you are making a suggestion to someone about something.

> **Alex**: I've had a hard day at the office. I quite fancy going out.
> **Meg**: I do too. *What about* going to the cinema?
> **Alex**: Good idea! I'll see what's on.

what about it?/how about it?

You use this expression in an informal context when you are asking someone if they agree with a suggestion which you have made.

> **Lucy**: You can have my spare room for a month if you give some help with childcare. *What about it?*
> **Alice**: Yes, thanks. It will be great to have somewhere to stay until I can move into my new flat.

what did I tell you?

You use this expression when you have previously warned someone that something bad or unfortunate might happen and then it did happen.

> **Joan**: Sally's just found out that they are all losing their jobs at the factory.
> **Mark**: *What did I tell you?* I said there was something going on there.

EVERYDAY EXPRESSIONS

what if?

You use this expression when you want to mention something that might happen, especially something bad or unhelpful.

Tom: We have to change planes in London and we don't have much time.
Ken: *What if* we miss our connection?
Tom: We'll just have to hope that we don't.

what's more

You use this expression when you wish to add something to what you have just said, often something very important or relevant.

Jill: I'm not taking a holiday this year. I'm very busy at work and, *what's more*, I can't really afford to go away.
Sue: Neither can I. I've just spent a lot of money on the house.

what's the use?

You use this expression when you want to stress that doing or saying something will have no effect.

Harry: I should try to warn Sue that Bill's not to be trusted.
Wendy: *What's the use?* She wouldn't believe you. She's madly in love with him.
Harry: She's going to get hurt.
Wendy: Well, there's nothing we can do.

what's up?

You use this expression to find out if something bad or unfortunate has happened. You can add **with** to find out why someone is upset, etc.

Jack: The local shop's not open. *What's up?*
Sue: There was a break-in last night and the owner got injured.

Interjections

why don't …?

You use this expression to make suggestions.

> **Kate**: It's a glorious day. *Why don't* we go to the beach?
> **Meg**: Good idea. I'll go and put a picnic together.
> **Kate**: And I'll go and fill the car up with petrol.

wonders will never cease!

You use this expression when you want to express great surprise. It is often used ironically.

> **Mary**: *Wonders will never cease!* I actually found a parking place in the town centre.
> **Jane**: You were lucky! Parking there's getting more and more difficult.

wouldn't you know it?

You use this expression when something unexpected has happened and caused problems or difficulties for you. Sometimes the expression is *wouldn't you just know it?*

> **Ben**: *Wouldn't you know it?* I usually arrive early at the station and the train is usually late. Today I was slightly later and the train was early.
> **Joe**: Did you miss it?
> **Ben**: Yes, I did. The train was just leaving the platform as I got there.

you could always

You use this expression when you are making a suggestion to someone. Other personal pronouns such as *I*, *he*, *she*, etc or a noun can be used instead of *you*.

EVERYDAY EXPRESSIONS

> **Bill**: The last train leaves quite early in the evening, but *you could always* stay tonight with me and get the first train in the morning. It leaves very early.
> **Sam**: Thanks for the invitation. I think I might just do that.

you'll never guess!

You use this expression when you are about to tell someone something very surprising or exciting.

> **Sally**: *You'll never guess* who I've just seen!
> **Anne**: I can't think who. Why don't you tell me?
> **Sally**: It was Rob Brown.
> **Anne**: I thought he was in prison for fraud.
> **Sally**: He was, but he's out. Apparently, he was innocent all along.

you never know

You use this expression when you think that it is just possible that something might happen, although it is very unlikely.

> **Jim**: *You never know*. Mike might pass the English exam, although he's not very good at English and some of the questions were very difficult.
> **Dave**: I would be very surprised if he passed. He didn't do much studying for it.

yuck!

You use this expression to indicate that something tastes unpleasant or disgusting.

> **Mary**: *Yuck!* This soup has far too much salt in it.
> **Sally**: So it does. It's made me very thirsty.

SENTENCES

This was not what I meant when I said
'I like nice short sentences'.

A SENTENCE is a group of words that can stand alone and make sense. It is a combination of two grammatical units – the **subject** and the **predicate**. Sentences can be divided into two categories, **minor** or **irregular sentences**, and **major** or **regular sentences**. You can further categorize them into **commands**, **declarations**, **imperatives** and **questions**.

So, why do you need to know about all these different kinds of sentences? Knowing about them will help in your written and spoken, formal and informal English. Easily spotting such sentences will help you to recognize in which contexts they are correct and for what purpose they should be used.

SENTENCES

MINOR SENTENCES

Minor sentences lack some of the grammatical features that are often thought to be characteristic of a sentence. For example, a minor sentence might not have a **subject** and a **predicate**. Examples include:

> Oh, no!; This way; Help!; Too true!; What a nerve!

Minor sentences are particularly common in **spoken English**

SUBJECT

The **subject** of a sentence refers to what the sentence is about, often the **person** or **thing** that carries out the **action** of the **verb**. The **subject** usually gives a clear idea of what the sentence is about.

The subject can be a **noun**;
> *Dogs* need a lot of exercise.
> *Paris* is the capital of France.

a **noun phrase**;
> *A heatwave* has been forecast.
> *Several happy customers* have complimented you.

a **pronoun**;
> *They* were found innocent.
> *We* won the battle.

a **subordinate clause**;
> *Who she was* remained a mystery.
> *Why he left* has not yet been revealed.
> *What he says* is not true.

an **infinitive**;
> *To do* that would be unforgivable.
> *To get* there is going to be very difficult.
> *To marry* young is her main aim.

Simple sentences

PREDICATE

The **predicate** refers to the part of a **sentence** or **clause** that gives information about the **subject**. It is basically all the parts of a clause or sentence that are not contained in the subject. It can either be a single verb or a number of elements. The italicized text in the following sentences shows the predicate.

> The little girl *fell*.
> The tired old man *slept soundly*.
> The tired old man *slept like a log*.
> Jane *fainted*.
> Peter *was rich and powerful*.
> Children *screamed loudly*.
> The lights *went out all of a sudden*.
> They *are leaving at the end of next week*.
> The child *threw the red ball to the dog in the park*.

dialogue and in reported speech in written English. In the example below, all but the first sentence are minor sentences. The first one is a **major sentence**. Those in blue italic are minor sentences.

> **Aunt**: I hear you've got a place in college. *How marvellous! Well done!*
> **Sue**: *I know! What a relief!*

By their very nature, minor sentences tend to be short. In spoken English even major sentences tend to be quite short.

SIMPLE SENTENCES

Short sentences of the kind common in informal spoken English often contain only one **clause**. (A clause is a meaningful group of words which, like a sentence, contains a **subject** and a **predicate**, but, unlike a sentence it may not stand alone and make sense. See **Clauses** pages 129–30.) Sentences with only one clause are called **simple sentences**. A simple sentence is a sentence made

OBJECT

Very often the **predicate** contains an **object**. The **object** of a sentence is the part of a sentence that is acted upon or is affected by the verb. It usually, but not always, follows the verb to which it relates.

A **direct object** refers to the person or thing that is directly affected by the action described by the verb.

A **direct object** can be a **noun**;

> The girl hit the *ball*.

a **pronoun**;

> She hit *him*.

a **noun phrase**;

> He has bought *a large Victorian house*.

a **noun clause**;

> I know *what he means*.

An **indirect object** usually refers to the person who benefits from an action, often by receiving something:

> Her father sent *the school* a letter.

The school is the **indirect object** and *a letter* is the **direct object**.

An **indirect object** can be preceded by the words *to* or *for*:

> Her father sent *the school* a letter.

It could be rephrased as:

> Her father sent a letter to *the school*.

And in this case the direct object would come before the indirect object.

up of one **clause**, with a single **subject** and **predicate**. Simple sentences are particularly common in informal spoken English, as is the case in all of the sentences in the piece of dialogue that follows below:

Jack: Will you take the job?
Bob: I don't know. I might do. I'm not sure.
Jack: You'd better make up your mind soon. The boss wants to know by tomorrow.

The following are examples of **simple sentences**:

The boy laughed.
He enjoyed the trip.
We liked the play very much.
They gave me a present yesterday.

COMPOUND SENTENCES

Compound sentences contain more than one **clause**. The clauses in compound sentences are linked by a **coordinating conjunction** such as *and*, *but*, or *or*. The individual clauses tend to be quite short. In the example below, the third and last sentences of Anne's reply to Sally are compound sentences:

Sally: Are you OK, Anne? You look tired.
Anne: I *am* tired. I had to get to work early today. *I got up at 6 o'clock and caught the early bus. It was either that or get a lift from Dad, but that would have been a lot of trouble for him.*

Sometimes compound sentences consist of just two **main clauses**, sometimes more than two. These clauses are linked by a **coordinating conjunction**, such as *and*, *but* or *or*, and the sentences formed in this way are known as compound sentences.

The following are examples of compound sentences:

She loved the children and she looked after them well.

SENTENCES

He left on time but the bus was late.
She will mend the dress or buy a new one.
I was sorry for him but I could not help him and I felt bad about that.
She played well but her opponent played even better and she lost the match.

COMPLEX SENTENCES

Complex sentences are less common in spoken English. The clauses in complex sentences are linked by a subordinating conjunction. There are many of these including *because*, *since*, *while*, *if*, and *unless*.

When they occur, the clauses tend to be few in number and quite short. Note that in informal spoken English there is nothing like the variety of sentence structures that you find in written English. In the following piece of dialogue sentences two and three in Peter's reply to Mike are complex sentences. The first sentence in Mike's reply to Peter is also a complex sentence.

Mike: Did Joe stay long at the party?
Peter: I've no idea. *He was still there when Kate and I left. We left after the dancing started.* We both hate dancing.
Mike: *Joe would stay on if there was dancing.* He loves showing off on the dance floor.

Longer sentences are often **complex sentences**. In **complex sentences** at least one of the clauses is a **main clause** but one or more of the clauses is a **subordinate clause** (*see* page 129).

A subordinate clause is connected to the main clause by a **subordinating conjunction** such as *although*, *because*, *before*, *since*, *unless*, *when*, *while* and *why*. Often the main clause comes before the subordinate, but sometimes the subordinate clause is put first.

The following are examples of **complex sentences**:

She danced while he played.
I left when they arrived.
The book was still where we had left it.
She cannot go unless her mother gives her permission.
Because his car broke down he arrived late at the wedding.
Wherever he goes, she goes.
Since you left he has been sad.

TYPES OF SENTENCE-STATEMENTS

Statements, declarative sentences

Sentences in the forms of **statements** tend to be short, often very short, as in the following piece of dialogue. All the sentences in the next example are statements:

Mary: I'm so bored. There's nothing to do. My friends are all on holiday. I'm going back to bed.
Mother: You can't do that. It's the middle of the afternoon. You can help me with the shopping. I need to go to the supermarket.
Mary: Oh, all right. I'll just get ready.

Exclamatory sentences

An **exclamation** is a sentence which is used to express some kind of emotion or reaction, such as excitement, surprise, annoyance, etc and often ends with an **exclamation mark** (!). Exclamations are particularly common in spoken English. They may take the form of **minor sentences** and some may even take the form of short **major sentences**. Often they consist of a single word. In the following pieces of dialogue all the sentences ending in exclamation marks are exclamations:

Jill: *Ouch! That hurt!*
Sarah: What's wrong?

Jill: I put my hand on that gate and got a splinter in my finger.
Sarah: *How painful!* You need to get it out right away.
Jill: I know. I'm trying to. *There! It's out! Thank goodness! What a relief!*

Jane: *Wow! What a fantastic view!* I must take a picture.
Sam: *How typical of you!* Instead of just enjoying the view you rush for your camera.
Jane: *What nonsense!* I am enjoying the view. If I take a picture I can enjoy it later too.

Directives, commands, imperative sentences

A **directive**, also known as a **command**, is a sentence which instructs someone to do something. Often the directive is not at all dictatorial and may even be more of a suggestion, rather than a command. Directives often end in **exclamation marks**. There is usually no **subject** in a directive and the relevant verb is in its basic or **infinitive** form (*see* page 177). The verb is in the **imperative mood** (*see* page 185).

Directives are particularly common in spoken English and some directives begin with the word *let* or the word *do*. In the following piece of dialogue all the sentences ending in exclamation marks, except *Hello!* and *Thanks!*, are **directives**. So is Bill's *Let me call for help*.

Ben: *Help me! Get me out of here!*
Bill: Hello! Is there someone down there?
Ben: Yes. I fell over the cliff and my foot's stuck in a rock.
Bill: *Let me call for help.* There's no signal on my mobile. I'll try that cottage over there.
Ben: Thanks! *Do hurry, please!* My foot really hurts.
Bill: I'll be as quick as I can. *Stay calm!*

Some **exclamations** in spoken English take the same kind of structure as **questions** although they are not really seeking information. They are really only seeking the listener's agreement. These **exclamatory questions** end in an exclamation mark. In the following piece of dialogue the two sentences ending in an **exclamation mark** (in blue italic) are exclamatory questions.

> **Mrs Jones**: *Isn't this weather wonderful!*
> **Mrs Black**: It certainly is. *Doesn't it make you feel cheerful!*
> **Mrs Jones**: Yes. Everyone is so much happier when it's sunny.

Questions, interrogative sentences

Questions are sentences that seek information. They often involve an **auxiliary verb**, such as *be*, *have*, or *do*; or a **modal verb** such as *can*, *might*, *could*, *would*, *should*, etc. (See **auxiliary verbs** and **modal verbs** pages 191–3). There are various ways of asking questions.

Yes/No questions

Some questions simply seek the answer *yes* or *no* or an equivalent of these and are known as **yes/no questions**. The **subject** and the **verb** are usually inverted so that the verb comes first and the verb is often an **auxiliary** one, as in:

> *Was he* the driver of the car?
> *Can you* hear me?

Sometimes more information is given in reply in addition to just *yes* or *no*. The answer may be uncertain or express doubt as in *I don't know*, *I've no idea*, *maybe*, *probably*, *probably not*, *not really*, etc. It could express a certainty that is more emphatic than *yes*, such as *definitely*, *absolutely*, *without a doubt*, etc. See the three short pieces of dialogue on the next page:

SENTENCES

Anne: *Is Tom still here?*
Mary: No. He left about an hour ago.
Anne: *Did he say why?* I was meant to meet him here.
Mary: I've no idea. I wasn't talking to him.
Anne: *Was he with anyone?*
Mary: Yes. He was with Jill.

Bill: *Could I use your computer to send an email?*
Joe: Sure. Go ahead.
Bill: *Can you let me have your password?*
Joe: I'll type it in for you. *Will you be long?*
Bill: No, Just a few minutes.

Jackie: *Is Mrs Jones very badly injured?*
George: Yes, unfortunately. I've still to hear from the doctors about her condition though.
Jackie: *Do you think she needs an operation?*
George: I'm guessing she does, but exactly what is going to be happening isn't clear yet. We just have to hope that she improves soon.
Jackie: *Can I do anything to help?*
George: Not really, but thanks for offering.

Alternative questions

Alternative questions require a reply that refers to choices given in the sentence. They contain the **conjunction** *or*, as in

Are you looking for a flat *or* a house?
Are you taking the bus *or* the train?
Do you leave this week *or* next week?
Is Mike Sue's brother *or* her cousin?

Wh-questions

Wh-questions begin with a word starting with *wh–*, such as *where*, *when*, *what*, *who*, *which*, *whose* and *why*. Let's also include *how* in this little group – although *how*, obviously does not begin with

WHO AND WHOM

The word *whom* is now quite rare in informal spoken English. It is becoming quite rare even in more formal contexts. It has been replaced by *who* although, strictly speaking, *who* should be the **subject** of a **verb** and *whom* the **object** of a **verb** or **preposition**.

Nowadays it is considered quite acceptable to say:

Who are you talking to?
Who did they attack?

Formerly the correct versions of these would have been:

To whom are you talking?
Whom did they attack?

See also page 315.

wh–. **Wh-questions** are seeking specific information and they are very common in spoken English. The answers can take the form of full sentences, especially in more formal contexts, but in informal spoken English they are often just clauses, phrases, or one word. Some examples of **wh-questions** are given in the three pieces of dialogue below.

Harry: *Where does John live now?*
Bill: In a flat in the city centre.
Harry: *When did he move?*
Bill: About two years ago.
Harry: I thought he loved this village. *Why did he move?*
Bill: Because his firm transferred him to the city branch.

Jane: *Who is that over there?*
Sue: The new marketing manager.
Jane: *What's his name?*

SENTENCES

Sue: Jim.
Jane: *Which firm did he work for before?*
Sue: An IT firm in Canada.

Mark: *Whose car is that?*
John: It's Sam's.
Mark: *Why did he leave it here overnight?*
John: It won't start.
Mark: *How will he get it home?*
John: A friend who's a mechanic is coming to try and fix it.

Tag questions

Tag questions contain a **question tag** and are extremely common in spoken English but less so in written English. A question tag is a very short phrase at the end of a sentence just before the question mark, as in:

These books are for sale, *aren't they?*

The addition of such a tag turns what would have been a statement into a question to which the answer is either *yes* or *no*. Note that question tags often use the **contracted form** of the **verb**:

aren't you?
wouldn't they?
isn't he?

You usually add a **positive question tag** to a negative statement when you expect a negative answer such as *no*, as in:

You haven't seen Alice recently, *have you?*

You usually add a **negative question tag** to a positive statement when you expect a positive answer such as *yes*, as in:

It was a really boring lecture, *wasn't it?*

You can add a **positive question tag** to a positive statement when you want to show particular surprise, interest, anger, etc, as in:

Jane's over forty, *is she?* She looks much younger.

If you are asking someone to do something you sometimes add a question tag, as in:

Look after my luggage for a few minutes, *will you?*

This makes the request sound more polite and less like a command. In the **question tag** you use the same tense of the **auxiliary** or **modal verb** (*see* pages 191–3) as you do in the statement and follow this with the relevant **personal pronoun**. In the following short pieces of dialogue the short phrases in blue italic type are question tags.

You're still at university, *aren't you*, Jim?
This is where you grew up, *isn't it*, Lucy?
You don't have a car, *do you?*
Sue used to work with Jack, *didn't she?*
The smoking ban hadn't come into force then, *had it?*
I'm not late, *am I?*
We can park here, *can't we?*
That's not long enough, *is it?*
Yes, but we should wait for Alice, *shouldn't we?*

THE COMMA IN TAG QUESTIONS

A **comma** is used to separate a **question tag** from the rest of a sentence, as in the following sentences:

It's a beautiful day, *isn't it?*
You do love him, *don't you?*
He still smokes, *doesn't he?*
She's not happy, *is she?*
We can still go, *can't we?*
They've won again, *haven't they?*
It isn't raining again, *is it?*

SENTENCES

Rhetorical questions

The expression **rhetorical question** sounds as though it should be a feature of literary English, but, in fact, rhetorical questions are quite a common feature of spoken English.

Rhetorical questions have the structure of questions and, when written down, end with question marks, but they do not expect or require answers. Frequently they are just expressing a strong feeling or attitude on the part of the speaker. The questions in the piece of dialogue below are all rhetorical questions:

Jill: Sally's always telling me what to do. *Who does she think she is?* She's so bossy. I wonder if she's like that with other people.
Sarah: *Who knows?* I've never met her.
Jill: *Are you kidding me?* You met her at my wedding.
Sarah: *How do you expect me to remember that?* It was fifteen years ago.
Jill: *How could you forget?* She's the one that fell into the wedding cake.
Sarah: I remember now!

Questions by tone of voice

Intonation often plays an important part in spoken English. Questions can be asked by uttering words in a questioning tone of voice, by making your voice rise slightly at the end of the sentence. The questions in the two short pieces of dialogue both come into this category.

Tom: *Your son has already graduated?*
Sam: Yes. He starts his first job tomorrow.

Jill: I used mnemonics to learn those lists.
Pam: *Mnemonics?*
Jill: Yes. It's a way of helping you memorize things using other familiar associations.

ANSWERS

We've touched on **questions** that will give an **answer yes** or *no*. In order to keep a conversation going we need to ask questions that give a longer answer than *yes* or *no*. Those questions need to include **interrogative pronouns** (for **pronouns**, *see* page 138) *what*, *which*, *who(m)* and *whose*; and **wh- words** such as *where*, *when*, *how* and *why*, the **interrogative adverbs** (*see* pages 122, 169). Chatty Bryan and quiet Jon have just met at a business conference. With **yes or no** questions Jon's replies have the potential to be minimal and the conversation is hard-going:

> **Bryan:** Hi. I'm Bryan from Oak Designs. *Have you come far?*
> **Jon:** No.
> **Bryan**: *Are you enjoying the conference?*
> **Jon**: Yes.
> **Bryan:** *Will you be attending the marketing lecture?*
> **Jon**: No.
> **Bryan**: OK ... [Silence] ... Is there anything about the conference that you are particularly enjoying?
> **Jon:** Chatting to people.
> **Bryan**: I can see that.

When Bryan asks questions that use **interrogative pronouns** or **adverbs** Jon's answers are a little bit longer and Bryan has more possible ways to keep the conversation going.

> **Bryan:** Hi. I'm Bryan from Oak Designs. *What* do you think of the conference so far?
> **Jon**: I think it's very well run.
> **Bryan:** Me too. I like how organized they are. *Who* do you work for?
> **Jon:** I own the company – a plastics moulding company.
> **Bryan:** Really? *What's* it like to be your own boss?
> **Jon:** The hours are terrible.

SENTENCES

> **Bryan:** I suppose they must be. And the holidays! *Where are you based?*
> **Jon:** Just outside Birmingham.
> **Bryan:** I'm Birmingham-based too – it's a great town. I live in Solihull now. I moved there from Norwich. *Which lectures will you be attending?* I'm going to the discussion on marketing.
> **Jon:** I'm going to the talk on 3D printing that's on tomorrow.
> **Bryan:** Oh really, *why* is that?
> **Jon:** Well, it's not something that there is a huge demand for just now, but I think that will change soon. I need to find out more about it.

Echo answer

There is also a very emphatic way of answering a question that is mostly a formal response but could also occur in informal speech. It is called an **echo answer**. In an echo answer, the person answering the question uses a phrase that uses some, or even all, of the words used in the question. This very emphatic response could perhaps be used to answer a very challenging or aggressive question, or it might be used in a formal situation like a courtroom or a meeting where you want to be very clear about an answer. In the example on the next page, *yes* or *no* could have been used to answer the question but the speaker has chosen to say something in a more deliberate or pointed way, perhaps with spoken emphasis on the verb: I *did* go, I *was* there, I *will* be going.

> **Tom:** Don't tell me you went to that meeting all on your own?
> **Sam:** *Yes, I did go to the meeting all on my own.* Is that a problem?

> **Pam:** I don't think you really wanted to volunteer for that project.
> **Jill:** *Actually, I really did want to volunteer.* Why would you say that?

CLAUSES

A **clause**, like a **major sentence**, is a meaningful group of words containing a **subject** and **predicate**. However, unlike sentences, not all clauses can stand alone and make sense. There are two main types of clause, **main clauses** and **subordinate clauses**.

Main clause

A **main clause** is one that can stand alone and make sense. Main clauses are extremely common both in written and spoken English. Every major sentence has to have at least one such clause:

He was at the office when I arrived.
I knew why he left.

Some sentences consist of more than one main clause connected by a **coordinating conjunction** such as *and*, *but* or *or*. Such sentences are known as **compound sentences**.

The following sentences consist of two **main clauses**:

I was very angry and *he knew it*.
You can apologize or *you can leave immediately*.

The following sentences consist of more than two **main clauses**:

She was intelligent and *she was very efficient* but *she had no luck in finding a job*.
We can get a flight today or *we can get one next week*, but *we cannot get one at the weekend*.

Subordinate clause

On the other hand, a **subordinate clause**, which begins with one of a wide range of **conjunctions**, such as *because*, *if*, *unless*, *while*, *before*, or a **relative pronoun**, such as *who*, *which*, *that*, cannot usually stand alone and make sense. It relies on the **main clause** to help it make sense.

In **replies** in spoken English, however, subordinate clauses can

SENTENCES

be used alone. In the piece of dialogue given below, Jo's replies are subordinate clauses, yet they make perfect sense because the omitted main clauses are suggested by the content of Jim's questions:

Jim: When did Sam leave for the airport?
Jo: *When Mum got home.*
Jim: Why did he leave so early?
Jo: *To avoid the evening rush hour.*

Relative clauses

A **relative clause** is a **subordinate clause** that provides information about someone or something. It functions a bit like an adjective. It begins with a **relative pronoun** such as *who*, *which*, *that*, *when* and *where*.

In relative clauses in spoken English the relative pronoun is often omitted. In the first short piece of dialogue below, the word *that* has been omitted after the word *film*. In the second piece of dialogue the word *that* has been omitted after the word *car*.

Sam: It is the most boring film *I've ever seen*.
Tom: Heavens! It must have been really bad.

Jane: I've seen a gorgeous house *I want to buy when I retire*.
John: Have you? Where is it?

Comment clauses

A **comment clause** is a short clause inserted into a sentence. Comment clauses are particularly common in spoken English. Sometimes their function is to show the attitude of the speaker to what is being said. Sometimes the comment clause is simply a **filler** in the sentence without really adding anything much to the meaning.

Bill: What's your doctor like?

John: *To be fair to him*, he's a great doctor. It's just that he can be really rude.

Sue: Jill Smith's just been appointed head of our department, *I'm sorry to say*.
Jean: Oh no! Isn't she the one you don't get on with?

PHRASES

A **phrase** usually refers to a group of words that work together to form a grammatical unit, although, in fact, a phrase may consist of just one word.

Noun phrase

A **noun phrase**, also called a **nominal phrase**, is a group of related words in which the main word is a **noun**, and which functions like a noun in a sentence or clause. Thus, *a very long black car* is a noun phrase in which the main word is the noun *car*.

A noun phrase can either act as the **subject**, **object** or **complement** of the sentence or clause.

Verb phrase

A **verb phrase** is a group of words that contain a verb, such as:

> I *can't see past the tree*.
> I *went outside*.
> He *walked to the park*.

A **phrasal verb** is different, *see* pages 207–19.

Adjective phrase

An **adjective phrase**, also called an **adjectival phrase**, is a group of related words in which the main word is an adjective and which functions like an adjective in a sentence or clause. Thus, *rather too old* is an adjectival phrases in which the main word is the adjective *old*.

SENTENCES

Adverb phrase

An **adverb phrase**, also called an **adverbial phrase** or an **adverbial**, is a group of related words in which the main word is an adverb and which functions like an adverb in a sentence or clause. Thus, *extremely frequently* is an adverb phrase in which the main word is the adverb *frequently*.

Preposition phrase

A **preposition phrase**, also called a **prepositional phrase**, is a group of related words in which the main word is a preposition and which functions like a preposition in a sentence or clause. Thus *on the table* is a preposition phrase in which the main word is the preposition *on*.

Participial phrase

A **participial phrase** is a group of related words in which the main word is a participle of a verb, either a **present participle**, as in the blue italic type in the following sentence:

Talking frankly about her experiences as a holiday rep, she frequently bursts out laughing.

Or a **past participle**, as in the sentence:
Amused by the comedian, we laughed uproariously.

This is a type of phrase that is you are more likely to encounter in written English than spoken English.

The words in blue italic in the following sentences are **participial phrases**:

Bored by the party, she went home early.
Living by himself, he was frequently lonely.
Relieved by the news, he smiled broadly.
Laughing happily, she went off to celebrate.
Built by his father, the house had been designed by him.

NOUNS AND PRONOUNS

I think this is what is meant by an abstract noun ...

IN SPOKEN and written English, **nouns** have the function of representing people, places, things, and ideas. You might have learned that nouns are **naming words**. Nouns can refer to physical things and also to abstract concepts and ideas. A **pronoun** is a word that can replace a noun or noun phrase. In the following paragraphs we'll discuss all the different types of nouns and pronouns.

NOUNS AND PRONOUNS

UNCOUNTABLE NOUNS

An **uncountable noun**, also called an **uncount noun**, is a noun that cannot usually be preceded by the word *a* or *an* and does not usually exist in the plural form. This is the opposite of **countable noun**, also known as **count noun**, a noun that can be preceded by the word *a* or *an* and can exist in a plural form.

In **informal spoken** English some **uncountable nouns** can act like countable nouns and take a plural. In the first sentence below the word *tea* is the **uncount noun**, and in the second sentence *milk* is an **uncount noun** and *sugar* is acting as a **count noun**, although it is usually an **uncount noun**. In the second the word *wine* is acting as a **count noun**, although it is usually an **uncount noun**.

> I'll just make *some tea*. Milk and sugar?
> No milk and *two sugars* please.
> *Two white wines* and one red please.

PLURAL FORMS OF NOUN

Regular plurals

The **plural form** of most **nouns** in English is formed by simply adding **s** or sometimes **es**. So we have:

cat – cats	march – marches
bush – bushes	road – roads
church – churches	table – tables
girl – girls	umbrella – umbrellas
house – houses	window – windows

In nouns which end in **a consonant followed by y** the plural form ends in *–ies*, as in:

baby – babies	history – histories
berry – berries	lady – ladies
candy – candies	story – stories
fairy – fairies	variety – varieties

Irregular plurals

Some nouns, however, form **irregular plurals** and unfortunately there is no pattern to learn for these – they just have to be memorized.

Some nouns with irregular plurals change the **vowel sound** in the singular form. So we have:

>   foot – feet   man – men
>   goose – geese   tooth – teeth
>   woman – women   mouse – mice
>   louse – lice   dormouse – dormice

Some plural nouns have a **completely different form from the singular** as:

>   die – dice   person – people
>   penny – pence

Some nouns **ending in f or fe** change the *f* to a *v*, as:

>   calf – calves   scarf – scarves
>   elf – elves   shelf – shelves
>   half – halves   wife – wives
>   leaf – leaves   wolf – wolves

but, for example, *belief* simply adds *s* and becomes *beliefs* and *roof* usually becomes *roofs* in the plural form. The word *hoof* can be either *hoofs* or *hooves* in the plural form.

The plural form of some nouns is the **same as the singular form**. (bear in mind we are not talking about **non-count** nouns here):

>   deer   sheep   salmon (and other types of fish)
>   fish   shrimp   series (and other words ending in -ies)
>   offspring

Some nouns are *already plural in form* and so do not change:

>   trousers   jeans
>   scissors

COMMON AND PROPER NOUNS

A **common noun** refers to something of which there are many examples and so is very common. The following words are examples of **common nouns**:

> apple, band, car, city, country, day, dog, man, month, planet, religion, street.

A **proper noun**, on the other hand, refers to something in particular, of which there is only one example. Unlike common nouns, **proper nouns** begin with a capital letter. Thus, the following words are examples of **proper nouns**:

> Granny Smith (a variety of apple), Beatles (the name of pop group), Buddhism (all religions are proper nouns), Volkswagen (trade name of a make of car), London, Sweden, Wednesday, Doberman (a breed of dog), Jack (name of a man), March, Mars (name of a planet), Marxism (ideologies or philosophies named after a person are also proper nouns), Scotland Street (a placename).

CONCRETE AND ABSTRACT NOUNS

A **concrete noun** refers to something that you can touch. The following are examples of **concrete nouns**:

> bag, carpet, door, flower, grape, hand, lake, monkey, orange, pan, road, shoe, window.

An **abstract noun** refers to something that you cannot touch. In other words, it refers to a quality, concept or idea. The following are examples of **abstract nouns**.

> anger, beauty, Christianity (religions are proper nouns and also abstract nouns), courage, danger, existentialism, fear, greed, happiness, loyalty, Marxism, patriotism, wisdom, youth.

Foreign plural forms of nouns

Some nouns in English have a plural form that follows the spelling rules of the foreign language from which they are derived, as in *stimulus* (*stimuli*). The following are examples of such words with the plural form in their original foreign language:

alga – algae	curriculum – curricula
alumnus – alumni	datum – data
amoeba – amoebae	fungus – fungi
antenna – antennae	genus – genera
bacterium – bacteria	larva – larvae
bacillus – bacilli	memorandum – memoranda
cactus – cacti	phenomenon – phenomena
criterion – criteria	stimulus – stimuli

Some nouns ending in **o** take **–es** instead of **–s** to become **–oes**:

echo – echoes	embargo – embargoes
hero – heroes	torpedo – torpedoes
potato – potatoes	veto – vetoes

Some nouns ending in **–is** drop the **–is** and add **–es**:

axis – axes	hypothesis – hypotheses
analysis – analyses	neurosis – neuroses
basis – bases	oasis – oases
crisis – crises	paralysis – paralyses
diagnosis – diagnoses	parenthesis – parentheses
ellipsis – ellipses	thesis – theses
emphasis – emphases	

Some nouns ending in **–ix** drop the **–ix** and add **–ices**:

appendix – appendices	matrix – matrices
index – indices	

A (very) few nouns add **–en** to pluralize.

ox – oxen   brother – brothers or (religious brothers) brethren
child – children

NOUNS AND PRONOUNS

Plural forms of compound nouns

If the final word of a *compound noun* is a *countable noun*, the plural form of the countable noun is used when the plural form of the compound noun is formed. So *swimming pool* becomes *swimming pools* in the plural, *sports field* becomes *sports fields* and *letter-box* becomes *letter-boxes*.

When a *compound noun* consists of a *countable noun* and an *adverb* the plural form of the countable nouns is used to form the plural of the compound word, as *passer-by/passers-by* and *looker-on/lookers-on*.

Compound nouns which are formed from *phrasal verbs* usually have a plural form which ends in *s*, as in *cover-up/cover-ups* and *make-over/make-overs*.

Summary

In the following sentences the words in blue italic are all plural forms of nouns.

>She answered my *queries* politely.
>There are several car *ferries* that we could take to the island.
>They've had to build two new *stadiums* for the Olympic Games.
>The field was full of *sheep* and a sheep had escaped through the broken fence.
>He doesn't get along with either of his *sons-in-law*.
>The last few protest meetings had record *turnouts*.
>Police say that there have been a number of *break-ins* in the area.
>The professor was responsible for some major *breakthroughs* in the treatment of cancer.
>Very few *circuses* here now have live animal acts.
>We need two *loaves* of brown bread.

PRONOUNS

A *pronoun* is a word that takes the place of a *noun* or *noun phrase* in a sentence.

Personal pronoun

A **personal pronoun** is a pronoun that is used to refer back to someone or something that has already been mentioned.

One

Formerly, *one* used to be quite commonly used in formal contexts instead of the personal pronoun *you*, as in

> *One* must not smoke in this area.
> *One* has no means of knowing what will happen.

However, use of *one* is now becoming very rare because to modern ears it sounds rather affected and unnatural. *You* has become commonly used in all but the most formal contexts. *One* is certainly not used in spoken English unless the speaker is being deliberately formal, for humorous effect.

I and me

The **personal pronouns** *I* and *me* can give rise to some problems. If you follow the rules of grammar the pronoun *I* is used as the **subject** of a sentence and the pronoun *me* as the **object**, as in:

> *I* want to buy a house.
> He drove *me* there.
> They gave it to *me*.

Many people are confused about when to use *I* and *me*. It is often wrongly assumed that the use of the word *me* is less polite than that of the word *I*, and that *I* is always the correct form.

It is actually ungrammatical to say or write *It is me*. To be grammatically correct, you should say or write *It is I*. However, it is now considered to be quite acceptable in all but the most formal contexts to say or write *It is me*. It is certainly the common way of saying it in spoken English.

People also get confused about expressions such as *between you and me*. They say *between you and I* which is grammatically wrong and a common error. The following sentences illustrate the use of *I* and *me*:

NOUNS AND PRONOUNS

There is a strong resemblance between him and *me*.
He and *I* disagreed about what should be done.
He didn't damage the car – it was *me*.
May my wife and *I* join you?
She plays against *me* in the next round of the tournament.

THE DROPPED SUBJECT-PRONOUN

Sometimes in spoken and informal English people will miss out a **subject-pronoun**, especially if it refers to themselves. This can help the flow and rhythm of conversation.

Haven't seen you in a while.   [*I* haven't seen you in a while.]
Hope you're well.   [*I* hope you are well.]
See you later.   [*I'll/We'll* see you later.]

You could also use these in a piece of informal writing such as a letter to a friend. **Stressed subjects**, however, are not dropped, for example:

Meg: Who broke this vase?
Mary: *I* broke it.

Replying *Broke it* would sound odd – we need a **subject-pronoun** or **noun** here to tell us who broke the vase. Subjects that are part of questions can be dropped sometimes if the speaker is talking directly about you:

Going shopping?   [*Are you* going shopping?]
Not going fishing today? [*Are you* not going fishing today?]

Sentences with a subject that refers to another person would sound very odd without a subject-pronoun:

Is he going shopping?   [Correct]
Is going shopping?   [Wrong]

PERSONAL PRONOUNS AND SEXIST LANGUAGE

Not so long ago, there was a distinct male bias in grammar. Words where gender is not known or not referred to – such as student, pupil, entrant, employee, fan, and worker – were always accompanied by a **masculine personal pronoun** such as *he or him*, or **masculine determiner** *his*. This was formerly standard practice:

> If a student fails the exam twice, *he* will be asked to leave the course.
> A police officer must never lose *his* temper.
> If an applicant is accepted for the course *he* will receive an application form in the post.
> Should an applicant be unsuccessful we will let *him* know immediately.

He or she ... or they

In recent times, it has been acknowledged that this tendency to use the masculine pronoun is **sexist**. Such sentences are better rephrased to avoid such discrimination. One of the easiest ways of doing this is to rewrite the whole sentence in the **plural form**, as in:

> If students fail the exam twice *they* will be asked to leave the course.
> Police officers must never lose *their* tempers.
> If applicants are accepted for the course *they* will receive an application form in the post.
> Should applicants be unsuccessful we will let *them* know immediately.

Sometimes people try to get round the problem by using *he or she* or *he/she*, *his or her* or *his/her*.

> If a student fails the exam twice, *he or she* will be asked to leave the course.
> A police officer must never lose *his or her* temper.
> If an applicant is accepted for the course *he or she* will receive an application form in the post.
> Should an applicant be unsuccessful we will let *him or her* know immediately.

NOUNS AND PRONOUNS

Using *he or she*, etc can sound or appear rather clumsy. Instead, the common way of coping with this problem, especially in spoken English, is to use *they*, *their* or *them*.

This use was previously considered grammatically wrong – and still is considered to be so by many – but it is particularly common in spoken English, and it is becoming increasingly common in written English, even in textbooks because it solves the problem of there not being a gender-neutral third-person pronoun in the language. See the following examples:

> If a student fails the exam twice, *they* will be asked to leave the course.
> A police officer must never lose *their* temper.
> If an applicant is accepted for the course *they* will receive an application form in the post.
> Should an applicant be unsuccessful we will let *them* know immediately.

everyone, everybody and no-one

The same was true of the pronouns **everyone**, **everybody** and **no-one**. If you were acting in accordance with the correct rules of grammar you had to say or write:

> Delegates must make *their* own way to the station on the morning of the trip and everyone has to bring *his* own lunch.

Now you can write, without committing a grammatical sin:

> ... everyone has to bring *their* own lunch.

Of course there are still many people who would never dream of going against grammar rules in this way. There is the argument though that changing a grammar rule (that everyone breaks anyway) and using *their*, *they* and *them* to refer to **singular genderless nouns** in informal English, is preferable to saying or writing something that could be deemed sexist.

ADJECTIVES

I want a fat-free, gluten-free, nut-free, sugar-free, dairy-free, vegetarian dish on a small, blue china plate. I'm not picky, I'm specific.

AN ADJECTIVE is a word that describes or gives more information about nouns or pronouns. An adjective is said to **qualify** a noun or pronoun because it limits the word it describes in some way by making it more specific.

So, qualifying the word *book* with the adjective *red* means that we know that we are concentrating on a *red book* and that we can forget about books of any other colour. Similarly, qualifying the word *car* with the word *large* means that we know that we are concentrating on a *large car* and that we can forget about cars of another size.

ADJECTIVES

Adjectives usually tell us something about the colour, size, quantity, quality or classification of a noun or pronoun.

In the following sentences the words in blue italic are adjectives:

> She wore a *white* dress.
> It was a *tiny* dog.
> They had *five* children.
> They were *sad* people.
> It was a *Victorian* house.

GRADABLE AND NON-GRADABLE ADJECTIVES

Gradable adjectives

Most adjectives are **gradable adjectives.** You'll also hear them called **qualitative adjectives**. This means that they refer to qualities that can vary in some way. It's perhaps easier to show this using examples than to describe. In the following sentences the words in blue italic are **gradable adjectives**:

> It was a *bright* shade of red.
> We were *happy*.
> It was a *hot* day.

VERY UNIQUE

A common error with the **non-gradable adjective** *unique* is to pair it with an **adverb of degree**:

> It was a *very unique* experience.

Unique means 'one of a kind' and so, strictly speaking, it is incorrect to talk as if you can have degrees of uniqueness, though you *will* hear 'very unique' said by fluent English speakers. It is not appropriate to say *very wool* or *very plastic*, or *very metal*. A thing either has those qualities or not, it can't have degrees of that quality.

Gradable adjectives can take a **comparative** and a **superlative** form. We'll go into this more later (*see* pages 152–4), but here is an example of the comparative and superlative forms of *small*.

> Bobby drove a *small* car. **[Gradable adjective]**
> Betty drove a *smaller* car. **[Comparative form]**
> Becky had the very *smallest* car of all. **[Superlative form]**

Gradable adjectives can be accompanied by an **adverb of degree** such as *very*.

Non-gradable adjectives

Some adjectives that do not take a **comparative** and **superlative** form, and cannot be modified by an **adverb of degree**, are called **non-gradable** or **classifying adjectives**:

> There was a *metal* fence round the garden.
> It was a *unique* experience.
> They need a *financial* system.
> The country has an *agricultural* economy.
> This is not a *medical* problem.
> This is an *urban* issue.
> We have *annual* meetings.

These adjectives identify the particular class that something belongs to. For example, if you take the noun *pain*, there are various kinds or classes of pain such as *mental pain*, *physical pain* and *emotional pain*. The adjectives *mental*, *physical* and *emotional* are all **classifying** adjectives.

Sometimes, confusion arises because some adjectives have both **gradable** and **non-gradable** definitions. The following words have a **measurable** (**gradable**) definition and also a different **unmeasurable** (**non-gradable**) definition, e.g.:

> I was an *emotional* wreck. **[Non-gradable]**
> Billy is a *very emotional* person and cries easily. **[Gradable]**

> Our electoral system is a *democratic* one. **[Non-gradable]**
> It was a *very democratic* process. **[Gradable]**

ADJECTIVES

> I work for the *Foreign* Office. **[Non-gradable]**
> The design looked *slightly foreign*. **[Gradable]**
>
> That is a *wooden* fence. **[Non-gradable]**
> He is a *very wooden* actor. **[Gradable]**
>
> I hate eating with a *plastic* spoon. **[Non-gradable]**
> Her heavy stage make-up makes her *slightly plastic* looking. **[Gradable]**

POSITION

Attributive adjectives

Attributive adjectives are placed immediately **before** the nouns which they qualify. In the following sentences the words in blue italic are attributive adjectives:

> The *blue* dress suited her very well.
> They lived in a *huge* house.
> We lived there for *six* years.
> They sell *delicious* cakes.

Post-modifiers

Adjectives which are **post-modifiers** (also known as **post-positives** or **postnominal**) go immediately **after** the noun which they qualify. This is comparatively unusual in English, though it is the norm in languages such as French and Spanish. Words that are used in this way can often be quite archaic or literary words, or words that are used in specific areas such as the military, royalty, religion or the law. Words that are borrowed from French can be used **post-positively**. In the following sentences the words in blue italic are post-modifiers:

> The president-*elect* takes over the presidency this week.
> The soldier is to appear before a court *martial*.
> They slept two *abreast*.
> Charles is the heir-*apparent*.
> There was food *aplenty* at the buffet.
> He is a chef *extraordinaire*.

ATTRIBUTIVE POSITION

Some **adjectives** are found only in the **attributive** position, meaning they come before the noun. The italicized words in the following list are examples of these:

> my *former* boss
> her *chief* reason for being here
> his *sheer* folly in doing that
> the *utter* beauty of the scene
> in a *commanding* lead
> the *searing* heat
> a *thankless* task
> a *fateful* meeting.

Some **pronouns** in English – *anything*, *anyone*, *anybody*, *everything*, *everyone*, *everybody*, *something*, *someone*, *somebody*, *nothing*, *no-one*, *nobody* – are always post-modified.

> Is there *anyone stronger* around who can lift this box?
> I wish I could find *something larger* that would fit me.
> The hotel didn't supply us with *anything luxurious*.
> Is there *no-one qualified* to teach this course?
> Is *anyone alive* down there?

PREDICATIVE ADJECTIVES

Predicative adjectives are joined to their relevant **nouns** by a linking **verb**. They are so called because they help to form the **predicate** (*see* page 115) of a **sentence** (*see* page 113). They typically come after the nouns they modify. They are shown, with linking verbs, in the text in blue italic below:

> The curtains in the bedroom *were blue*.
> The dog *was huge*.
> We *were hungry*.
> The result *is still uncertain*.

ADJECTIVES

Some adjectives are followed by a **preposition** such as *to*, *of* or *with*. In the following sentences the words in blue italic form a predicative adjective plus preposition:

> She is *allergic to* eggs.
> He is *afraid of* his boss.
> The house is *devoid of* charm.
> The task was *fraught with* danger.
> She is *reliant on* her parents.
> She is *good at* tennis.

See pages 220–60 for more on **prepositions** and the words that go with them.

COLOUR ADJECTIVES

Colour adjectives identify the colour of something, as in *black*, *red*, *yellow*, *purple* and *brown*.

In order to give a more precise description of a colour you can precede the colour adjective with a word such as *dark*, *pale*, *bright*, *light*, *deep*. The words in blue italic in the following sentences are examples of this:

> She has *light brown* hair.
> He wore a *dark blue* shirt.
> It was a *bright green* hat.
> She wants a *deep purple* dress.

If you wish to be less precise about the colour of something you can add the suffix *–ish* to the relevant colour, as in *greenish*, *yellowish*.

EMPHATIC ADJECTIVES

Emphatic adjectives are adjectives which you place in front of a noun to emphasize your feelings about something or to emphasize the degree of something, as in *absolute*, *pure*. In the following sentences the words in blue italic are emphatic adjectives:

The play was an *utter* disaster.
The film was *pure* magic.
He is an *utter* sweetheart.
The whole thing was a *positive* delight.
The campaign was a *total* success.

ORDER OF ADJECTIVES

If several **adjectives** are used to qualify a **noun** they tend to be placed in a certain order.

The usual order is:

- adjectives relating to **qualities** – such as *pretty*, *bright*, *happy*, *hot*
- adjectives relating to **size** – such as *little*, *large*, *small*, *tiny*, *enormous*
- **verb participles** used as adjectives – such as *exciting*, *depressing*, *broken*, *disappointed*, *worried*
- adjectives relating to **colour** – such as *orange*, *blue*, *green*, *red*, *white*
- adjectives relating to **nationality or region** – such as *French*, *German*, *British*, *American* or *northern*
- adjectives relating to **classification** – such as *wooden*, *Victorian*, followed by adjectives relating to purpose or use such as *dining table*.

The following sentences show the usual sequence of adjectives:
   They live in a *little white* house.
   She wore a *beautiful, short, black* dress.
   There was a *large, deep, circular pond* in the garden.
   The roses were growing in the *small, enchanting Italian country* garden.
   They lived in an *ugly, depressing city* suburb.
   They sat round a *large, polished, mahogany dining* table.

COORDINATE AND CUMULATIVE ADJECTIVES

We are told that in a list of adjectives we should put **commas** between **coordinate adjectives**, but not between **cumulative** adjectives. However, it can be tricky telling them apart.

Coordinate adjectives separately modify a noun. You can rearrange them and it still sounds fine.

> The skirt was made of *grey*, *striped*, *coarse* material.
> The skirt was made of *coarse*, *grey*, *striped* material.

Also, if you can put *and* in between adjectives and it still sounds OK, then these are coordinate adjectives.

> The skirt was made of *coarse* and *grey* and *striped* material.

A **cumulative adjective** is very important to a noun's meaning and so you can't change its position. It has to precede the noun.

> They sat round a *mahogany dining* table. [Correct]
> They sat round a *dining mahogany* table. [Wrong]
> They sat round a *mahogany and dining* table. [Wrong]

Even if the cumulative adjective appears in a list with coordinate adjectives it doesn't need a comma.

> I need to see *cold hard* cash before I'll part with my car. [Cumulative]
> She loved her *new cotton* trousers. [Cumulative]
> It was a *rainy*, *windy* winter night. [Coordinate]
> A *dusty*, *cold*, *damp*, *abandoned* house. [Coordinate]
> He's a *tired*, *hungry*, *grumpy* baby. [Coordinate]

INTERROGATIVE ADJECTIVES

The adjectives *which* and *what* are known as **interrogative adjectives**. They are used to ask questions about the nouns which they qualify. In the following sentences the words in blue italic are interrogative adjectives:

Which book would you like to borrow?
What school did you go to?
Which dress did you choose in the end?
What restaurant have they gone to?

WHICH OR WHAT?

Sometimes (as in the above examples) it is OK to swap *what* for *which* and it does not create a sentence that is incorrect:

Which book would you prefer; the mystery or the romance?
What book would you prefer; the mystery or the romance?

However, swapping *which* for *what* doesn't always work:

What are you looking for? **[Correct]**
Which are you looking for? **[Wrong]**

Which are you looking for? is only correct if we're responding to being presented with a choice.

Customer: Do you sell wood, tile or vinyl flooring?
Shop assistant: Well, *which* [kind] *are you looking for?*

COMPOUND ADJECTIVES

Compound adjectives are made up of two or more words, usually separated by a hyphen. In the following list the words in blue italic are compound adjectives:

a *grey-haired* man
a *black-and-white* cat
an *air-conditioned* office
a *kind-hearted* woman
a *first-class* hotel.

ADJECTIVES

ADJECTIVES USED AS NOUNS

Sometimes adjectives can be used as **nouns**, especially when they are preceded by the definite article. In the following sentences the words in blue italic are adjectives used as nouns. It is sometimes considered **offensive** to use this construction, such as *the disabled*, as it can sound as though you are just lumping people together rather than considering them as individuals:

> There are few opportunities for *the unemployed* around here.
> *The poor* seem to keep getting poorer.
> *The old* are often lonely.

Sometimes **colour adjectives** function as nouns without the definite or indefinite article:

> *Yellow* is meant to make people feel more optimistic.
> *Blue* is her favourite colour.
> He always wears *black*.

ADJECTIVE OR ADVERB?

Some words can be used both as **adjectives** and **adverbs**. Which part of speech they are is obvious from the context in which they appear. The word *early* is an **adjective** in the first of the following sentences and an **adverb** in the second.

> We caught the *early* train.
> The train left *early* and we missed it.

COMPARATIVE FORMS OF ADJECTIVES

Many adjectives have a **comparative form** used to indicate that something has more of a quality than something else. It is mostly qualitative adjectives that take comparative forms, although a few colour adjectives can also do so.

Some adjectives add *–er* to the absolute form to form their comparative form such as *braver* and *louder*. Some other adjectives are preceded by the word *more* to form their comparative form such as *more beautiful* and *more suitable*.

Comparative forms of adjectives

Comparative and number of syllables

Which is the correct form of the comparative to use is often largely a matter of length. Adjectives which consist of one syllable, such as *loud*, usually add *–er* to make *louder*.

When a one-syllable adjective ends in a single vowel followed by a single consonant, the consonant is doubled before the *-er* ending is added, as in *big*, *bigger*.

Some adjectives which consist of two syllables form their comparative by adding *–er*. This is especially true of adjectives which end in *–y*, such as *merry/merrier*, but it is also true of some other two-syllable adjectives such as *clever/cleverer* and *quiet/quieter*. In other cases, such as *famous* or *careful*, the comparative form is formed with *more*, as in *more famous*, *more careful*.

In some cases the comparative of a two-syllable adjective can be formed either by adding *–er* to the positive or absolute form or by preceding this with *more*. Thus the word *gentle* can have the comparative form *gentler* or *more gentle* and the word *pleasant* can have the comparative form *pleasanter* or *more pleasant*.

Adjectives which consist of three or more syllables usually have comparative forms using *more*, such as *more dangerous*. Some three-syllable adjectives which begin with the prefix *–un* can form their comparative forms by adding *–er*, such as *unhappy/unhappier*, *unlucky/unluckier*.

The above are regular ways of forming the comparative of adjectives. The following words in blue italic are examples of these:

It was a *brighter* day.
He is *younger* than his wife.
The child is *quieter* than her brother.
She gets *lovelier* each year.
This essay is far *more interesting*.
This is a *politer/more polite* way of saying the same thing.
This is certainly a *pleasanter/more pleasant* way of spending the day.
That is the *likelier/more likely* solution.
That is an even *more ridiculous* idea.

ADJECTIVES

Irregular comparatives

The adjectives *good* and *bad* have the irregular comparative forms *better* and *worse*, as in *a good day/a better day* and *a bad experience/a worse experience*.

No comparative form

Some adjectives have only an absolute form and do not normally have a comparative (or superlative) form. These include *mere*, *perfect*, *real*, *right*, *unique* and *utter*.

SUPERLATIVE FORMS

You can also describe something by saying that something has more of a quality than anything else of its kind. In order to do this you use the **superlative form** of an adjective. The regular superlative form of an adjective is formed in the same way as the comparative form, except that the comparative ending *–er* is replaced by the superlative ending *–est*, and the word *more*, which is used to form the comparative, is replaced by the word *most*. Thus, in the following sentences the words in blue italic are examples of the superlative form of adjectives:

> I want the *largest* size.
> It was the *longest* journey I've ever taken.
> It was the *most disappointing* news that I had had all year.
> This is the *quietest* room in the hotel.
> He is certainly the *cleverest* student.
> The rose is the *loveliest* flower.

Irregular superlatives

The adjectives *good* and *bad* have the irregular superlative forms *best* and *worst*, as in *a good day/the best day* and *a bad experience/the worst experience*.

No superlative form

Some adjectives have only an absolute form and do not normally have a superlative (or comparative) form. These include *automatic*, *authentic*, *closed*, *metal*, and *wrong*.

DETERMINERS

OK, I need to determine your opinion, her opinion, his opinion – maybe even my opinion – on what words are the possessive determiners.

A DETERMINER is a word that is used in front of a noun or pronoun to give some information about it. Formerly, **determiners** were classified as **adjectives**. However, unlike adjectives, determiners do not, strictly speaking, 'describe' a noun or pronoun.

REFERRING AND QUANTIFYING

Determiners refer to things and they quantify things. If a determiner refers to something it shows you who or what is being discussed: *the cup*, *my home*, *that chair*. And if a determiner quantifies something it tells you how much or how many of something is being discussed: *some*

DETERMINERS

coffee, *forty stones*, *less water*. They also have a few more qualities. Let's look at the **articles** first. They are among the most commonly used words in the English language.

DEFINITE AND INDEFINITE ARTICLES

The **definite** and **indefinite articles** are often categorized as **determiners**.

Definite article

The **definite article** is *the* and it can be used in various ways.

Referring back

It can be used in a sentence to refer back to a person or thing that has already been mentioned or identified.
In the following examples *the* is used in this way:

> Mrs Brown gave birth to a boy. *The* boy was called John.
> I was asked to choose a restaurant and *the* restaurant I chose was The Olive Tree.
> Father bought a new dog. *The* dog is a Labrador.

The only one of its kind

The **definite article** can also be used to identify someone or something as the only one of its kind. In the following sentences *the* is used in this way:

> He is reading *the* Bible.
> Tourists often visit *the* Tower of London.
> She has been declared *the* new prime minister of the UK.

A whole class or group

The **definite article** is used to refer to a whole class or group of things or people. In the following sentences *the* is used in this way:

> Lions belong to *the* big cats.
> Because of a long-lasting family feud *the* Smiths did not speak to *the* Simpsons at John and Jane's wedding.
> Efficiency is meant to be a national trait of *the* Germans.

A unique quality

Less commonly, the **definite article** can be used to indicate the unique quality of someone or something. In this context *the* is emphasized and is pronounced *thee*. In written form it will often be italicized. In the following sentences *the* is used in this way:

> In the sixties it was *the* restaurant to go to in London.
> It is currently *the* city venue for fashionable wedding receptions.
> The musical is *the* show to see this Christmas.

Indefinite article

The form of the **indefinite article** is either *a* or *an*. *A* goes with words that begin with a **consonant sound** such as *a desk, a plant, a tiger, a zoo, a yellow top*. *An* goes with words that begin with an initial vowel sound such as *an army, an entry, an elephant, an hour, an object*.

The **indefinite article** can be used in various ways.

One

It can be used in the same way as the adjective *one*. In the following sentences *a/an* is used in this way:

> The town is exactly *a* mile away.
> We waited *an* hour for the bus to come.
> *A* year ago we were happy, but things have changed.

A specific person or thing

The **indefinite article** is also used to refer to or single out a specific person or thing. In the following sentences *a/an* is used in this way:

> Jim married *a* girl called Mary from the next village.
> The family had *a* black cat called Sooty.
> Sue is going out with *a* young man called Tom.

DETERMINERS

A OR AN?

The **indefinite article** has the forms **a** and **an**. Although these words are very small they can cause a great deal of confusion. The form **a** is used before words or abbreviations that are pronounced with an initial consonant sound, as in *a box*; *a garden*; *a UFO*; and *a wall*.

The form **an** is used before words that begin with an initial vowel sound, as in *an apple*; *an igloo*; *an IOU* and *an ostrich*. Remember that it is the sound of the initial letter and not the spelling that determines whether the indefinite article should be **a** or **an**.

The form **a** is used before words beginning with the letter **u** when these are pronounced as though they began with the consonant **y**, as in *a unit* and *a union*.

The form **an** is used before words beginning with the letter **h** where this is not pronounced, as in *an heir* and *an hour*. Formerly the form **an** was commonly used before words beginning with the **h** sound which began with an unstressed syllable, as in *an historic victory* and *an hotel*, but in modern usage the form **a** is used in such cases, as in *a historic victory* and *a hotel*.

An indefinite meaning

The **indefinite article** is also used with an indefinite meaning, in the same way that *any* is. In the following sentence *a/an* is used in this way:

> He was as big as *a* house.
> *An* island is a piece of land entirely surrounded by water.
> *A* paediatrician is a doctor who specializes in children's illnesses.

'For'

The **indefinite article** is also used in the following way, with the word 'for' implied but omitted before it:

>The grapes are £3 *a* kilo.
>The gardener will charge you £12 *an* hour.
>The cake is £2 *a* slice.

DEMONSTRATIVE DETERMINERS

Demonstrative determiners are used to point out or indicate the nouns which they qualify.

The **demonstrative determiners** are *this*, *that*, *these* and *those*, as in *this book*, *that house*, *these flowers* and *those girls*.

In the following sentences the blue italic words are examples of **demonstrative determiners**:

>*This* cake is absolutely delicious.
>I do admire *those* flowers.
>I used to live in *that* house.
>*These* students are all taking the exam.
>I love *this* dress, but I can't afford it.
>Who is *that* man over there?
>Why are *those* people wearing hats?
>*These* trees are huge.
>*Those* red grapes are delicious.
>*These* green grapes are sour.

POSSESSIVE DETERMINERS

When you wish to indicate that something belongs to someone or something or that it is connected in some way with someone or something, you use the **possessive determiners** *my*, *our*, *your*, *his*, *her*, *its*, *their*. Formerly, **possessive determiners** were commonly known as **possessive adjectives**. In the following sentences the blue italic words are **possessive determiners**:

>I would like *my* book back, please.
>Where are *your* children?

DETERMINERS

Dad let me borrow *his* car.
He was brushing *his* teeth.
She looks very like *her* mother.
Unfortunately, the dog broke *its* leg in the accident.
The children loved *their* new bikes.

INDEFINITE DETERMINERS

The **indefinite determiners**, also called **general determiners**, are used to qualify nouns or pronouns when you are talking about people or things in a general or indefinite way, without identifying them.

The indefinite or general determiners include:

all, *any*, *both*, *each*, *either*, *every*, *few*, *little*, *less*,
many, *much*, *more*, *neither*, *no*, *several*, *some* and
neither.

These are indicated in blue italic in the following sentences:

Any room in the hotel will do.
Both students are to blame.
Neither house is really suitable.
Either bus will take you to the village.
Every car has been damaged.
Many books were destroyed in the fire.

WATCH OUT

DON'T use two **referring determiners** together:
   The dress is in *my* shop. **[Correct]**
   The dress is in *the my* shop. **[Wrong]**

DO use *of* between a **quantifier** and another determiner:
   They were talking to *some of my* family. **[Correct]**
   They were talking to *some my* family. **[Wrong]**

Few patients have survived such an operation.
No facts are known yet.
Some gardens are beautifully kept.
Several buses go into the centre of town.
Little information has been released.
We have *enough* children to start a new class.
He does not have *enough* knowledge.
He has no *more* work to do.
There have been *more* accidents on that stretch of road.
Are there *any* jobs available?

NUMBER DETERMINERS

Numbers when they are used before a noun are sometimes classified as **determiners**, and sometimes as **adjectives**. Numbers such as *one*, *two*, *ten*, *twenty*, etc are called **cardinal numbers**, while numbers such as *first*, *second*, *tenth*, *twentieth*, etc are called **ordinal numbers**.

In the following sentences the words in blue italic are **cardinal numbers**:

We only have *one* chance to succeed.
There are *seven* people in the house.
More than *sixty* soldiers died in the battle.
There are *five hundred and fifty* pupils in the school.

In the following sentences the italicized words are **ordinal numbers**:

This is the *third* time he's been in prison.
This is the little girl's *fourth* birthday.
They're celebrating their *twenty-fifth* wedding anniversary.

DETERMINERS AND NOUNS

Take care with **determiners** and **uncountable nouns**.

Some determiners are restricted to certain types of noun. You can't use *a* or *an* with an uncountable noun.

Advice is an **uncountable noun**. A similar word to advice is *tip* except *tip* is a **countable noun**. Compare the following:

DETERMINERS

I'll give you *a tip* about painting.
I'll give you *some tips* about painting.
I'll give you *some advice* about painting.
[Wrong] I'll give you *an advice* about painting.

Milk is an **uncountable noun**. *Lemon* can be a **countable noun** (the fruit) or an **uncountable noun** (the flavour or juice). *Drop*, *spot*, and *slice* are **countable nouns**. Compare the following:

I'd like a *drop of/spot of* milk in my tea.
I'd like a *slice of lemon* in my tea.
I'd like *some milk* in my tea.
I'd like *some lemon* in my tea.
I'd like *a milk* in my tea. [**Wrong**. Milk is uncountable, you would never say *a milk* or *some milks*.]
I'd like a lemon in my tea. [**Wrong**. Saying this would mean you want a whole lemon in your tea!]

Sugar is an **uncountable noun** BUT you *could* say:
I'd like *a sugar* in my tea.
I'd like *one sugar* (*two sugars*, etc) in my tea.

This is a fairly informal usage, where *a sugar* or *one sugar* is short for *one spoonful of sugar* or a *sugar lump* or *sugar cube*.)

Take care with **determiners** and **plural nouns**:

Brian has *many* badges in his collection. **[Correct]**
Brian has *some* badges in his collection. **[Correct]**
Brian has *much* badges in his collection. **[Wrong]**

You could use *much* in this way:

There is *much variety* in Brian's badge collection.

as *variety* is an **uncountable noun** and *much* refers to a non-specific abundance of something.

ADVERBS

Barry was very versatile – he could panic in several different ways.
This week he was desperately, silently, hopelessly and impossibly panicking.

THE MAIN function of an **adverb** is to give more information about a **verb**. An **adverb** is said to **modify** a verb because it limits the word it describes in some way. Thus, modifying the verb *walk* with the adverb *quickly* means that we know that we are concentrating on walking quickly and that we can forget about walking in any other way.

MODIFYING

So, we know that adverbs modify **verbs**. **Adverbs** can also modify: other **adverbs**, as in *extremely suddenly*; **adjectives**, as in *gravely ill*; **prepositions**, as in *just after dinner*; and **conjunctions** as in *exactly what he said*.

ADVERBS

HOPEFULLY

Changes in the language are frequently met with great opposition, at least until people get used to them, or until the loudest of the objectors are no longer with us. The opposition to the introduction of *hopefully* with the meaning 'it is to be hoped that' was particularly forceful. The following sentences use *hopefully* with that meaning.

> Hopefully, we'll get there in time for dinner.
> Hopefully, I will be able to go on holiday this year.

Its traditional meaning had been 'with hope', as in:

> We waited hopefully for their arrival until it became clear that they were not coming.

Even now, people still grumble about it, although *hopefully* in its more modern sense is now regarded as quite acceptable, except perhaps in very formal contexts. The arguments against the acceptance of *hopefully* in its more recent meaning were not convincing. Much was made of the possibility of ambiguity occurring, especially when the adverb is placed immediately before the verb, as in:

> They will hopefully wait for us although we're going to be a bit late.

However, the *hopefully* in the sentence above is much more likely to mean 'it is to be hoped that' and, if there are genuine possibilities of ambiguity, you can change its position to the beginning of the sentence.

An **adverb** is usually a single word. When a group of words performs the same function as an adverb it is known as an **adverbial phrase** or **adverbial** (*see* page 132).

IRREGULAR ADVERBS

Most adverbs can be formed by adding –ly to the end of an adjective, but the following cannot:

adjective	adverb
good	well
fast	fast
hard	hard
late	late
early	early
daily	daily
straight	straight
wrong	wrong [although wrongly is acceptable]

TYPES OF ADVERB

There are various types of adverb – adverbs of time, frequency, duration, place, manner and degree, as well as interrogative adverbs.

Adverbs of time

Adverbs of time indicate when something has happened. They include words such as *then*, *now*, *afterwards*, *before*, *later*. In the following sentences the italicized words are adverbs of time:

> I'll see you *soon*.
> They haven't seen him *lately*.
> It was her birthday *today*.
> I wasn't married *then*.
> We'd never met *before*.
> *Afterwards* we had afternoon tea.

Adverbs of frequency

Adverbs of frequency indicate how frequently something happens. They include words such as *often*, *always*, *never*, and *seldom*.

In the following sentences the italicized words are adverbs of frequency:

ADVERBS

It *always* snowed at Christmas there.
We *rarely* meet these days.
He *never* drinks alcohol.
She is *forever* criticizing him.
We play tennis together *regularly*.
The patient is being monitored *constantly*.
We *usually* have dinner at 8pm

Adverbs of duration

Adverbs of duration indicate how long something lasts or occurs. They include words such as *always*, *briefly*, *permanently*, *indefinitely*.

In the following sentences the italicized words are **adverbs of duration**:

She is living with her grandmother *temporarily*.
He has been suspended from his job *indefinitely*.
I haven't known her *long*.
We will stay here *overnight*.
She's *always* lived here.
They stopped *briefly* to fill the car with petrol.

Adverbs of place

Adverbs of place are used to indicate where something happens or takes place. They include such words as *here*, *there*, *near*, *downstairs* and *indoors*. In the following sentences the italicized words are **adverbs of place**:

He has gone *overseas*.
They live *nearby*.
She went *inside*.
He walked *alongside*.
They are travelling *northward*.
We waded *ashore*.
The child doesn't live *here*.
He held the banner *aloft*.
We met *midway*.

Adverbs of manner

Adverbs of manner indicate how something happens or the circumstances in which something happens. They are frequently formed by adding *–ly* to an adjective and they include *carefully, easily, hurriedly, plainly, quickly, safely, suddenly, willingly*. A few of them end in *–wise, –ways* or *–wards*.

In the following sentences the italicized words are **adverbs of manner**:

She was *neatly* dressed.
He smiled *vaguely*.
They spoke *eloquently*.
I behaved *foolishly*.
We waited *patiently*.
You are needed *urgently*.
She acted *independently*.
He moved *sideways*.

Adverbs of degree

Adverbs of degree are used to indicate the degree to which an action is performed. Many of them are formed by adding *-ly* to an adjective and they include *fairly, moderately, remarkably, very* and *partly*.

In the following sentences the italicized words are **adverbs of degree**:

I enjoyed the film *immensely*.
She was *hugely* impressed by the efforts of the children.
They were only *moderately* enthusiastic about the project.
She was *slightly* hurt by the remark.
They were *partly* responsible for the error.
Her father was a *supremely* successful businessman.

Adverbs of emphasis

A small group of **adverbs of degree** are known as **adverbs of emphasis**. These are formed from **emphatic adjectives** and include *absolutely, entirely, really, utterly* and *positively*.

SPLIT INFINITIVE

At one time the avoidance of the split infinitive was taught in schools as being one of the most important rules of grammar. There are still people who regard it almost as a grammatical sin to split an infinitive. The battle still rages, although many now have no idea of what it is all about.

A split infinitive occurs when the infinitive or base form of a verb (*see* page 177) has an adverb or adverbial phrase put between the word *to* and the relevant verb. A famous and much-quoted example is *to boldly go*, from the introduction to the TV series *Star Trek*. If you were determined to avoid splitting the infinitive you'd have to say *boldly to go* or *to go boldly*.

The problem with avoiding split infinitives is that you can end up with a piece of written English that sounds unnatural – or worse – with a meaning that is altered. For example, the sentence:

> He went home to quietly think about his options.

means the man is thinking about things in a reflective, contemplative way. If we rewrite the sentence as:

> He quietly went home to think about his options.

we are talking about the quiet manner in which he travelled home. If we rewrite this sentence as:

> He went home to think quietly about his options.

it reads better than the last one, but what was so hard to understand about the first usage? It's hard to come up with a sensible reason why any usage should be forbidden if it is clear and understandable. And if it is hard to think of a reason to keep a rule, inevitably that rule will die out.

It takes a long time for grammar changes to become generally accepted, but we can safely say that the rule against the split infinitive has had its day.

HYPHENS

Remember that the hyphen is normally used in certain adverbs, sometimes to avoid ambiguity, as in *a well-established method*, *a half-organized scheme* and *the best-known writer of travel books about that area*.

Do not use a hyphen to separate an adverb from an adjective or participle if the adverb ends in *–ly*, as in *a highly successful fashion designer* and *an immaculately dressed young man*.

The italicized words below are **adverbs of emphasis**:

> We *totally* disagree with you.
> I was *utterly* devastated by the news.
> I *quite* agree.
> She *positively* adores him.

Interrogative adverbs

Interrogative adverbs are among the **wh-words** which are used to ask **wh-questions** (*see* page 122) and include *when, where, how* and *why*.

The italicized words below are **interrogative adverbs**:

> *When* did you last see him?
> *Where* was the money hidden?
> *How* are you feeling?
> *Why* was he there?

GRADABLE AND NON-GRADABLE

If an adverb is **gradable** it means you can use another adverb in front of it to show it has a certain degree of a certain quality. The other adverb that shows the extent of the degree is known as a **degree adverb** and the following words are examples:

almost, a bit, barely, completely, extremely, fairly, greatly, pretty, really, rather, slightly, very.

ADVERBS

> He drove a fairly *small* car.
> She cooked a very *delicious* meal.
> We lived in a very *old* house.

You can't use **degree adverbs** with **non-gradable adjectives** (page 145) since non-gradable adjectives refer to a particular type or an absolute quality.

> He drove a *diesel* car.
> She cooked an *Italian* meal.
> We lived in a *wooden* house.

Non-grading adverbs are words such as *completely*, *totally* and *absolutely*. They emphasize absolute qualities. These *can* be paired with **non-gradable adjectives**.

> The cat was *absolutely* dead – no mistaking it.
> His idea was *virtually* unique.
> The play was *utterly* excellent

DEGREE ADVERBS, NON GRADABLE ADJECTIVES

The commonly used adverb *really*, and the adverbs *fairly* and *pretty* are regularly used with both **gradable** and **non-gradable** adjectives, e.g.:

> It's a fairly unique car.
> That's a really excellent idea.

CONJUNCTIONS

A conjunction links one group of words to another.

A CONJUNCTION is a **linking word** used to join words, word groups or **clauses** (see pages 129–31). There are two types of conjunction, **coordinating conjunctions** and **subordinating conjunctions**.

COORDINATING CONJUNCTIONS

Coordinating conjunctions are conjunctions which join elements which are of equal status. These units may be words, word groups or main clauses. **Coordinating conjunctions** include *and*, *but*, *or*, *yet* and, in pairs and often for emphasis, *both … and*, *either … or*, *neither … nor*.

CONJUNCTIONS

AND and BUT

It is no longer considered an error to start a sentence with *and* or *but*. This is quite a recent change and one that has probably arisen because people started to ask 'why not?' ... and there isn't a satisfactory reason behind the rule. However, do not overdo it. Starting a sentence with *and* or *but* is best reserved for those occasions when you want to draw particular attention to something or to emphasize something. A whole string of sentences starting in this way is going to sound very tedious.

In the following sentences the words in blue italic are **coordinating conjunctions** which link words:

>She's an artist *and* a writer.
>He is an intelligent *and* enthusiastic young man.
>He was tall, dark *and* handsome.
>She was poor *but* happy.
>It was a small *but* comfortable house.
>She was elderly *but* extremely fit.
>They worked slowly *but* confidently.
>You can serve fruit *or* cheese at the end of the meal.
>Did you *or* your husband witness the crime?
>Is that good *or* bad news?
>The teacher was firm *yet* fair.
>They are either stupid *or* naïve.
>She is either foolish *or* deceitful.
>They are neither skilled *nor* experienced.

In the following sentences the words in blue italic are **coordinating conjunctions** which link **main clauses**:

>He has asked Anne to marry him *and* she has accepted.
>The students live in Leeds *and* they travel here every day.
>He was born in England *but* lives in Australia.

They can stay here *or* they can go home.
Students can either live in flats *or* they can live in halls of residence.

SUBORDINATING CONJUNCTIONS

Subordinating conjunctions are used to link a subordinate clause or dependent clause to the main clause. Subordinating conjunctions may introduce an adverbial clause, a comparative clause, a relative clause, or a noun clause. For all of these, *see* the section on clauses, pages 129–31.

Subordinating conjunctions introducing adverbial clauses

These are clauses which have a function in a sentence similar to that of an adverb (*see* pages 163–70) or an adverbial phrase (*see* page 132). They add information about time, place, concession, condition, manner, purpose and result.

Subordinating conjunctions introducing adverbial clauses of time

These include *after*, *before*, *since*, *when*, *whenever*, *while*, *until*, *as soon as*. In the following sentences the words in blue italic form a conjunction introducing an adverbial clause of time:

> *As soon as* the babysitter comes we'll set off.
> I smile *whenever* I see the child's happy face.
> I'll wait *until* your friend comes.

Subordinating conjunctions introducing adverbial clauses of place

These include *where*, *wherever*, *everywhere*. In the following sentences the word in blue italic is a conjunction introducing an adverbial clause of place:

> I forget *where* I left the package.
> *Wherever* the actor goes, photographers follow.

Subordinating conjunctions introducing adverbial clauses of purpose

These include *in order (to)*, *to*, *so as to*, *so that*. In the following sentences the words in blue italic form a conjunction introducing an adverbial clause of purpose:

CONJUNCTIONS

> **ONE CONJUNCTION FOR TWO CLAUSES**
> A common error by English learners is to use two conjunctions to join two clauses. Only one is required. You'll notice the sentences below are correct with either of the conjunctions chosen, just not at the same time.
>
> *Because* it is hot *so* I have turned off the heating. **[Wrong]**
> *Because* it is hot I have turned off the heating. **[Correct]**
> It is hot *so* I have turned off the heating. **[Correct]**
>
> *Since* I got there first *and* I got a table all to myself. **[Wrong]**
> *Since* I got there first, I got a table all to myself. **[Correct]**
> I got there first *and* I got a table all to myself. **[Correct]**

We left the party early *so as to* catch the last bus home.
In order to get there on time we'd have to leave now.
I saved money all year *so that* I could afford to go on holiday to South Africa.

Subordinating conjunctions introducing adverbial clauses of reason

These include *because*, *since*, *as*, *in case*. In the following sentences the words in blue italic form a conjunction introducing an adverbial clause of reason:

We need to leave very early *in case* the traffic is very heavy on the motorway.
Because it's raining heavily we'll have to cancel the picnic.
Since he committed the crime he should accept the punishment.

Subordinating conjunctions introducing adverbial clauses of result

So that comes under this category. The words *so* and *that* can be separated, *so* coming before an adjective or adverb in the main clause and *that* being the first word in the subordinate clause. In the following sentences the words in blue italic form a conjunction introducing an adverbial clause of result:

> He hit his opponent *so* hard *that* he knocked him out.
> He spoke clearly *so that* everyone heard every word.

Subordinating conjunctions introducing adverbial clauses of condition

These include *unless*, *if*, *provided (that)*, *providing*, *as long as*. In the following sentences the words in blue italic form a conjunction introducing an adverbial clause of condition:

> I'll go *provided* you come with me.
> *As long as* you're happy I'm happy to do what you ask.
> *If* he stays I'm leaving.

Subordinating conjunctions introducing adverbial clauses of manner

These include *as though*, *as if*, *as*, *like*. In the following sentences the words in blue italic form a conjunction introducing an adverbial clause of manner:

> He walked *as though* he were in pain.
> She smiled broadly *as if* she were very happy.

Subordinating conjunctions introducing adverbial clauses of concession

These include *although*, *though*, *even though*, *whereas*, *while*, *whilst*. In the following sentences the words in blue italic form a conjunction introducing an adverbial clause of concession:

> She still loves him *although* he treated her badly.
> *Even though* I dislike him personally I admire his work.
> *While* Mary is an excellent cook neither of her sisters can even boil an egg.

VERBS

Apparently this lesson is about 'doing' words so I'm hoping it's a bit like PE.

THE VERB is usually the most important part of a sentence. Verbs fulfil a number of functions in sentences, such as **tense** and **mood**. It is sometimes stated that a verb is a '**doing word**'. To some extent this is true, and it is an easy way to remember the function, but it is not the full story.

'DOING' AND 'BEING' WORDS

Verbs *are* '**doing**' words' in the sense that they express action. In the following sentences the words *walk* and *listen* are both **verbs**:

> They always *walk* to school.
> Please *listen* carefully.

However, verbs can also be said to be '**being**' words, in that they indicate a condition or a state. In this situation they do not actually refer to an action, but simply act as a connection between the **subject** (*see* page 114) and the other parts of the sentence that relate to it. In the following sentences the words *is* and *seems* are both **verbs**:

She *is* a very beautiful woman.
He *seems* an honest man.

INFINITIVE

The **infinitive**, or **base**, is the form of a verb when it's used without any indication of person, number or tense. There are two forms of the infinitive. One is the **to infinitive** form, as in:

She wanted *to sing*.
They refused *to go*.
I'd like *to help*.
They wished *to leave*.
The child has nothing *to do*.

The other form of the **infinitive**, without *to*, is sometimes called the **base infinitive**. This form consists of the base form of the verb without *to*, as in:

We saw him *fall*.
She watched him *go*.
They watched him *walk*.

TENSES

Regular verbs follow a set, regular pattern. In order to understand what this pattern involves, you need to know something about **tenses**. The word **tense** is a noun referring to the *time* at which an action takes place. (The word *tense* is also an adjective with the meaning *anxious*, and though reading about verbs may well make you anxious, there is no connection between the two uses!)

VERBS

Present tenses

If the action is taking place **now** the verb is in the **present tense**, as in:

> They *live* next door to us.
> He *hates* to eat sprouts.
> We *make* cakes in the kitchen.

The **simple present tense** uses the **base** form, also known as the **infinitive** form, as in *walk*, *run*, or *go*:

> I *walk* in the country at the weekend.
> I *run* each day
> I *go* to town on the bus every morning.

The **continuous present tense**, also called the **progressive present tense**, is formed using the present tense of the verb *to be* and the present participle of the main verb ending in *–ing*. It frequently occurs in **contracted forms**, especially in spoken English. It is used when you are talking about something that is happening while you are speaking or when you are referring to an action continuing over a period of time and not complete at the time when you are referring to it.

Some learners mix this up with the **simple present tense**. Sometimes these mistakes occur because of the influence of what happens in their own native language.

In the following sentences the words in bold in the sentences are all verbs in the **continuous present tense** (In contracted forms the pronoun is included, as in *He's*.)

> *Joe's walking* to work.
> *He's* not *driving*?
> Why *is* Sam *laughing*?
> Jack *is winning* the match.
> We *are making* cakes.

Past tenses

If the action has taken place in the past, the verb is in the **past tense**, as in:

>The children *played* in the park yesterday.
>She *chose* a simple wedding dress.
>I *heard* a strange noise.
>In time she *forgave* him.

The **simple past tense** is used to refer to a regular or repeated action that took place in the past.

>I *ate* peaches in the field.
>I *took* a swimming class.

The **continuous past tense** is used to refer to a continuing action that took place in the past and is now complete. It is also used to refer to an event in the past that occurred during the course of another event:

>This time last week we *were lying* on a beach in the sun.
>I *was working* on my computer.
>We *were* still *sitting* in our cars when the police arrived.
>I *was cleaning* my flat until midnight last night.

The **present perfect tense**, also known as the **perfect tense**, is another tense which refers to the past. It is formed using the **present tense** of the verb *have* and the **past participle** of the main verb.

It is used to refer to an action that began in the past but continues into the present time:

>I *have looked* everywhere for it.
>He *has lived* in France for over thirty years.
>Floods *have destroyed* thousands of books in the warehouse.

Future tense

If the action referred to is likely to happen in the future the verb is in the *future tense*, as in:

> She *will be* very pleased to see you.
> They *will take* a look at your report tomorrow.

In spoken English the future tense is usually formed by using will and the infinitive form of the verb, as in:

YOU *SHALL* GO TO THE BALL

The verbs *will* and *shall* are used to form the *future tense*. Formerly, the verb *shall* was always used with *I* and *we* and *will* was always used with *you*, *he/she/it* and *they*. There was an exception to this. *Will* was used with *I* and *we*, and *shall* was used with the other personal pronouns when a firm intention was being expressed, as in:

> 'You shall go to the ball,' said the Fairy Godmother to Cinderella.

In modern usage *will* is now commonly used in most relevant contexts.

Will and *shall* appear in the contracted form *'ll*, as in:

> I'll go with you.
> They'll get the information tomorrow.

At one time, this contracted form was found only in spoken English, or in very informal written English. Nowadays, in accordance with the new spirit of informality that has spread through the language, this contracted form is used in some more formal contexts. It should still be avoided in the most formal contexts. *See also* will/shall page 316.

He *will go*.
She *will leave*.
They *will read*.

Contracted forms of this are very common in spoken English, as in the short pieces of dialogue below:

We have to leave now or *we'll be* late.
He'll get here soon.
She'll feel better after a sleep.

Note that the **simple present tense** is sometimes used with an adverb or adverbial to refer to a time in the future and this use is common in spoken English.

In the following sentences the words in italic are verbs in the **simple present tense** referring to the future:

We *leave* very early tomorrow morning.
The play *starts* in less than an hour.

PARTICIPLES

Participles are formed from **verbs** and have a few jobs; one of which is that you can sometimes use them as **adjectives**. This might be easier to understand from some examples:

Infinitive	Past participle	Present participle
to rise	the *risen* bread	the *rising* tide
to break	the *broken* arm	the *breaking* news
to walk	a *walked* dog	a *walking* stick
to track	a *tracked* route	a *tracking* device

Past participle

The **past participle** is used with parts of the verb *have* to form the **perfect tense**, also known as the **present perfect tense**, as in:

They *have bought* a new house.
She *has taken* her child to the doctor.

VERBS

> ### I'M LOVING IT
> In modern, informal usage you will sometimes hear, the **present continuous tense** used where the **present tense** would do:
>
> > I am liking this music!
> > I am loving this doughnut!
>
> The **present tense** would be sufficient here:
>
> > I like this music!
> > I love this doughnut!
>
> This usage of the **present continuous tense** is colloquial, currently used for emphasis or comical effect, though its use is spreading.

In the first sentence, *bought* is the past participle of the verb *buy* and in the second *taken* is the past participle of the verb *take*.

The past participle is also used to form the **pluperfect tense**, also known as the **past perfect tense**, as in:

> We *had brought* a packed lunch with us.
> He *had hidden* the jewels in a cave.

In the first sentence *brought* is the past participle of the verb *bring* and in the second *hidden* is the past participle of the verb *hide*.

Present participle

The **present participle** is formed by adding *–ing* to the **infinitive** or **base form**, as in *walking*. The present participle is used with parts of the verb *be* to form the **present continuous tense**, as in:

> We *are walking* to work.
> You *are snoring*.

Participial phrases

A **participial phrase** is a group of related words in which the main word is a **participle** of a verb, either a **present participle**, as in the following sentence:

Walking along the beach, he thought deeply about his future.

Or a **past participle**, as in the sentence:

Impressed by the results, she invested in the company.

The words in italic in the following sentences are **participial phrases**:

Bored by the party, she went home early.
Living by himself, he was frequently lonely.
Relieved by the news, he smiled broadly.
Laughing happily, she went off to celebrate.
Built by his father, the house had been designed by him.

MISRELATED PARTICIPLE

Sometimes participles are either wrongly or ambiguously placed. These are often known as **misrelated participles**, although some people also call these **dangling participles**, as in:

In the distance we could see, driving through the mountain pass, a small group of soldiers.

This sentence is potentially ambiguous. Are *we* driving through the mountains or is it *the small group of soldiers* that are doing the driving? It is important that you attach the participle to the appropriate noun to avoid confusion and remove any possibility of ambiguity, as in:

Driving through the mountain pass, we could see in the distance a small group of soldiers.

VERBS

GERUND: THE –ING FORM OF THE VERB

The part of a verb ending in **–ing** can either be a **present participle** or it can be a **verbal noun**, also known as a **gerund**. It depends on the context. In the sentence:

>I am *walking* in the park.

the word *walking* is a **present participle**, while in the sentence:

>*Walking* is an excellent form of exercise.

the word *walking* is a **verbal noun** or **gerund**. In this sentence the verbal noun or gerund *walking* is the **subject** of the sentence, but a verbal noun or gerund can also be the **object** of a sentence, as in:

>He has taken up *walking* in order to get fit.

Possessive case

There is one aspect of **gerunds** that causes particular problems. According to traditional grammar, **nouns** or **pronouns** which qualify verbal nouns or gerunds should be in the possessive case. This means that the sentence:

>My parents strongly object to *my* smoking in their house.

is, according to traditional grammar, considered correct, whereas the sentence:

>My parents strongly object to *me* smoking in their house.

is considered wrong. Likewise, the following sentence:

>Apparently, her mum does not like *your* going round there.

is, according to traditional grammar, considered correct, whereas the sentence:

>Apparently, her mum does not like *you* going round there.

is considered wrong.

The trouble is, that to many people it sounds more natural to use the second version of each of the above sentences. The result is that more and more people are opting for the second usage. It is another of those cases in modern English where what sounds natural is taking precedence over what has been accepted as grammatically correct. However, at this time, this use is best confined to spoken English and informal written English.

MOOD

Mood is one of the categories into which verbs are divided. It gets its name from the fact that it was thought to show the attitude or viewpoint that a particular verb indicated.

Imperative mood

The **imperative mood** is particularly common in spoken English as it is used to give orders or instructions, or to make a request. These are all a common feature of spoken English. The sentences that follow are in the imperative mood.

> *Give* me two of those brown loaves, please.
> *Get* down from that tree, Sam!
> *Leave* the window open, Alice.

Indicative mood

The **indicative mood** of a verb is used to make a factual statement, such as the italic words in the following sentences:

> The parking restrictions *apply* on working days.
> It *snowed* last night.
> The plane *leaves* at 7am.
> I *start* my new job tomorrow.
> We *give* generous discounts to members of staff.
> We *are losing* money on this venture.

Subjunctive mood

The **subjunctive mood** was originally a term used in Latin grammar where it was used to express a wish, supposition, doubt, improbability or other non-factual statement. The subjunctive mood in English is used to express **hypothetical statements**, as in:

VERBS

If I *were* you I would forget all about it.

The word *were* is in the subjunctive mood. The subjunctive mood is also used in certain formal clauses beginning with *that*, as in:

I demand *that she pay* me in full immediately.
I respectfully request *that he depart* at 9am sharp.

As far as most verbs are concerned, the subjunctive form of the verb is the same as its basic form except that the third person singular leaves off the *–s* ending, e.g. *pay* instead of *pays*.

However, the verb *be* has the past tense subjunctive *were* and its present subjunctive is *be*.

IF I WERE YOU ... I'D AVOID THE SUBJUNCTIVE

Because many people nowadays are not familiar with the word **subjunctive**, and, even if they are, do not understand what it is, its use is fading, except in very formal contexts.

If you are writing something formal and do not wish to use the subjunctive you can always use the verb *should* instead, as in the sentence

The judge recommends that he should be imprisoned.

rather than

The judge recommends that he be imprisoned.

VOICE

Voice, with reference to verbs, has nothing to do with the vocal cords. Instead, it refers to two ways of looking at the action of verbs. Verbs which take an object, called *transitive verbs*, (*see* page 189) can either be in the *active voice* or the *passive voice*.

Active and passive voice

A verb is said to be in the **active voice** when the subject of the verb performs an action. The following sentences are all in the active voice.

> The farmer drove the truck.
> The chef cooked the meal.
> Mary baked a cake.
> The pills cured the illness.

A sentence with a verb in the **active voice** actually identifies the person who was responsible for the action so there is little possibility of vagueness or ambiguity, as in:

> Jack broke the window.

A verb is said to be in the **passive voice** when the subject is acted upon, rather than when it does the acting. The following sentences are all in the passive voice.

> The truck was driven by the farmer.
> The meal was cooked by the chef.
> The cake was baked by Mary.
> The illness was cured by the pills.

A sentence with a verb in the **passive voice** can describe an action without identifying the person who is responsible for it and this leaves room for vagueness or ambiguity, as in:

> The window was broken.

The **active voice** is much more commonly used than the passive voice and this is especially true of spoken English where the action is usually more immediate and the sentences are simpler. The **passive voice** is more likely to be used in rather formal literary English or in technical or scientific writing. It is occasionally used in spoken English, but overuse of the passive can make speech sound rather formal and unnatural.

VERBS

USING THE PASSIVE VOICE

Verbs in the *active voice* create the action of a piece of writing. They are more direct and more forceful and they are often clearer and shorter.

Sentences with verbs in the *passive voice* are often less direct, and can be longer and less clear. Sometimes they can slow the action down. Research shows that readers take longer to understand sentences with verbs in the passive voice than with verbs in the active voice.

However, do not be afraid of the passive voice. Some people treat it as if it has to be avoided at all costs. This is not true.

You might want to report some kind of action which you know has been committed without knowing who committed it, as in:

The car was stolen early this morning.

This sounds better than:

Someone stole the car early this morning.

Use the passive voice sparingly until you have reasonably well-honed writing skills, but it can be a useful device.

If you are writing something of an academic nature or if you are writing something that is meant to be informative, do not use phrases in the passive voice too often.

The phrases in the passive voice that follow, for example, are too vague to be appropriate in that kind of writing:

It is now widely believed that …
It has been shown by research that …
Studies show that …

See also pages 345–7.

TRANSITIVE VERBS AND INTRANSITIVE VERBS

Transitive verbs

Only transitive verbs are affected by voice (*see* pages 186–8). Transitive verbs are verbs which can take a direct object. In the sentence:

> The men *love* their children.

the noun children is a direct object and the verb love is transitive. In the following sentences the italicized words are transitive verbs:

> We *know* the truth.
> They *hate* the climate here.
> I *chose* the blue curtains.
> You *will adore* him.
> She *crossed* the street.

Intransitive verbs

In the following sentences the verbs in italic are intransitive because they do not take an object.

> Snow *fell* yesterday.
> The situation *improved*.
> A figure *appeared*.
> She *blushes* easily.
> They *work* hard.
> He *died* yesterday.

Either

Many verbs can be either transitive or intransitive according to context. In the sentence:

> They both *play* the piano. [Transitive]
> The children *play* on the beach every day. [Intransitive]
> They *climb* the highest mountains. [Transitive]
> The paths *climb* steeply. [Intransitive]

VERBS

AUXILIARY VERBS

An **auxiliary verb** is a verb which is used with a **main verb** to form certain **tenses**, and to form **negative remarks** or **questions**. The main auxiliary verbs, sometimes known as the **primary auxiliary verbs**, are *be*, *have* and *do*, although these verbs can also be used as main verbs. Parts of the verb *to be* can be used as auxiliary verbs with the **–ing form** of a main verb to form the **continuous present tense**, as in:

> Doctors *are trying* to save her life.
> He *is driving* the bus.

Parts of the verb *to be* can be used as auxiliary verbs with the **past participle** of a main verb to form the **passive voice**, as in:

> The house *is built* on rock.
> The child's face *is covered* with mud.

Parts of the **verb *to have*** can be used as **auxiliary verbs** with the **past participle** of the **main verb** to form the **present perfect tense**:

> We *have cleaned* the house.
> She *has lost* her watch.

And to form the **past perfect tense**, as in:

> He *had missed* the bus.
> You *had already left* the room.

Parts of the verb *to do* can be used as **auxiliary verbs** with a **main verb** to add **emphasis** to the main verb, as in:

> She *does* still live there, I'm certain.
> It was obvious that they *did* steal the money.

The auxiliary verbs, *be*, *have* and *do* are often used to form **negative sentences**, as in:

> He *is not* working.
> She *has not* survived.
> They *did not* tell the truth.

190

Modal auxiliary verbs

Auxiliary verbs are also often used to form **questions**, as in:

Is the elevator working?
Has he found the money yet?
Do you believe him?

In spoken English, and informal written English, auxiliary verbs are particularly common in the **contracted form**. So *you are* becomes *you're*; *I have* becomes *I've*; *we have* becomes *we've*; *does not* becomes *doesn't*; *did not* becomes *didn't*; *you have* becomes *you've*, *he is* and *he has* become *he's*; *I am* becomes *I'm*, and so on. *Is not* becomes *isn't*; *has not* becomes *hasn't*; *did not* becomes *didn't*, and so on.

We've cleaned the house.
She's lost her watch.
He'd missed the bus.
You'd already left the room.
He *isn't* working.
She *hasn't* survived.
They *didn't* tell the truth.

MODAL AUXILIARY VERBS

A **modal auxiliary verb** is an auxiliary verb that is used with a main verb to help it express a wide range of meanings including probability, possibility, ability, permission, suggestions, requests, offers, invitations, promises, etc.

The modal auxiliary verbs are *can, could, may, might, will, would, shall, should, must, ought to, be able to, need to*. Unlike **primary auxiliary verbs** (*see* page 190) modal auxiliary verbs have only one form (*can, could, may*, etc). Also, unlike primary auxiliary verbs, modal auxiliary verbs cannot act as **main verbs**.

Some **modal auxiliary verbs** are often found in **contracted forms** *I'll* for *I will*; *I'd* for *I would*; *that'd* for *that would*; *can't* for *cannot*; *couldn't* for *could not*, and so on.

In the following sentences the words in italic in the sentences are all modal auxiliary verbs:

I *COULD OF* SWORN THAT WAS CORRECT

We've touched a few times on how, occasionally, it is OK to break the prescriptive rules of English grammar. Mostly these rule-breaks have gradually developed over decades (or even centuries), and with sensible reasons, to become an accepted (or almost-accepted) standard.

The English language changes over time, and will continue to change, especially if the established rules make little sense, or if they are widely misunderstood and there isn't a good enough reason to preserve the usage. The majority usage will almost always win – and there is not a lot you can do to stop that.

Well, what we will next describe is a mistake that is happening more and more regularly, which breaks a perfectly good rule, purely because one word sounds like another. There is a very common tendency for people to use *could of*, *should of*, *would of*, *must of*, etc, instead of the correct form of **modal auxiliary verb** (page 191) *could have*, *should have*, *would have*, *must have*, etc.

This usage is grammatically wrong. Speakers who say or write this are replacing a **verb** with a **preposition** – words with completely different functions. It makes no sense to use *of* instead of *have*, except that they sound similar. The misuse has come about probably through the mishearing of the **contracted** forms *could've*, *would've*, *should've*, etc. Of course, except in very formal contexts, it is absolutely fine to use modal verbs in contracted forms – but *could of* is as loathed by some as it is widely used by others. Those who know the use is wrong find it enormously irritating, so if you want to appear fluent do *not* use the word *of* instead of the verb *have* as part of a modal verb.

But will it become standard usage one day?

Could I borrow your car, Dad?
Can you play the piano, Pat?
We *couldn't* find any courgettes.
I'd like to have some more time.
Would you like me to drive?
That'd be good.
I *wouldn't* if I were you.
Will you help me carry these boxes upstairs, Joe?
Mary *might* have got here already.
You *must* all hand in your assignments next Monday.
Should we wait for Mary?
That *shouldn't* be a problem.
We *ought to* get there by four o'clock.
I really *need to* be home by ten.

REGULAR VERBS

Spelling rules for regular verbs

1. To form the **present tense** when the infinitive or base form ends in **–ch**, **–ss** or **–x**, **–es** is added rather than just **–s**, as in: *march/marches* and *toss/tosses*. When the base form ends in **–y** – the **y** changes to **i** before the **–es** is added, as in: *try/tries* and *cry/cries*.

2. The **present participle** of regular verbs is formed by adding **–ing** to the infinitive or base form, as in: *laugh/laughing* and *walk/walking*. To form the **present participle** when the infinitive or base form ends in **–e**, the **e** is removed from the infinitive or base form before adding **–ing**, as in: *manage/managing* and *rummage/rummaging*. [Note that *ageing* can also be correctly spelled *aging*.]

3. In regular verbs the ending **–ed** is added to the infinitive or base form of the verb in order to form the **past tense** and the **past participle**. Therefore *worked* is the past tense of the verb *work*.

    If the verb already ends in **e** then only **–d** is added. Therefore *loved* is the past tense of the verb *love*.

    When the infinitive or base form ends in **–ch**, **–ss** or **–x**; **–ed** is

VERBS

added, as in: *march/marched* and *toss/tossed*. When the infinitive or base form ends in *–y*, the **y** changes to **i** before *–ed* is added, as in: *try/tried* and *marry/married*.

4   When a verb consists of **one syllable** and ends in a **single consonant** which is preceded by a **single vowel**, you double the consonant when adding *–ed* to form the past tense or past participle, or *–ing* to form the present participle, as in: *drop/dropped/dropping* and *pat/patted/patting*.

5   When a verb consists of **more than one syllable** and ends in a **single consonant** preceded by a **single vowel**, you double the consonant if the word is pronounced with the stress on the last syllable to form the past tense or past participle and the present participle. Examples include *refer/referred/referring* and *transmit/transmitted/transmitting*.

There are some exceptions to this rule. One of them concerns the letter **l**. For this *see* **rule 6** below. Other exceptions include *worshipped/worshipping* and *handicapped* where you double the **p** even though the stress is on the first syllable.

6   When the verb ends in *–l*, then you double the letter **l** when forming the past participle or past tense or when you add *–ing* to form the present participle, even when the stress is *not* on the final syllable, as in: *travel/travelled/travelling* and *level/levelled/levelling*. American English does not follow this rule. It has *traveled/traveling* where British English has *travelled/travelling*.

7   Another feature of regular verbs is that the **third person singular** of their present tense is formed by adding *–s* to the infinitive or base form, as in: *He plays football*; *It seems obvious*.

> Note that some of these spelling rules do not apply ONLY to regular verbs, but they do cause particular problems with reference to them.

Regular verbs

Common errors involving regular verbs

- Forgetting to remove the –e from infinitive or base forms before adding –ing when forming the present participle: for example writing *judgeing* instead of *judging*.

- Forgetting to double the final consonant when forming the past tense or present participle of verbs such as *rot* or *pet*. Do not write *roted* or *peting*. These are wrong. *Rotted* and *petting* are the correct forms.

- Forgetting to double the final consonant in the past tenses or present participles of such words as *prefer* and *commit*. Do not write *prefered/prefering* or *commited/commiting*. These are wrong. *Preferred/preferring* and *committed/committing* are the correct forms.

- Forgetting to double the –r in the past tense and present participle of the verb *occur*. These should be spelled *occurred* and *occurring*. A word of warning – while you are trying to remember to double the letter **r**, you need to remember to still include two of the letter **c**!

- Mistakenly doubling the –r in the past tense of the verb *offer*. *Offerred* is wrong because the stress on *offer* is not on the last syllable. *Offered* is correct.

- Mistakenly doubling the –p in the present participle of the verb *develop*, as in *developping*. *Developping* is wrong because the stress on *develop* is not on the last syllable. *Developing* is correct.

- Forgetting to double the –l when forming the past participle or present participle of verbs such as *travel* and *level*. Do not write *marveled* or *appaling*. These are wrong. *Marvelled* and *appalling* are the correct forms.

- Forgetting to double the –p in *worshipped/worshipping*. This is an exception to **rule 4** on page 194. The form with the single letter **p** is correct use in American English (*worshiped/worshiping*).

- Doubling the *–t* in the past participle, past tense and present participle of the verb *benefit* as in *benefitted/benefitting*: These are wrong because the stress is not on the *last* syllable of the word *benefit*. They should be spelled *benefited* and *benefiting*.

IRREGULAR VERBS

As you might expect from their name, irregular verbs do not follow the pattern of regular verbs. They fall into several different categories, the rules of which are listed below.

Rules for irregular verbs

1. In some irregular verbs the **past tense** and the **past participle** both take the same form as the infinitive or base form, as in: *cut/cut*, *bet/bet*, *hit/hit* and *put/put*.

2. Some irregular verbs have **two past tenses** and **two past participles**, both sets having the same form, as in: *burned/burnt*, *dreamed/dreamt* and *spoiled/spoilt*.

3. Some irregular verbs have **past tenses** and **past participles** which have the **same form** as each other and do not end in *–ed*, as in: *hold/held/held*, *keep/kept/kept* and *teach/taught/taught*.

4. Some irregular verbs have a **past tense** which, in common with those of regular verbs, ends in *–ed* or *–d*, whichever is relevant. However in this category the verb has **two possible past participles**, one of which is the same as the past tense and the other of which takes a different form. For example, the verb *show* has the past tense *showed* and the two past participles *showed* and *shown*, and the verb *prove* has the past tense *proved* and the past participles *proved* and *proven*.

5. Some irregular verbs have a **past tense** and a **past participle** which are **different from each** other and **different from the infinitive** or base form. For example the verb *draw* has the past tense *drew* and the past participle *drawn*, the verb *grow* has the past tense *grew* and the past participle *grown*, and the verb *swim* has the past tense *swam* and the past participle *swum*.

HELP!

If you have read through all this and feel completely overwhelmed, do not worry and do not feel inadequate. It's not you. It's them! **Irregular verbs** are acknowledged to be one of the most difficult aspects of English grammar. There is only one thing you can do with them: you have to grit your teeth and learn them. It will be worth it in the end. A list of irregular verbs can be found on pages 201–6.

Common errors involving irregular verbs

- Many of the errors involve the verbs which have been assigned to point 5 on the previous page. Some errors involve using the **past participle** form of one of these verbs wrongly when it is the **past tense** that is the correct form in the context, as in:

    I *swum* (**past participle**) in the lake yesterday. [Wrong]
    I *swam* (**past tense**) in the lake yesterday. [Correct]
    The phone only *rung* (past participle) once. [Wrong]
    The phone only *rang* (past tense) once. [Correct]

- Some errors involve using the **past tense** form wrongly when it is the **past participle** that is the correct form in the context, as in:

    The ship *had sank* (**past tense**) off the coast of Ireland. [Wrong]
    The ship *had sunk* (**past participle**) off the coast of Ireland. [Correct]

- Using *beat*, the *past tense* of the verb *beat*, in contexts where the **past participle** *beaten* should be used, as in:

    We've *beat* (**past tense**) them three times this season. [Wrong]
    We've *beaten* (**past participle**) them three times this season. [Correct]

- Using **bit**, the past tense of the verb **bite**, in contexts where the past participle **bitten** should be used, as in:

    Her dog **has bit** (**past tense**) the postman. [Wrong]
    Her dog **has bitten** (**past participle**) the postman. [Correct]

VERBS

5 Using *gotten* instead of *got* as the past participle of the verb **get** in British English is currently considered wrong as in:

> They *have gotten* very friendly just recently. [American English]
> They *had gotten* what they deserved. [American English]
> They *have got* very friendly just recently. [British English]
> They *had got* what they deserved. [British English]

This usage is growing in popularity because of the influence of American media.

6 Using **dove** instead of **dived** as the past tense of the verb **dive** in British English is currently considered wrong. In American English both **dove** and **dived** are acceptable.

> The boy *dove* into the pool. [American English]
> The boy *dived* into the pool. [American English/British English]

7 One of the most common errors involves the verb **do**. People frequently misuse **done** (**past participle**), as in:

> He *done* wrong and should be punished. [Wrong]
> He *has done* wrong and should be punished. [Correct]
> He *did* wrong and should be punished. [Correct]

VERB AGREEMENT

Verb agreement is also known as **concord** and refers to the fact that a verb must 'agree' with the appropriate **subject** in **number**. The word **number** is used to indicate whether the form of a word refers to one thing or more than one thing. Number agreement indicates that a singular noun is usually accompanied by a singular verb, as in:

> The bus to the city *runs* every two hours.

While a plural noun is usually accompanied by a plural verb, as in:

> Buses to the city *are* not very reliable.

Common errors involving number agreement

Usually two singular nouns joined together with *and* take a plural verb, as in:

> Tom and Jane *are* going to the party.

However, when the subject is made up of two or more singular nouns connected by a phrase which, in some way, emphasizes the 'togetherness' of the nouns, such as *together with*, *as well as*, *with* and *plus*, the verb takes the singular form, as in:

> The boy's father, together with his elder sister, is going to visit him in hospital.

Formerly it was the case that, when the subject takes the form of a singular noun linked to a plural noun by *of*, as in *a number of issues*, this had to be accompanied by a singular verb, as in:

> A number of serious issues *has* to be taken into consideration.

If you used a plural verb in this context it was considered wrong. Nowadays, many people use a plural verb in such a situation, especially in spoken English, as in:

> A number of serious issues *have* to be taken into consideration.

EITHER OR ... NEITHER NOR

Remember that if there is a combination of singular and plural subjects in the *either ... or* construction, the verb agrees with the noun nearest to it, as in:

> *Either* my brother *or* my parents are giving me a lift to the airport.
> *Either* his friends *or* his cousin is to blame for the damage to his car.

The same is true of the *neither ... nor* construction, as in:

> *Neither* my sisters *nor* my brother has been invited.

VERBS

In other words, they make the verb agree with the nearest noun, in this case *issues* rather than *number*. Since this sounds more natural it is becoming more and more common, although it is grammatically wrong.

Take care with **group** or **collective nouns**, such as *committee*, *family*, *government* and *jury*. They can cause problems in relation to verb agreement. Some of these can be accompanied by either a **singular** or **plural verb** depending on the context. It all depends on whether you wish to emphasize the **unity** of the relevant noun, or whether you wish to emphasize the **individual components** that go to make up the noun.

If you wish to emphasize the unity of the relevant noun you would opt for a **singular verb**. If you wish to emphasize the individual components that go to make up the noun you would opt for a **plural verb**.

For example, if you are thinking of the family as a unit you might say:

> The family *is* the most important influence in a young child's life.

If you are considering the components of a family you might say:

> His family *are* coming from various parts of the world to celebrate his eightieth birthday with him.

This distinction can be very difficult to understand. It can sometimes be difficult to decide which meaning you have in mind. Most people go on instinct or on what they think sounds best. In American English such group or collective nouns are treated as singular.

Remember that **indefinite pronouns**, such as *anyone*, *someone*, *everyone* and *no one*, should be accompanied by a singular verb, as in:

> Everyone *is* welcome to attend the opening party.
> Either of the flats *is* suitable.
> Neither of them *has* a job.

IRREGULAR VERB LIST

In the following list of irregular verbs the **past tense** and the **past participle** both take the **same form as the infinitive** or base form:

infinitive	past tense	past participle
bet	bet	bet
burst	burst	burst
cast	cast	cast
cost	cost	cost
cut	cut	cut
hit	hit	hit
hurt	hurt	hurt
let	let	let
put	put	put
set	set	set
shed	shed	shed
shut	shut	shut
slit	slit	slit
split	split	split
spread	spread	spread

Some irregular verbs have **two past tenses** and **two past participles which are the same**. These include:

infinitive	past tense	past participle
burn	burned, burnt	burned, burnt
dream	dreamed, dreamt	dreamed, dreamt
dwell	dwelled, dwelt	dwelled, dwelt
hang	hanged, hung	hanged, hung
kneel	kneeled, knelt	kneeled, knelt
lean	leaned, leant	leaned, leant

VERBS

infinitive	past tense	past participle
leap	leaped, leapt	leaped, leapt
learn	learned, learnt	learned, learnt
light	lighted, lit	lighted, lit
smell	smelled, smelt	smelled, smelt
speed	speeded, sped	speeded, sped
spill	spilled, spilt	spilled, spilt
spoil	spoiled, spoilt	spoiled, spoilt
weave	weaved, woven	weaved, woven
wet	wetted, wet	wetted, wet

Some irregular verbs have **past tenses** that **do not end in −ed** and have the **same form as the past participle**. These include:

infinitive	past tense	past participle
bend	bent	bent
bleed	bled	bled
breed	bred	bred
build	built	built
cling	clung	clung
dig	dug	dug
feel	felt	felt
fight	fought	fought
find	found	found
flee	fled	fled
fling	flung	flung
get	got	got
grind	ground	ground
hear	heard	heard
hold	held	held

Irregular verb list

infinitive	past tense	past participle
keep	kept	kept
lay	laid	laid
lead	led	led
leave	left	left
lend	lent	lent
lose	lost	lost
make	made	made
mean	meant	meant
meet	met	met
pay	paid	paid
rend	rent	rent
say	said	said
seek	sought	sought
sell	sold	sold
send	sent	sent
shine	shone	shone
shoe	shod	shod
sit	sat	sat
sleep	slept	slept
slide	slid	slid
sling	slung	slung
slink	slunk	slunk
spend	spent	spent
stand	stood	stood
stick	stuck	stuck
sting	stung	stung
strike	struck	struck
string	strung	strung
sweep	swept	swept

VERBS

infinitive	past tense	past participle
swing	swung	swung
teach	taught	taught
tell	told	told
think	thought	thought
understand	understood	understood
weep	wept	wept
win	won	won
wring	wrung	wrung

Some irregular verbs have **regular past tense** forms but **two possible past participles**, one of which is regular. These include:

infinitive	past tense	past participle
mow	mowed	mowed, mown
prove	proved	proved, proven
sew	sewed	sewed, sewn
show	showed	showed, shown
sow	sowed	sowed, sown
swell	swelled	swelled, swollen

Some irregular verbs have **past tenses** and **past participles** that are **different from each other and different from the infinitive**. These include:

infinitive	past tense	past participle
arise	arose	arisen
awake	awoke	awoken

Irregular verb list

infinitive	past tense	past participle
bear	bore	borne
begin	began	begun
bid	bade	bidden
bite	bit	bitten
blow	blew	blown
break	broke	broken
choose	chose	chosen
do	did	done
draw	drew	drawn
drink	drank	drunk
drive	drove	driven
eat	ate	eaten
fall	fell	fallen
fly	flew	flown
forbear	forbore	forborne
forbid	forbade	forbidden
forgive	forgave	forgiven
forget	forgot	forgotten
forsake	forsook	forsaken
freeze	froze	frozen
forswear	forswore	forsworn
give	gave	given
go	went	gone
grow	grew	grown
hew	hewed	hewn
hide	hid	hidden
know	knew	known
lie	lay	lain
ride	rode	ridden

VERBS

infinitive	past tense	past participle
ring	rang	rung
saw	sawed	sawn
see	saw	seen
rise	rose	risen
shake	shook	shaken
shrink	shrank	shrunk
slay	slew	slain
speak	spoke	spoken
spring	sprang	sprung
steal	stole	stolen
stink	stank	stunk
strew	strewed	strewn
stride	strode	stridden
strive	strove	striven
swear	swore	sworn
swim	swam	swum
take	took	taken
tear	tore	torn
throw	threw	thrown
tread	trod	trodden
wake	woke	woken
wear	wore	worn
write	wrote	written

PHRASAL VERBS

A PHRASE usually refers to a group of words that work together to form a grammatical unit (see pages 131–2). A **clause** or **sentence** can usually be broken down into **phrases**. A **phrasal verb**, however, is a verb that consists of two or three words. They can be made up of a **verb** followed by an **adverb**; *or* they can consist of a **verb** followed by a **preposition**; *or* they can consist of a **verb** followed by an **adverb** *and* a **preposition**.

WHAT'S THE PROBLEM?

Learners of English often find phrasal verbs quite problematic. Why should this be? Well, for a start, they are numerous

PHRASAL VERBS

and, in addition, there is not a predictable pattern to tell you which verb might go with which preposition or adverb. Native speakers achieve their familiarity with phrasal verbs through repeated use and hearing of these phrases every day of their lives, and a little bit of intuition is involved too. Another difficulty is that phrasal verbs frequently do not mean what they seem to mean (*see* **Figurative or literal meaning** on page 212) which makes them harder to learn. Examples of phrasal verbs are given in the sentences below with the phrasal verb in italics.

In this first group of sentences the **phrasal verbs** all consist of a **verb** followed by an **adverb**:

> We *sat down* and waited.
> She *slipped on* the ice and fell over.
> They *set off* just before dawn.
> When does the plane *take off*?
> It's time to *go in*.
> The price of property here will *go up*.
> *Come up* now, please.
> Winter will *set in* soon.
> Our holiday plans have *fallen through*.
> *Lie down* and try to sleep.
> The car had *moved off*.
> He hopes to find a permanent job and *settle down*.
> The child *curled up* and went to sleep.
> The caller *rang off* before I got to the phone.

In the next group of sentences the **phrasal verbs** all consist of a **verb** followed by a **preposition**:

> They *walked through* the forest.
> We *drove through* the city at midnight.
> You should *call on* your new neighbour.
> The child *fell into* the water.
> My father finally *got over* his illness.
> The workers *asked for* more money.

He originally *came from* London.
She was *living with* her parents at the time.
We had *pored over* all the holiday brochures.
He is *embarking on* a new career.
We *banked on* your support.
She *brought up* her children alone.
He *turned down* the job offer.

In this last group of sentences the **phrasal verbs** all consist of a **verb** followed by an **adverb** and a **preposition**.

Tiredness *crept up on* her as she drove and she decided to stop for some coffee.
We'll have to *come up with* another source of funding.
It is time they *did away with* these out-dated laws.
He must *face up to* the possible consequences of his action.
I refuse to *put up with* our noisy neighbours any longer.
You are bound to *come up against* a few problems in the course of this task.
The children *get up to* a lot of mischievous tricks when the teacher leaves the room.
He *ran off with* his best friend's money.
It all *comes down to* money in the end.

POSITION OF THE OBJECT IN PHRASAL VERBS

When a **phrasal verb** is used in a **transitive** situation (*see* page 189) you sometimes have a choice as to where to place the **object**. In the following sentences the italicized words represent the phrasal verb. In the first of each pair of examples the direct object follows, and in the second of each pair the direct object comes before the second word of the phrasal verb.

We *filled up* the water jug with cold water from the kitchen tap.
We *filled* the water jug *up* with cold water from the kitchen tap.

PHRASAL VERBS

> He'll never *live down* this terrible scandal.
> He'll never *live* this terrible scandal *down*.
>
> The quarrel *tore apart* the entire family.
> The quarrel *tore* the entire family *apart*.
>
> She is *putting away* the dishes in the cupboard.
> She is *putting* the dishes *away* in the cupboard.
>
> The boxer *knocked out* his opponent in the first round.
> The boxer *knocked* his opponent *out* in the first round.
>
> The mayor is *handing over* trophies to the winners now.
> The mayor is *handing* trophies *over* to the winners now.

How do you decide where to put the noun or noun phrase? It is often a matter of taste, or a matter of which form you think sounds better. Sometimes which sounds best depends on the length of the noun phrase.

Pronoun objects

When the object is a **pronoun** – such as *him*, *her*, *it* – it usually comes before the second word of the phrasal verb.

In the following sentences the italic words show **phrasal verbs** and their **pronoun objects**:

> I gave my letter of complaint to the manager, but she immediately *handed it over* to her assistant.
> When he broke off the engagement he wanted her to keep the ring, but she *gave it back*.
> It was Jim who thought of the idea, but it was Jack who *put it forward* to the committee.
> The little girl was injured in the playground and the teacher is trying to find the child who *knocked her over*.
> The young man was knocked out and doctors took several minutes to *bring him round*.

PHRASAL OR SINGLE VERB?

There is a growing tendency to use a phrasal verb where a single verb will do. For example, for a long time people were content to use the verb *meet* on its own. This was true of informal contexts, as in:

> I'm *meeting* Rebecca for lunch tomorrow.

But it was also true of more formal contexts, as in:

> The board of directors plan to *meet* their management staff next week.

In recent years, however, people have begun to use the phrasal verb *meet with* instead of just the verb *meet*, as with:

> I'm *meeting with* Rebecca for lunch tomorrow.

and, more especially, in formal contexts:

> The board of directors plan to *meet with* their management staff next week.

British English has acquired this use from American English. Objectors to it say that the use of *with* with *meet* is unnecessary. Nevertheless, the phrasal verb *meet with* seems to be here to stay.

This use is also spreading to other verbs. For example, some people are no longer content to *consult* a professional about something. They prefer to *consult with* a professional, as in:

> He thinks that he has been dismissed unfairly and he has been advised to *consult with* his lawyer.

> I need to *consult with* my team and get back to you about those changes.

PHRASAL VERBS

FIGURATIVE OR LITERAL MEANING?

One of the difficulties with phrasal verbs is that they frequently do not mean what they seem to mean. You can know perfectly well the meaning of the individual words that make up the phrase, and yet be unable to understand the meaning of the phrase. As is the case with many idioms, many phrasal verbs are used **figuratively** and it is often not easy to deduce this figurative meaning from the **literal** meaning of the words making up the phrase.

Some figurative meanings of phrasal verbs are more difficult to deduce than others. Some are quite easy:

> The children will *come through* that door very soon.

The literal meaning of the phrasal verb *come through* in the above sentence means just what it says, that the children will exit from the door soon. However, in the sentence:

> It was a miracle that so many soldiers *came through* the war alive.

the phrasal verb *came through* is not used exactly literally in that sentence, but is used in a way that is only a short step from the literal meaning. The sentence is referring to soldiers who survived a war.

In the sentence

> He *got over* the fence with difficulty and hoped there were no guard dogs around.

got over obviously refers to someone literally climbing over a fence to get to the other side.

In the sentence

> He never *got over* his brother's sudden death and missed him all his life.

got over refers to recovering from something bad that has

happened. The phrasal verb is not being used exactly literally, but it is close enough to the literal meaning to be easily deducible in context.

There are a great many examples of phrasal verbs of this kind – not quite literal in meaning but fairly easy to understand in context. Some are a step forward in difficulty from the two phrasal verbs mentioned above, but still relatively easily deducible, and they certainly do not usually cause any problems to native speakers.

These include *look down on* and *look up to.* The phrase *look down* means that you literally lower your eyes in order to see what is below you. Similarly, the phrase *look up* means that you literally raise your eyes in order to see what is above you.

There is a bit more to their literal meanings when you add the prepositions *on* and *to* respectively. The phrasal verb *look down on* can also mean that you think that someone is much less important than you are and so is inferior to you, as in:

>She *looks down on* students who didn't go to a private
>school like her.

The phrasal verb *look up to* means that you respect and admire someone as though they were much more important or better than you, as in:

>He is a well-known artist as well as being a teacher and
>many of the students *look up to* him.

The phrasal verb *look forward* means literally that you are looking at what is straight in front of you. If you add *to* to the phrase, as in *look forward to*, you are pleased or excited about something that you expect to happen sometime soon, as in:

>The little girl is really *looking forward to* her friend's
>birthday party.

The literal meaning of the phrasal verb *look through* should present no difficulties, as in:

PHRASAL VERBS

We *looked through* the window at the rain.

While its figurative meaning as applied to newspapers, reports, etc, is fairly obvious from the context, as in:

I have to *look through* the report before the meeting.

When used of something that is done to people, however, things become more complicated. If you *look through* someone you look at them as though you have not noticed them, often because you are deliberately ignoring them because you are angry with them, as in:

As she came towards me I was about to speak to her but she *looked right through me* and walked on.

Learners can be easily confused when the meaning of a phrasal verb seems quite easy to understand and then turns out not be. There may be an unexpected overtone or nuance that changes the meaning quite considerably. Take the sentence below:

Mark's *gone off with* Jane on a camping holiday.

Now, we know nothing whatsoever about Mark and Jane or their relationship, and we do not need to know. All we are told is that they have gone on a camping holiday together.

On the other hand, if the sentence is simply

Mark's *gone off with* Jane.

then we have grounds for some suspicion as to why he has gone off with her, and if the sentence then becomes

Mark's *run off with* Jane.

then our suspicion appears to be well-founded. It would seem that Mark and Jane have been having a relationship and they have decided to live together. It is amazing what you can learn from a little phrasal verb!

COMPLEX PHRASAL VERBS

A small selection follows of fairly complex **phrasal verbs** which have been formed from common **verbs**. There are many, many more, but this selection will show you phrasal verbs in action, so to speak. Most of these phrasal verbs have meanings which are more than just the sum of their parts. In other words, you cannot deduce their overall meaning just from knowing the meaning of the individual words.

come

come down on
If you *come down on* someone or something you criticize or punish them for something they have done, as in:
> The head teacher said that she will come down heavily on bullies.

come down with
If you *come down with* a disease or an infection you develop or begin to have it, as in:
> I am coming down with flu.

come up with
If you *come up with* an idea, plan, etc, you think of it, often having thought about it for a considerable time, as in:
> They have finally come up with funding to pay for the project.

cut

cut back on
If you *cut back on* something you reduce the extent of it, often because you cannot afford to spend so much money on it, as in:
> We're going to cut back on the amount we spend on socializing.

cut down on
If you *cut down on* something you try to reduce the amount of it that you use, or reduce the number of times you do it, as in:
> I'm cutting down on sugar to lose weight.

do

do away with
If you *do away with* something you get rid of it or abandon it, as in:
> They've introduced a new system and done away with the old one.

Do away with can also be used informally to mean 'to kill someone', as in:
> She looked so angry that I thought she was going to do away with me!

PHRASAL VERBS

do out of
If you *do* someone *out of* something you stop them having it, as in:
> The workers felt that they had been done out of a day's holiday.

get

get along with
If you *get along with* someone you find it easy to be with them and to enjoy their company, as in:
> It's good that all the members of the team get along with each other.

get away with
If you *get away with* something you are not punished or scolded for doing it, as in:
> He gets away with being really lazy because the boss likes him.

get behind with
If you *get behind with* something you are late or slow in doing it:
> The landlord is angry because we're getting behind with the rent again.

get down to
If you *get down to* something you start doing it seriously and paying a lot of attention to it, as in:
> We really must get down to thinking of ways to save money.

get out of
If you *get out of* something you avoid doing something which you do not want to do, as in:
> He's been asked to speak at the meeting but he's trying to get out of it.

get round to
If you *get round to* doing something you do something that you have been intending to do for some time, or that you should have done before, but have been too busy or unwilling to do, as in:
> I haven't got around to getting a new car yet.

get through to
If you *get through to* someone by telephone you are able to contact them and speak to them, as in:
> Telephone reception isn't good here. I wasn't able to get through to my office.

Get through to can also mean to succeed in getting someone to understand something, although this may be difficult, as in:
> He didn't seem to understand how urgent the situation was, but I finally got through to him.

get up to
Get up to is used in informal

contexts. If you *get up to* something you do something naughty, as in:
  Those kids are giggling and I'm sure they're getting up to mischief.

go
go along with
If you *go along with* someone, you go with them somewhere, as in:
  She wants me to go along with her to the party.

If you *go along with* a ruling, decision, etc, you accept it and obey it:
  Although he could have appealed against the court's ruling he decided to go along with it.

If you *go along with* someone or with their idea, policy, etc, you accept it or agree with it, as in:
  Most of the managers go along with our proposals.

go back on
If you *go back on* something, you do not do what you promised or agreed to do, as in:
  She has gone back on her promise.

go in for
If you *go in for* a competition of some kind you take part in it, as in:
  I'd like to go in for the marathon.

If you *go in for* a particular kind of work you make it your job or career, as in:
  She wants to go in for medicine if she passes her exams.

go off
If someone *goes off* someone or something it means they cease to like them or it, as in:
  My sister has gone off her best friend since they quarrelled.

go off with
If someone *goes off with* something they take something that belongs to someone else, usually without permission, as in:
  I showed a customer a rather valuable book and I later discovered that he had gone off with it.

go through with
If you *go through with* something you continue doing it until it has been completed or achieved, as in:
  The government's proposal to raise taxes was so unpopular that they did not go through with the scheme.

keep
keep in with
If you *keep in with* someone you remain friendly with them, usually

PHRASAL VERBS

because this may help you to get something you want, as in:
> Keep in with Anne, I'm certain she's going to be made head of department.

keep on at
If you *keep on at* someone you repeatedly ask or tell them something so that they get upset, as in:
> Her supervisor kept on at her about working harder.

keep out of
If you *keep out of* something you avoid being involved in a difficult situation, as in:
> If the two sisters start arguing with each other, keep out of it.

keep up with
If you *keep up with* someone you stay in contact with them, as in:
> We promised to keep up with each other after we left university.

make
make off with
If you *make off with* something you steal something and take it away, as in:
> The dog leapt onto the table and made off with the roast beef.

make up for
If you *make up for* something you do something that tries to put right a bad situation, as in:
> He bought his mother a beautiful, expensive new vase to make up for breaking her favourite one.

make up with
If you *make up with* someone you become friends again following an argument, as in:
> I made up with Brian following that big argument we had last week.

pull
pull out of
If you *pull out of* something you get out of a difficult situation, as in:
> We're pulling out of the market because it's no longer profitable.

put
put down to
If you *put* something *down to* something you think or say that something is caused by something, as in:
> The firm put the slump in their profits down to the recession.

put in for
If you *put in for* something you apply for it, as in:
> There's a more senior job coming up soon and I'm putting in for it.

put up to
If you *put* someone *up to* something

you encourage them to do something foolish, dangerous or wrong, as in:
> Her friends put her up to stealing a packet of sweets from the shop.

put up with
If you *put up with* something or someone you accept an unpleasant situation or person without complaining, or tolerate someone or something, as in:
> They can't put up with their noisy neighbours any longer.

stand
stand up for
If you *stand up for* someone or something you defend or support them when they are under an attack of some kind, as in:
> Marge stood up for me when I was getting all the blame.

stand up to
If you *stand up to* someone you refuse to be bullied by them and are able to resist their attacks or demands, as in:
> He did his best to stand up to the bully but it was not easy.

take
take up on
If you *take* someone *up on* something you accept an offer or a suggestion that they have made to you:
> I'm busy tonight but I'll take you up on dinner next week if you're free.

walk
walk away from
If you literally *walk away from* someone or something you just move away from them by walking:
> He walked away from me while I was still talking.

If you figuratively *walk away from* a situation you do not try to deal with it but leave it or ignore it, as in:
> After their last quarrel he felt that their friendship was at an end and the time had come to walk away from it.

walk in on
If you *walk in on* someone you enter somewhere unexpectedly and see them, or several people, doing something private or secret which may embarrass you or them, as in:
> I walked in on my aunt when she was changing her clothes.

walk off with
If you *walk off with* something you win something, such as a trophy, very easily, as in:
> They easily walked off with first prize

PREPOSITIONS

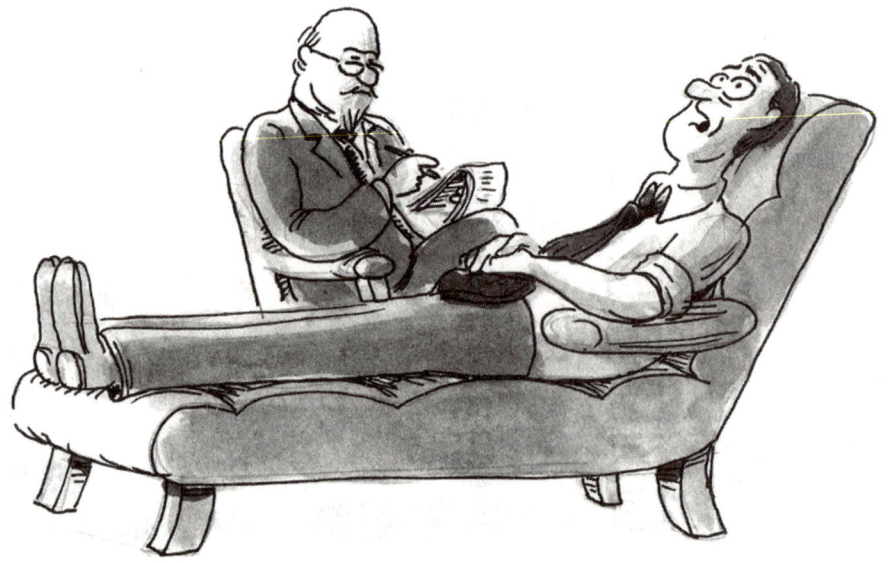

You know, certain things make me feel really guilty sometimes. But the worst bit is, I don't know if I feel *guilty for*, *guilty at*, *guilty about*, or *guilty of* them.

A PREPOSITION is a kind of linking word which is used to show the relationship between a noun or pronoun and the rest of a sentence. The preposition usually comes before the noun it refers to or 'governs'. There are two types of preposition, **simple prepositions** and **complex prepositions**.

SIMPLE PREPOSITIONS

Simple prepositions are often very short words, such as *at*, *by*, *in*, *of*, *off*, *on*, *to* and *up*, but also include such words as *among*, *before*, *behind*, *during* and *through*.

In the following sentences the words in italic are all **simple prepositions**:

The cakes are *on* the table.
The cat is *up* the tree.
She sleeps *during* the day.
They left *before* dawn.
We arrived *after* dinner.
I will stay there *for* three weeks.
He is a young man *of* great talent.
She carried a bag *with* a black handle.
I will go *with* them.
He was sacked *for* theft.
I paid *by* cash.
We had to leave *without* Mary.
They were *against* the scheme.

COMPLEX PREPOSITIONS

Complex prepositions consist of two or three words. These include *ahead of*, *because of*, *instead of*, *on account of*, *by means of* and *on behalf of*.

In the following sentences the words in blue italic form **complex prepositions**:

She attended the conference *in spite of* illness.
He had to retire *on account of* his age.
They are not rich *in terms of* money.
They have a dog *in addition to* the three cats.

COMMON ERRORS

You might think that, as parts of speech go, prepositions look fairly harmless. This is probably because many of them are so short – you might not think that such tiny words could cause much in the way of trouble. However, small is not always innocent. Just think of the discomfort that mosquitoes can cause! Prepositions may be short but they are certainly not problem-free.

SENTENCES ENDING IN A PREPOSITION

You may have learned in school that prepositions should not be put at the end of sentences. The rule was adopted from Latin: a Latin sentence cannot end in a preposition. However – and this may make some people unhappy – that is not a good reason for English to follow suit.

Avoiding putting a preposition at the end of a sentence or clause can lead to the language sounding unnatural. Compare the following sentences:

> This is the kind of behaviour *up with which* the company *will not put*.
>
> This is the kind of behaviour the company *will not put up with*.

The first one sounds odd. No one would ever say this, and you would rewrite the sentence to avoid that structure before you would ever choose to write it that way. The most sensible thing to do with regard to prepositions is to put them where they sound most natural. For example:

> What on earth are the children up *to*?
>
> There's nothing you can do, so it's not worth fretting *about*.

Sometimes the best place to place a preposition depends on whether the context is formal or informal. In ordinary informal contexts you would write or say:

> Which hotel did you stay *in*?

In a formal written context you might choose to write:

> *In which* hotel did you stay?

There is a lot more to consider about prepositions than worrying about whether to end a sentence with them, as this chapter explains.

Omitting prepositions, such as *to*, is a common error among learners when speaking English. For example, they may say:

> *I'm going* station now. **[Wrong]**

instead of

> *I'm going to the* station now. **[Correct]**

or

> We're going *cinema* now. **[Wrong]**

instead of

> We're going *to the cinema* now. **[Correct]**

It is easy to understand why such mistakes arise because English is not at all a consistent language. For example, it is quite correct to say:

> I'm going *home* to feed my cat. **[Correct]**

But it is also correct to say:

> I've got a cat *at home*, so I need to go and feed him. **[Correct]**

Many problems associated with prepositions tend to centre not on the prepositions themselves, but on their relationships. It is the function of prepositions to show how some elements in sentences relate to other elements, and it is not always easy to decide which preposition connects what to what. This is a particular problem for learners of English as a foreign language or as a second language.

WORD PAIRS

Some words cause particular problems because they can hook up with more than one preposition. For example, the verb *agree* can be accompanied by *to*, *with* or *on*, while the adjective *responsible* can team up with *to* or *for*. The A–Z list which follows, although it is by no means comprehensive, will give you guidance on some of these.

PREPOSITIONS

absent
absent from
You are said to be *absent from* a meeting or place when you are not there, as in:
> The actor was absent from last night's performance because he was ill.

present at
The opposite of *absent from* is *present at*, as in:
> There were 300 people present at the protest meeting.

absolve
absolve from
Absolve is mostly used in formal contexts, in law or religion. If you *absolve* someone *from* or *of* blame you say publicly or officially that they are not guilty of a crime or act of wrongdoing, often one that they have been accused of:
> He has been absolved from all blame in connection with the accident.

You can be absolved from a duty:
> The judge absolved him from his duties at court.

absolve of
Absolve of is mostly used in religious contexts.
> The priest absolved him of his sins.

accustomed
accustomed to
If you are *accustomed to* something it is something that you do regularly or are very familiar with, as in:
> Their teenage children were accustomed to the amenities of city life and found life in a country village very boring.

It is a more formal way of saying 'used to', as in:
> They were accustomed to the intense heat.

in the habit of
Another way of saying *accustomed to* is *in the habit of*, as in:
> She's in the habit of going for a run after work every evening.

accuse/charge
accuse of
If you believe that someone has done something wrong you can *accuse* them *of* wrongdoing, as in:
> He was accused of taking the money.

If you use the noun *accusation* this is often followed by the preposition *against*, as in:
> He appears to have made false accusations against her.

charge with
Another way to say the same thing

is to say *charge with*. If the police formally accuse someone of a crime they *charge* them *with* it, as in:
  The police charged him with burglary.

press charges against

If you use the noun *charge* this is often followed by the preposition *against*:
  The police decided to press charges against him.

adhere
adhere to

Adhere to is mostly used in formal contexts. If you *adhere to* a rule or an agreement you do what it says you should do or in other words you obey it, as in:
  We expect all pupils to adhere to the school's rules.

afraid/frightened
afraid of

If you are *afraid of* something you feel fear because you think you might be hurt or harmed, as in:
  The children are afraid of the dark.

frightened of

You can also say that you are *frightened of* something, which has the same meaning as *afraid of*:
  The man is frightened of dogs because he was once bitten by one.

agree/disagree/approve
agree to

If you *agree to* something you say that you will allow it to happen, as in:
  They agreed to our plan right away.

If you *agree to* do something you say that you will do it, as in:
  He agreed to clean the car at the weekend.

agree with

You are said to *agree with* someone about something if you both have the same opinion or feeling about it, as in:
  I hardly ever agree with my brother but I think he's right about this.

If you approve of something, such as a suggestion or a plan, you can be said to *agree with* it, as in:
  I agree with his proposals for a wind farm.

Less commonly *agree with* can be used to indicate that something is good for you, as in:
  The warmer climate agrees with him and his health has improved.

agree on

If people discuss and reach a decision about something you can say that they *agree on* it, as in:
  The couple have got their families to agree on a date for the wedding.

PREPOSITIONS

in agreement
If you want to use the noun *agreement* in this context this is also followed by the preposition *with*, as in:
> If we're all in agreement with each other, we can move on.

disagree with
The opposite of agree with is to *disagree with*, as in:
> The politicians disagreed with each other about the way forward.

alternative
alternative to
When used to describe a course of action the adjective *alternative* refers to something that can be done or used instead of something else, as in:
> The police are recommending an alternative route to the city centre.

Alternative can also be used as a noun taking the preposition *to*:
> There's no alternative to hard work when it comes to passing exams.

answer
answer for
If you have to *answer for* something you are responsible for it and have to explain how it came to happen, as in:
> The team's manager will have to answer for their appalling performance.

If you say that you *can't answer for* someone else who is not present it means that you cannot say what they are likely to think or do, as in:
> I'm in favour of the scheme but I can't answer for my colleagues.

answer to
If you *answer to* someone in authority it means that you have to explain to them why you have acted in the way you did, as in:
> I'm not going to tell you why I'm late. I only answer to the head of the department.

anxious
anxious about
If you are *anxious about* something you are worried about it for some reason and think about it all the time, as in:
> The students are anxious about their exam results.

anxious to
If you are *anxious to* do something you want very much to do it, as in:
> She is anxious to get a job so she can start saving some money.

anxious for
Anxious for can sometimes be used

to mean 'worried about', as in:
   Their son is doing a dangerous job and they're anxious for his safety.

However, *anxious for* can also indicate that you want very much to have something or that you want it to happen, as in:
   They are anxious for their house alterations to get finished.

apart
apart from

You use *apart* immediately followed by *from* when you are referring to an exception of some kind, as in:
   I like all kinds of films apart from horror.

   Apart from my sister, everyone in our family has summer birthdays.

Apart from can also be used to mean 'as well as', as in:
   Apart from their large townhouse in London they have a flat in Paris.

appeal
appeal against

If you *appeal against* a decision or a judgment you ask for it to be reconsidered and changed, as in:
   He was found guilty but his defence team have appealed against the verdict.

appeal

Note that in American English *appeal* is used without a preposition following it, as in:
   They have appealed the verdict.

appeal to

If you *appeal to* someone for something you make a request for some kind of help, as in:
   Police have appealed to the public for information regarding the break-in.

If something *appeals to* you, you like it and find it attractive or interesting, as in:
   The idea of getting married at a beach resort really appeals to me.

apply
apply for

If you *apply for* something you make a formal request to be considered for something such as a job, a place at college, etc, as in:
   There's a job vacancy but you have to apply for it by Tuesday of next week.

apply to

Apply to means 'to concern or affect someone or something', as in:
   This warning doesn't apply to people who are already following the rules.

approve/disapprove
approve of

If you *approve of* an action, suggestion, etc, you think it is a

PREPOSITIONS

good thing and are pleased with it, as in:

> His parents approved of his decision to go to university.

disapprove of

The opposite of *approve of* is *disapprove of*, as in:

> Many people disapproved of the bad language in the play.

arrive/reach
arrive at

If you *arrive at* a place you come to it after a journey, as in:

> We arrived at the party just as everyone else was going home.

arrive in

If the place at the end of your journey is a country or a town you use *in* instead of *at* with *arrive*, as in:

> The ferry was delayed and we did not arrive in France until after dark.

reach

Note that the verb *reach* without a following preposition can often be used instead of *arrive at*, as in:

> We hope to reach the hotel before nightfall.

ashamed
ashamed of

If you are *ashamed of* something you have done you feel guilty or embarrassed because you think it was wrong or unacceptable in some way, as in:

> He was really ashamed of shouting at his mother last night.

You can also be *ashamed of* yourself when you feel this kind of guilt, as in:

> He felt ashamed of himself for shouting at his mother last night.

ask
ask after

If you *ask after* someone you ask how they are, if they are well, etc:

> Nigel always asks after you whenever I see him.

attached
attached to

If you are *attached to* someone or something you like them very much and have often known or owned them for a long time, as in:

> The children are very attached to their grandfather.

aware/unaware/conscious
aware of

If you are *aware of* someone or something you know that they exist or are present, as in:

> She was suddenly aware of footsteps behind her.

Word pairs

unaware of
The opposite of *aware of* is *unaware of*, as in:
> He was quite unaware of the time until he heard the clock strike midnight.

conscious of
The expression *conscious of* means much the same as *aware of*, as in:
> He was conscious of someone staring at him.

unconscious of
The opposite of *conscious of* is *unconscious of*, as in:
> He seemed totally unconscious of the fact that people were laughing at him.

bank/rely/depend
bank on
If you *bank on* something happening you *rely on* it happening and hope that you will get some advantage from it happening, as in:
> I'm running late and I'm banking on the train being late. It usually is.

rely on/depend on
Bank on is slightly more informal than *rely on*. You can also use *depend on* in this way.
> He's relying on his experience in the army being relevant to his application to join the police.
> I always depend on you to make sure I'm on time.

because/owing/due
because of
If something happens *because of* something it happens as a result of it, as in:
> The football match had to be cancelled because of a flooded pitch.

DUE TO
Due to is sometimes used as an alternative to *because of* (*see* entry above) and *owing to*. Although it is grammatically wrong to do so, this usage is becoming widespread because the difference between *due to* and *owing to* and *because of* is quite difficult to understand. *Due to* is adjectival and means 'caused by', while *because of* and *owing to* are prepositional, as in:
> Everyone agreed that it was an error *due to* lack of experience.
> Cancellations *due to* bad weather are expected.

PREPOSITIONS

owing to
The phrase *owing to* is a slightly more formal than *because of*, as in:
> We had to postpone our holiday owing to my mother's illness.

due to
Due to is sometimes used as another way to say *because of*. This is very commonly used now, but used to be considered ungrammatical. *See the box on page 229.*
> I missed the play due to my illness.

become
become of
You use the phrase *become of* to refer to what has happened to someone or what they are doing now, as in:
> He was at primary school with me and I often wonder what became of him.

begin
begin by
If you *begin by* doing something you do it first before doing anything else, as in:
> I think we'll begin by putting the kettle on for a cup of tea.

begin with
If you *begin with* something you deal with it first before carrying out other tasks, as in:
> Assembly in that school always begins with a prayer.

believe
believe in
If you *believe in* something such as magic, fairies or ghosts, you feel sure that these exist.
> The children still believe in Father Christmas.

The same is true if you *believe in* God, as in:
> She believed in God but did not attend church.

The phrase *believe in* can also be used to mean that you have confidence and trust in someone and are sure that they will be successful, as in:
> It is important to believe in yourself and be confident.

If you *believe in* something can also mean you are in favour of it or support it because you think that it is right, as in:
> He believed in equality for women.

belong
belong to
If something *belongs to* someone, they own it, as in:
> That car over there belongs to my neighbour.

If you *belong to* something, such as a club, organization, group or category, you are a member of it, as in:
> They all belong to the local tennis club.
> They belonged to the English aristocracy.

benefit
benefit from
If you *benefit from* something you get some form of advantage from it, as in:
> Lower paid workers should benefit from the new tax rules.

blame
blame for
If you *blame* someone *for* something you say that they are responsible for something bad:
> The driver of the other car blamed him for the accident.

The noun *blame* is also paired with the preposition *for*:
> I got the blame for the error in the accounts.

blame on
The expression *blame* something *on* someone used to be considered unacceptable by many users, but now things have changed and this use has become quite widespread:
> I wasn't even here when the vase broke. Don't blame it on me!

If you want to use the noun *blame* to convey this meaning you say or write:
> They tried to put the blame on me although I was completely innocent.

bored
bored with
If you are *bored with* something you no longer find it interesting, as in:
> He says he's bored with his job and wants to leave.

bored of
The expression *bored of* is sometimes used in speech or very informal pieces of writing, as in:
> I'm bored of this programme.

capable/incapable
capable of
If you are *capable of* something or doing something, you are able to do it or are liable to do it:
> I really didn't think that he was capable of playing the piano like that.

incapable of
The opposite of *capable of* is *incapable of*, as in:
> She had thought herself incapable of speaking in public.

PREPOSITIONS

Incapable of is often used in quite formal contexts.

care
care for
If you *care for* someone who is sick, disabled, old, very young, etc, you look after them and make sure that they have the things they need, as in:
  She employs someone to care for her elderly mother during the day.

If you say you *don't care for* something, it means you don't like it, as in:
  I don't care for red wine.

care about
If you *care about* something you think that it is important and you are concerned about it, as in:
  If you cared about the environment you would recycle your rubbish.

If you *care about* someone or something you really like them or love them, as in:
  He asked his mother to come and stay with them because he really cared about her.

centre
centre on
If something *centres on* something it is the focus or centre of attention or activity, as in:
  The greater part of the bankers' discussion centred on the downturn in the world economy.

centre around/round
The phrase *centre around* or *centre round* is now frequently used instead of *centre on*. This is disliked by some language commentators on the grounds that the word *centre* is too precise to be used with the imprecise words *round* or *around*. The phrases *centre around* or *centre round* are more likely to be tolerated by precise users if they are used with reference to something generalized rather than something specific, as in:
  Most of her hobbies centre around the great outdoors.

commitment/committed
commitment to
If you show *commitment to* someone or something you show loyalty to them, as in:
  His commitment to the project was rewarded with a bonus.

committed to
The expression *be committed to* can have much the same meaning:
  She was so committed to her charity work that she spent all her free time volunteering.

Word pairs

communicate

communicate to

If you *communicate* something *to* someone you tell them about it:

She had to communicate news of the factory's closure to the workforce.

communicate with

If you *communicate with* someone you exchange information with them, as in:

We communicate regularly with each other by email.

compare

compare to or with

When you compare two things you often do so as a comment on their differences or similarities. In this context you can say *compare with* or

COMPARE TO OR WITH?

When commenting on the similarity or dissimilarity of two objects of the same type or categorization, formerly the correct usage was considered to be the phrase *compare with*:

Compared with the Alsatian, a dachshund is a tiny dog.

Compare to was considered the correct usage to compare objects of a dissimilar type or categorization:

Compared to cats, dogs are so much more friendly.

Both are now considered interchangeable and *compare to* is now found more often and is considered the preferred use. The difference between the use of the two phrases is not at all clear to most speakers. We find, repeatedly, that when the distinction between what is considered 'correct' and what is considered 'wrong' is slight or difficult to understand, then that rule eventually dies out. *Compare with* and *compare to* are both considered acceptable in this context:

Compared with last year, our profits are up 13 per cent.
Compared to last year, our profits are up 13 per cent.

PREPOSITIONS

compare to:
> He always feels he is being compared to/with his older brother.

compare to

When you are only commenting on the similarity between two things and saying that they are like each other, then *compare to* is the correct phrase, as in:
> He is a very good actor but you certainly cannot compare him to Robert de Niro.

See also the box on page 233.

compatible

compatible with/incompatible with

If something is *compatible with* something else the two things are able to exist together or can be used together without any problems being caused, as in:
> Having such a high pressure job isn't compatible with the demands of family life.

The opposite of this is *incompatible with*, as in:
> The new head's approach to education is totally incompatible with the deputy head's approach.

complain

complain about

If you *complain about* something you think that there is something wrong with it and you say that you are not satisfied with it, as in:
> The food in the restaurant was so bad that several people complained about it.

complain of

If you *complain of* something it can mean that you say that you are annoyed or upset about it, as in:
> The man who was arrested complained of ill-treatment.

It can also mean that you have a pain in part of your body or that you are feeling ill, as in:
> The child is complaining of a pain in her stomach.

complain to

If you *complain to* someone you tell them that you are not satisfied with something or that someone or something has made you annoyed or upset, as in:
> The speakers I bought are faulty and I'm going to complain to the manager of the shop where I bought them.

compliment

compliment on

When you *compliment* someone *on* something you say something pleasant in praise of their

appearance, ability, etc, to show that you admire them, as in:
> Several people complimented her on her new hairstyle.

composed
composed of
If something is *composed of* some parts, substances, people, etc, it is made up of them, as in:
> The exam is composed of two units: an oral test and a written test.

The phrase *be composed of* is similar in meaning to that of *consist of*, but it is often used in more formal contexts. See *consist of*.

concerned
concerned about/for
If you are *concerned about* something you are worried about it, as in:
> She is concerned about environmental issues.

The phrase *concerned for* also means worried about, as in:
> Many young people are concerned for the future of the planet.

concerned with
If something is *concerned with* something it deals with it or is about it, as in:
> The book is concerned with changes in society after the Second World War.

conditional
conditional on
If something is *conditional on* something it means it will only happen or be done if something else happens or is done first, as in:
> His offer to buy their house is conditional on a substantial reduction in the price.

This phrase is found in fairly formal or commercial contexts.

conducive
conducive to
If something is *conducive to* something it makes it possible or more likely to happen, as in:
> The resort was very noisy and hardly conducive to a relaxing time.

The phrase *conducive to* is used in fairly formal contexts.

confidence
confidence in
If you *have confidence in* someone you feel sure that they are going to do something well or are going to succeed in something that they are trying to do, as in:
> He has to undergo a long and difficult operation to fix his heart but he has complete confidence in the surgeon.

PREPOSITIONS

confident
confident of
If you are *confident of* something you feel sure that it will happen or that you will achieve it, as in:
> He seems to be confident of getting the job.

concentrate
concentrate on
If you *concentrate on* something you give it most of your attention rather than attending to other things, as in:
> They usually spend a lot of time playing sports but this year they are having to concentrate on their studies.

conform
conform to
If something *conforms to* something such as a rule or guideline, it obeys or follows it, as in:
> Planning permission was refused because the plans of the building did not conform to regulations.

You can also use *conform with* in this context, as in:
> The proposed skateboarding park must conform with safety regulations.

Conform to can also mean 'to agree with or match', as in:
> He doesn't conform to my idea of a doctor: he's so young!

You can also use *conform with* in this context, as in:
> He did not conform with her idea of a prospective husband.

connect
connect with/to
When the verb *connect* means 'to join' it can be followed either by *to* or *with*, as in:
> The proposed road would connect our town with the city.

> Our property is connected to theirs by a narrow winding lane.

connect with
If the verb means 'to notice or show a link or relationship between someone or something', *connect* is followed by *with*, as in:
> Police have failed to connect him with the crime.

consent
consent to
If you *consent to* something, you agree to it or give your permission for it to happen, as in:
> She consented to his suggestion that she go into a care home.

consist
consist of
If something *consists of* two or more

things or people, it is made up of them, as in:

> The football team consists of pupils from two different schools.

> The mixture consists of flour, milk, eggs and flavouring.

The phrase *consists of* means the same as *be composed of* but it is not used in the passive.

content
content with
If you are *content with* something you are quite happy or willing to have it or accept it, as in:

> She seems to be content with a very quiet life.

content to
If you are *content to* do something you are happy or willing to do it, as in:

> He was content to work overtime every week as long as he got paid for his extra hours.

contrast
contrast with
If two things *contrast with* each other they show a marked difference when they are compared with each other, as in:

> The children's colourful coats contrasted with the stark whiteness of the snow.

convinced
convinced of
If you are *convinced of* something you are sure that it's true, as in:

> She was convinced of his honesty despite her friend's warning that he had deceived her.

cope
cope with
The phrase *cope with* is similar in meaning to *deal with*, but the situation involved is often more difficult, or more of a problem, as in:

> She has to cope with a full-time job on top of looking after her children and elderly parents.

correspond
correspond to
If something *corresponds to* something it is very similar to or the same as something or it is the equivalent of it, as in:

> The title of advocate in the Scottish legal system corresponds to the title of barrister in the English one.

correspond with
If you *correspond with* someone you write letters to them and receive letters from them, as in:

> They have never met but they have corresponded regularly with each other since they were childhood pen pals.

critical

critical of

If you are *critical of* someone or something you point out their faults or bad points, as in:
> Several parents were critical of the school's policy towards bullying.

culminate

culminate in

If something *culminates in* something it finishes in that particular way, as in:
> The evening culminated in an impressive fireworks display.

Culminates in is a formal way of saying *ends in*.

deal

deal with

If you *deal with* something or someone you take the necessary action to achieve a result or solve a problem, as in:
> The manager will deal with the customer's complaint.

If a book, speech, etc, *deals with* a subject it is about that subject, as in:
> The article deals with homelessness.

decide

decide on

To make up your mind about something or to choose someone or something after thinking carefully, as in:
> She spent ages worrying about what to wear to the party and finally decided on her little black dress.

decide upon

Decide upon has the same meaning as *decide on* but it is often used in more formal contexts.

delight

delight in

If you *delight in* something (often something that upsets someone else) you take pleasure in it or enjoy it, as in:
> He delights in collecting coins, banknotes, stamps and postcards from all over the world.

delighted with

If you are *delighted with* something you are very pleased and happy about it, as in:
> I'm delighted with my new dress.

depend

depend on

If something *depends on* something else it is directly affected by that, as in:
> Where we go on holiday this year depends on how much it will cost.

If you *depend on* someone or something you need their support in order to survive, as in:
> She depends on an allowance from her parents to pay her bills at university.

dependent
dependent on
If you are *dependent on* someone you depend on their support for your survival, as in:
> The magazine is dependent on local advertising for its funding.

deprive
deprive of
If you *deprive* someone *of* something you stop them from having it, especially something that they really ought to have, as in:
> The laws are there to stop people being deprived of their rights.

deter
deter from
If something *deters* you *from* doing something it stops you from doing it, as in:
> They put a fence round the old tree to deter children from climbing it.

detract
detract from
If something *detracts from* something it makes it seem less good or attractive, as in:
> The ruins of the old factory detract from the beauty of the area.

devoid
devoid of
If something is *devoid of* something it is completely lacking in it, as in:
> The house is comfortable enough but it is completely devoid of style.

devoted
devoted to
If you are *devoted to* someone you love them very much or are very loyal to them, as in:
> She's devoted to her grandchildren and always buys them special treats.

different
different from
Different can be followed by the prepositions *from*, *to* and *than*. In British English *different from* is the most acceptable construction, especially in formal contexts, as in:
> Her attitude to work was quite different from his.

different to
Different to is found in informal, especially spoken, contexts, as in:
> Their lifestyle is completely different to mine.

PREPOSITIONS

different than

Different than is frequently used in American English, but this construction is not considered correct in British English, although it is becoming more common. *Different than* is considered more acceptable if it is followed by a clause, as in:

> It looks no different than it did a decade ago.

dispose
dispose of

If you *dispose of* something you throw it away or give it to someone, as in:

> You must remember that some things can be recycled when you are disposing of your household waste.

distract
distract from

If you *distract* someone *from* something you take their attention away from something, as in:

> It's dangerous to talk to the driver because you'll distract him.

dressed
dressed in

If you are *dressed in* something, you are wearing it, as in:

> The children were all dressed in their school uniform.

The phrase *clothed in* means the same, but it is usually found in more formal contexts, as in:

> The king and queen were clothed in scarlet robes trimmed with ermine.

end
end in

If something *ends in* something it finishes in that particular way, as in:

> The night ended in triumph as he took home three awards.

Culminate in is a more formal way of saying this.

end with

If something *ends with* an event, etc, that event marks the finish of something, often being the last of a series, as in:

> The choir sang a selection of well-known songs, ending with the national anthem.

engaged
engaged in

If you are *engaged in* something you are busy doing something or are very much involved in something, as in:

> They are engaged in the difficult process of selling their house.

Engaged in is usually used in quite formal contexts.

engaged to

If you are *engaged to* someone you have said that you will marry them, as in:

> Sue has just got engaged to Tom and they are planning a June wedding.

engrossed
engrossed in

If you are *engrossed in* something you are so interested in it that you concentrate on it and do not notice anything else, as in:

> She was so engrossed in the film that she did not hear me talking.

envious
envious of

If you are *envious of* someone, you wish that you had something that they have or do, as in:

> She is envious of her brother because he is old enough to stay out late.

If you are *envious of* something that someone has, you wish that you had it, as in:

> They were envious of the luxury house that their friends lived in.

escape
escape from

If you *escape from* a dangerous place or situation you succeed in getting away from it, as in:

> They escaped from poverty by managing to emigrate.

except

The word *except* introduces the person or thing that a general statement does not apply to, as in:

> You can borrow any of the books except this one.

except for

It is sometimes followed by *for*, as in:

> We will all be there except for Jim.

exception
with the exception of

When you are mentioning someone or something that is an exception you often use the phrase *with the exception of*, as in:

> The whole family went with the exception of my aunt, who was feeling ill.

An *exception* is someone or something that a general statement of some kind does not apply to.

faith
faith in

If you have *faith in* someone, you trust them absolutely or have complete confidence in them, as in:

> She has great faith in her counsellor.

If you lose *faith in* someone, you

PREPOSITIONS

no longer trust them or have confidence in them, as in:

> The workers are losing faith in their management team and are worried about their jobs.

faithful

faithful to

If you are *faithful to* someone or something you remain loyal to them and continue to give them your support, as in:

> The politician remained faithful to his principles and refused to vote with his party on the issue.

If you are *faithful to* a husband or wife, etc, you are in a monogamous relationship with them, as in:

> He promised in his wedding vows to be faithful to his wife.

unfaithful to

The opposite of *faithful to* is *unfaithful to*, as in:

> He did not want to be unfaithful to his wife.

familiar

familiar to

If something is *familiar to* you, you know it well, as in:

> Although her face is familiar to me I cannot remember her name.

familiar with

If you are *familiar with* something, you know or understand it well, as in:

> She was brought up in this area so she must be familiar with it.

fond

fond of

If you are *fond of* someone you like them very much and may even love them, but usually not in a romantic way, as in:

> John and the girl next door are very fond of each other, but there has never been any suggestion of romance between them.

free

free of

If something or someone is *free of* something they do not have any of it or contain any of it, as in:

> The room is now free of dust.
> The patient is now free of pain.

free from

The expression *free from* means the same as *free of* and is used in much the same way, as in:

> Yesterday the doctors thought she had measles but today she is free from all the usual symptoms.

friend

friends with

If you are *friends with* someone that person is your friend, as in:
> I have been friends with Anne since our schooldays.

friendly with

If you are *friendly with* someone you like each other and enjoy spending time together, as in:
> She is friendly with several of the women who have children at her daughter's school.

full

full of

If something is *full of* people or things it contains a very large number of them, sometimes to the extent that it can hardly contain any more, as in:
> The cellar was full of rubbish.

filled with

If something is *filled with* people or things it is *full of* them, as in:
> She was trying to smile although her eyes were filled with tears.

glad

glad about

If you are *glad about* something you are pleased and happy about it, as in:
> We have discovered that we can get a flight from our local airport and we're very glad about that.

glad for

If you are *glad for* someone you are pleased that they have got something or done something, as in:
> Our son has got the job he applied for and we're so glad for him.

glad of

If you are *glad of* something you are happy that you have it and you are grateful for it, as in:
> He's had to work overtime a lot recently, but he was glad of the extra money so near to Christmas.

glad to

If you are *glad to* do something you are willing and keen to do it, as in:
> I'll be glad to look after the children for you this afternoon.

graduate

graduate from

If you *graduate from* a university or college you get a degree from it, often a first degree, as in:
> Many young people now have difficulty in getting jobs when they graduate from university.

grateful

grateful for

If you are *grateful for* something

PREPOSITIONS

you are happy to have it and feel that you want to thank someone for it, as in:
>We are very grateful for all the donations to our charity.

grateful to

If you are *grateful to* someone for something you feel that you want to thank them for it, as in:
>We are so grateful to everyone who has given us their support.

guilty

guilty about

If you feel *guilty about* something you feel bad and ashamed because you know that you have done something bad or wrong, as in:
>I feel guilty about forgetting your birthday.

guilty at

The phrase *feel guilty at* means the same, as in:
>They feel guilty at not inviting him to their party.

guilty for

The phrase *feel guilty for* means the same, as in:
>I feel guilty for telling a lie.

guilty of

If you are *guilty of* something you have done something bad, wrong or criminal, as in:
>The jury found him guilty of theft.

>He's guilty of being far too generous.

half

half/half of

You can use either *half* or *half of* to refer to an amount that is one of two equal parts that make up a whole. You can use *half of* instead of *half* in front of a noun or noun group beginning with a determiner, although *half* is the more common, as in:
>He has done half his work for today.

>The child ate only half her lunch.

>She has been in and out of hospital for half of her adult life.

>Her father was overseas with the army for half of her childhood.

You use *half of* not *half* in front of pronouns, as in:
>I haven't finished my essay but I've done half of it.

>More than half of our foreign students went back to their own countries after graduating.

You use *half* not *half of* in front of words such as *hour*, *kilo*, *metre*, etc, as in:
>It will take us half an hour to get there.

>I need half a kilo of flour for this recipe.

harmful
harmful to
If something is *harmful to* someone or something it has a bad effect on them, as in:
> Exhaust fumes from cars are harmful to the environment.

hear
hear of/hear about
If you *hear of* something you find out about it, as in:
> She's heard of a job that would suit her very well.

You can also use *hear about* in this sense, as in:
> We only heard about her promotion yesterday.

heard
heard of
You can use *heard of* to show that you have knowledge about someone or something, as in:
> Have you heard of a town called Tring?

hope
hope for
You use *hope for* when you want something to happen and think that it is possible, as in:
> She's hoping for some sunshine on her wedding day.

hope of
If there is *hope of* something happening you want it to happen and think that it might, as in:
> Doctors have hope of a cure in the near future.

> Their army outnumbered ours and there was no hope of victory.

inferior/superior
inferior to
If someone or something is said to be *inferior to* someone or something else, they are not as good or they are of poorer quality, as in:
> You shouldn't feel inferior to them just because they have more money than you do.

superior to
The opposite of this is *superior to*, as in:
> The team that is playing this week is far superior to the one that played last week.

inquire
inquire into
If you *inquire into* something you ask questions in order to get information about it, as in:
> The police are inquiring into the company's profits because they suspect the owner of fraud.

insist

insist on

If you *insist on* doing something you say very firmly that you will do it, as in:

> She insisted on getting a taxi to the airport although we offered to drive her there.

intention

intention of

If you say that you have every *intention of* doing something, you mean that you definitely plan to do it, as in:

> He says that he has every intention of finishing his project today.

If you say that you have *no intention of* doing something, you mean that you are definitely not going to do it, as in:

> They say they've done nothing wrong and they have no intention of apologizing.

interfere/meddle

interfere in

If you *interfere in* something you get involved in it and try to influence it or change it in some way although it's not really your business, and other people do not want you to get involved, as in:

> The new owner promised that he would not interfere in the day-to-day running of the business.

The expression *meddle in* means much the same, as in:

> I resent the fact that my son tries to meddle in my financial affairs.

interfere with

If something *interferes with* something it prevents it from happening successfully or as planned, as in:

> The bad weather interfered with their plans.

involved

involved in

If you are *involved in* something you take part in it, often very actively, or are connected with it, as in:

> Police suspect that he was involved in the robbery.

> My son is very involved in sport at school.

involved with

If you are *involved with* something it means that you take part in it, often very actively, as in:

> She is involved with the local church.

If you are *involved with* someone it can mean that you are working with them or spending time with them, or that you are connected with them in some way, as in:

He feels that he wants to be more involved with his children.

However, it can also mean that you are having a romantic relationship with someone, as in:
We think she's involved with a man from her work.

irrespective/regardless
irrespective of
Irrespective of means 'having no effect on a situation' or 'having no importance or relevance', as in:
The competition is open to all local artists, irrespective of age.

regardless of
Irrespective of means much the same as *regardless of*, as in:
Our aim is for all students with suitable academic qualifications to get a college education, regardless of financial situation.

lack
lack of
If there is a *lack of* something there is either not enough of it or a complete absence of it, as in:
Because of a lack of funds, we have no option but to close the youth club.

lean
lean on
Lean on has several meanings. Literally it means to rest on something or someone for support, as in:
She leant on her son's arm as they walked slowly up the road.

Lean on can also mean to rely or depend on someone for support, as in:
She's a single mother with three young children and she leans quite heavily on her parents.

Lean on also has a more sinister side and can mean to try to influence or persuade someone by threatening them in some way, as in:
The blackmailer leant even harder on his victim in the hope of getting more money.

liable
liable for
If you are *liable for* something then you are legally responsible for something or for the cost of something, as in:
He doesn't earn enough to be liable for income tax.

liable to
If someone or something is *liable to* do something they are likely to do it, as in:
The kitchen door is liable to slam shut if there's a wind blowing.

If you are *liable to* something you are likely to be affected by it, as in:

That area is liable to flooding sometimes, so don't buy a house there.

loyal
loyal to
If you are *loyal to* someone or something you are faithful to them and always give them your support, as in:
> Some of the soldiers remained loyal to their leader after the mutiny.

disloyal to
The opposite of *loyal to* is *disloyal to*, as in:
> The soldier was accused of being disloyal to his regiment.

masquerade
masquerade as
If you *masquerade as* someone you pretend to be that person, as in:
> The thief masqueraded as a security guard in order to get into the staff area.

meet
meet with
If you *meet with* something it happens to you or you experience it, as in:
> You can expect your wind farm proposal to meet with a lot of local opposition.

There is a modern tendency, especially in business circles, to use *meet with* where *meet* is perfectly adequate, as in:
> We plan to meet with their representatives next week.

merge
merge into
If one thing *merges into* another the difference between them gradually fades and it's difficult to separate them, as in:
> The grey clouds merged into the grey sea.

merge with
If a firm should *merge with* another the two firms join together and form a single firm, as in:
> Our small PR company is to merge with a large city firm.

mindful
mindful of
If you are *mindful of* something you remember about it and take it into consideration when you do something, as in:
> You must be mindful of your responsibilities as group leader.

> Mindful of the dangers of sudden avalanches in the region, we decided to ski elsewhere.

model
model on
If you *model* yourself *on* someone you try to act like them because you admire them and want to be like them, as in:
> She tried to model herself on her favourite artist.

native
native to
If an animal or plant is *native to* somewhere, that is where it exists naturally and its natural habitat is there, as in:
> The orchids are native to South America.

near
near to
If something is *near to* something it is a very short distance away from it, as in:
> Their house is quite near to the village.

Near to can also be used to mean that someone or something is almost in a particular state, as in:
> His wife was very near to giving birth when they arrived at the hospital.

close to
Close to can be used in both these meanings, as in:
> Our new flat is close to the city centre.

> The firm is close to bankruptcy.

need
in need of
If you are *in need of* something you require it or it is necessary that you have it, as in:
> We are in need of extra funding to finish the project.

need for
If there is a *need for* something it is necessary or must be done, as in:
> There is no need for everyone to go.

next
next to
If something is *next to* something it is physically by its side, as in:
> The houses were right next to each other.

object
object to
If you *object to* something, you do not approve of it or you do not agree with it, as in:
> Local residents are sure to object to the new parking restrictions.

A more formal way of saying this is *raise objections to*, as in:
> They have not yet raised any objections to the proposed new scheme.

oblivious
oblivious of/to
Some people still object to the

PREPOSITIONS

use of *oblivious to*, insisting that *oblivious of* is the only correct form. However, the use of *oblivious to* is increasing, partly because it is the preferred option in American English. It can no longer be regarded as wrong, although it still raises some objections.

Both *oblivious of* and *oblivious to* originally meant 'no longer aware of' or 'forgetful of', as in:
   Longing for a swim after the long, hot drive, and oblivious of the warning she had received about strong currents, she plunged into the waves.

Now both expressions are often used to mean 'simply unaware of something', as in:
   Oblivious to the passage of time, she suddenly realized that darkness had fallen and she was still far from home.

obsessed
obsessed by
If you are *obsessed by* someone or something you think or worry about them all the time, finding it difficult to think about anything else, as in:
   She's totally obsessed with fashion and spends most of her salary on cosmetics and designer clothes.

obsessed with
You can also use *obsessed with* in the same way, as in:
   He's obsessed with football and loves to watch his favourite team in action.

opportunity
opportunity for/to
If you have the *opportunity for* something it is possible for you to get it or achieve it, as in:
   The company's owner saw the offer as an opportunity for expansion.

This can also be expressed using the *opportunity to* do something, as in:
   It was a once-in-a-lifetime opportunity to travel to other parts of the world.

opposite
opposite of
If something or someone is the *opposite of* something or someone else, they are completely different from each other in some way, as in:
   She is quiet and studious, quite the opposite of her fun-loving sister.

opposed
opposed to
If you are *opposed to* something then you strongly disapprove of it, as in:
   Many of the town's residents are opposed to the idea of a new out-of-town supermarket.

opt
opt for
If you *opt for* something you choose it rather than something else, as in:
> She was offered a place at Oxford, but for family reasons she's opted for a university nearer home.

pleased
pleased about
If you are *pleased about* something you are happy about it, as in:
> Our daughter is getting married to a really nice man and my husband and I are very pleased about it.

pleased with
If you are *pleased with* something you like it and are satisfied with it:
> She was very pleased with the Christmas present from her aunt.

pleasure
take pleasure in
If you *take pleasure in* something you enjoy it, as in:
> He took pleasure in playing golf.

pore
pore over
If you *pore over* something you look at it for a long time and read it carefully, as in:
> Three of us pored over the map but we couldn't find the village.

prefer
prefer to
If you *prefer* something or someone *to* something or someone else, you like it better and would rather have it, as in:
> I prefer country life to life in the city, but I have to live in the city for work.

preferable
preferable to
If something or someone is *preferable to* something or someone else they are considerably better, more suitable, etc, as in:
> To me train travel is preferable to air travel.

prevent
prevent from
If something *prevents* you *from* doing something it stops you from doing it, as in:
> Heavy traffic prevented us from getting there in time.

prior
prior to
Prior to is a formal way of saying 'before', as in:
> Prior to his retirement he was chief executive of a large textile business.

PREPOSITIONS

prohibit
prohibit from
If something or someone *prohibits* you *from* doing something you are not allowed to do it, as in:
> The new law prohibits people from smoking in here.

Prohibit from is often used in the passive in formal contexts, as in:
> Members of the public are prohibited from touching any of the museum exhibits.

protest
protest against
If you *protest against* something you say that you strongly disagree with and disapprove of something, often saying so publicly in company with other people who have the same opinion, as in:
> A large crowd gathered in the city's main square to protest against the proposed changes to the Human Rights Bill.

protest at
If you *protest at* something, you say that you strongly disagree with and disapprove of something, as in:
> Many people have protested at the government's handling of the economy.

proud
proud of
If you are *proud of* someone you think that they have done something good and you admire them, as in:
> She is proud of her son for having done so well in his exams.

If you are *proud of* something you are very pleased to have it or to have done it, as in:
> She's very proud of getting a place in the school football team.

provide
provide for
If you *provide for* someone you give them the things, such as food and clothing, that they need to live on:
> She works hard in order to be able to provide for her children.

react
react to
If you *react to* something you behave in a particular way as a result of it, as in:
> She reacted with joy to the news that her daughter had given birth to a girl.

> How do you think the stock market will react to the news that unemployment is rising?

The noun from *react* is *reaction*. If

you have a *reaction to* something it affects you in some way, as in:
   She had a very bad reaction to the antibiotics which they gave her.

recover
recover from
If you *recover from* an illness or a bad or unpleasant situation you get well again or return to your previous state, as in:
   She is recovering from a nasty virus.

refer
refer to
If you *refer to* someone or something you mention or speak about them, as in:
   She's clearly very fond of her grandfather and constantly refers to him in her conversation with others.

reflect
reflect on
If you *reflect on* something you think about it very carefully and deeply, as in:
   Unsure what to do after finishing school, he reflected on all his options.

reflect upon
Reflect upon is a slightly more formal version of this.
   I am disappointed in you. I think you should go a home and reflect upon what you said and did.

refrain
refrain from
If you *refrain from* doing something you do not let yourself do it even though you may want to, as in:
   Please refrain from eating or drinking in the library.

Refrain from is used in quite formal contexts.

rely
rely on/upon
If you *rely on* someone or something you need their support in order to survive, be successful, etc, as in:
   She was an actress and relied on her parents' financial support.

   The country can no longer rely on tourism alone to ensure its future.

Rely upon is a slightly more formal version of this.

remind
remind of
If someone or something *reminds* you *of* someone or something, they make you remember or think of that person or thing because they are similar in some way, as in:
   She reminds me very much of

PREPOSITIONS

her mother at that age, both in temperament and looks.

renege
renege on
If you *renege on* a promise or an agreement, you do not do what you promised or agreed to do, as in:
> We had plans to work with a local company, but they have reneged on their agreement with us.

resistant
resistant to
If something is *resistant to* something it is not affected or damaged by it, as in:
> We need to use a metal that is resistant to rust.

responsible
responsible for
If you are *responsible for* doing something it is your job or duty to get it done and you may be blamed if something goes wrong, as in:
> As the person responsible for company security, he may lose his job for allowing unauthorized visitors into the building.

If you are *responsible for* someone it is your job to look after them or take care of them and you may be blamed if something goes wrong, as in:

> Each nursery assistant is responsible for four children.

Responsible for also means causing something, as in:
> Building faults were responsible for subsidence of the houses.

restrict/limit
restrict to/limit to
If you *restrict* the size, amount, extent, etc, of something *to* something, you do not allow anything larger, greater, etc, than that, as in:
> We restrict the number of people allowed in the hall to 400.

> Membership is restricted to people over 60.

Limit to is also used in this way, as in:
> They are going to limit the time each gym member can spend on the rowing machine to 20 minutes.

result
result from
If something *results from* something it is caused by that, as in:
> Some of the damage results from the fire and some from the water used to put it out.

result in
If something *results in* something it

causes that to happen, as in:
> The building of the factory resulted in a great many new jobs for the people in the surrounding area.

retire
retire from
If you *retire from* something you stop doing something, often because you have reached a particular age or because you are ill, as in:
> He decided to retire from professional football after injuring his leg very badly in the cup final.

revert
revert to
If you *revert to* something you start doing something again that you used to do in the past, as in:
> After he came out of prison his behaviour improved for a time but he has now reverted to his old ways.

rich
rich in
If something is *rich in* something it contains a lot of it, as in:
> They eat a diet that is rich in calcium.

> The area is rich in history.

rob
rob of
If you *rob* someone *of* something you steal something from someone or take something away from someone, as in:
> The thieves robbed the gallery of its best artworks.

> His injury on the track robbed the athlete of a gold medal.

satisfied
satisfied with
If you are *satisfied with* something you are pleased with it and cannot find fault with it, as in:
> I am quite satisfied with the new arrangements.

sceptical
sceptical about
If you are *sceptical about* something you have doubts about whether it is true or whether it is likely to happen, as in:
> He says that he is very sceptical about our chances of winning.

sceptical of
Sceptical of means the same as *sceptical about*, as in:
> We are sceptical of her claim that she is related to the dead man.

sensitive
sensitive to
If you are *sensitive to* someone else's feelings, needs, etc, you are aware

of them and are able to understand them, as in:
  He is sensitive to the family's grief, especially since it is not long since his own father died.

If someone or something is *sensitive to* something they are easily affected or damaged by it, as in:
  The child is very sensitive to the heat and comes out in a rash if she gets too hot.

  The student is very sensitive to any form of criticism and needs to learn not to over-react to constructive criticism.

separate
separate from
If you *separate* something or someone *from* something or someone, you divide them into two parts or sections, as in:
  The recipe says that I must separate the egg whites from the egg yolks.

  It was school policy to separate the girls from the boys for most sporting activities.

If something *separates* something *from* something else, it is between them so that they are not right next to each other, as in:
  A large hedge separates our garden from our next-door neighbour's garden and gives us each some privacy.

share
share out
If you *share* something *out* you divide it between two or more people, as in:
  The birthday cake was shared out among all the guests at the party.

share with
If you *share* something *with* someone you have it or use it together with another person or other people, as in:
  She shares a flat with three girls that she was at school with.

sick
sick of
If you are *sick of* someone or something they bore you or they have been irritating you for some time and you are tired of them, as in:
  I think we're both sick of all the talent shows on TV.

Sick of is used in informal contexts.

similar
similar to
If something is *similar to* something it is like that thing but not the same as it, as in:
  Their house is quite similar to ours.

similarity between

If you want to use the noun *similarity* to convey the same idea it is followed by *between*, as in:

   There is a similarity between our houses.

similarity to

Similarity can also be followed by *to*, as in:

   In that photograph she has a striking similarity to her grandmother.

smell
smell of

If something *smells of* something it has the smell or odour of that thing, as in:

   The room smells of flowers fresh from the garden.

sorry
sorry about

If you are *sorry about* something, you feel sad and ashamed about it, as in:

   I am sorry about my behaviour the other day.

sorry for

You can also use *sorry for* in this context, as in:

   She's sorry for being late, but the traffic was very heavy because of an accident on the motorway.

If you are *sorry for* someone you feel pity or sympathy for them, as in:

   She feels really sorry for homeless people and tries to help by working as a volunteer at the local shelter.

strive
strive for

If you *strive for* something you try very hard to get it, as in:

   She strives for perfection, but is rarely successful.

subject
subject to

Subject (with the stress on the first syllable) *to* has various meanings. If someone or something is *subject to* something bad or unpleasant, they are likely to be affected by it, as in:

   They have just announced that most train schedules are subject to delay.

If something is *subject to* something happening, it depends on that thing happening for it to take place, as in:

   The construction of a new hotel on the outskirts of town is subject to planning permission.

If something is *subject to* a law, rule, etc, it must obey that law, rule, etc, as in:

   Working conditions for part-time

employees are now subject to new regulations.

Subject to can also be a verb which means 'to make someone experience something unpleasant', as in:
We were subjected to noise from the building site next to our hotel.

In the case of the verb *to subject*, the stress is on the second syllable.

substitute
substitute for
If something is a *substitute for* something else it is used instead of it, as in:
She uses an artificial sweetener as a substitute for sugar.

If someone is a *substitute for* someone else they do the job that that person usually does, as in:
He is playing today as a substitute for the injured goalkeeper.

succeed
succeed in
If you *succeed in* doing something, you do or achieve what you set out to do, as in:
He succeeded in passing all his exams.

suffer
suffer from
If you *suffer from* something you are usually affected by something unpleasant such as disease, pain, etc, as in:
The country was still suffering from the effects of the recession.

susceptible
susceptible to
If you are *susceptible to* something you are very likely to be affected or influenced by it, as in:
These plants are particularly susceptible to disease.

suspicious
suspicious of
If you are *suspicious of* someone, you do not trust them and think that they may have done something wrong, as in:
I'm rather suspicious of Anne's new boyfriend.

If you are *suspicious of* something you think that it may be dishonest, illegal, etc, although you do not have any proof, as in:
The policeman was suspicious of the car driver's explanation and he wondered if the car was a stolen car.

sympathize
sympathize with
If you *sympathize with* someone you

feel sorry for them and understand the problems they have, as in:
> I can sympathize with the people looking for work because I've been unemployed several times in my life.

tamper
tamper with
If you *tamper with* something you make changes to it without being asked to, often with the intention of deliberately damaging it, as in:
> His rival tampered with his car engine and caused him to crash.

tendency
tendency to
If someone or something has a *tendency to* do something they are likely to do it, as in:
> I have a tendency to worry, I can't help it.

think
think over
If you *think* something *over* you consider it very carefully before reaching a decision, as in:
> They have offered him the job, but he has asked for some time to think it over.

think through
If you *think* something *through* you think about a possible course of action very carefully, considering all the things that might happen, as in:
> I wasn't surprised their plan failed, because it was obvious that they simply hadn't thought it through.

think up
If you *think* something *up* you create it in your mind, often something inventive or imaginative, as in:
> One of the prisoners of war thought up a clever escape plan.

together
together with
Together with can mean in addition to something else, as in:
> You need to produce your passport together with your birth certificate.

Together with can also be used to refer to someone who is also involved in something, as in:
> Jim, together with Tom, climbed to the very summit of the mountain.

true
true to
If you are *true to* someone or something you remain loyal to them and continue to give them your support, whatever happens, as in:
> Even after several serious defeats on the battlefield the troops remained true to their leader.

PREPOSITIONS

If you are *true to* your word or promise, you act or behave as you promised to do, as in:

> She was true to her word and repaid the money I lent her by the end of the month.

wait

wait for

If you *wait for* someone or something you stay where you are until they arrive, as in:

> I'm outside the cinema waiting for my son, but he's a bit late.

> We're waiting for the bus.

If you *wait for* something to happen you are expecting it to happen, as in:

> He is waiting for a flat to become vacant.

wait on

If you *wait on* someone you bring food and drink to them at their table, especially in a restaurant, as in:

> The young woman who waited on us in the restaurant was very polite.

Wait on is sometimes used to mean 'to look after someone's needs', as in:

> My son has the flu and expects me to wait on him, even though I'm very busy.

Wait on is also used informally in British English to mean *wait for*, as in:

> We are waiting on Jack to finish work.

Many people disapprove of this last use and it should not be used in formal contexts.

CONFUSABLE WORDS

Hands up who cringes every time Mr Baxter says *supposably*.

THE ENGLISH language has a huge vocabulary. This is obviously a good thing because it means that you have a wide choice of words to express what you want to say. However, it also means that it is very easy to get confused when you are trying to select the right word for what you want to express.

PROBLEMS

There are various well-known potential problems when it comes to making the right choice of word, but you can only try to avoid them if you know about them. Our aim is to try to bring some of these possible stumbling blocks to your

CONFUSABLE WORDS

attention. There are three categories of words which cause particular confusion. They are **homophones, homographs, homonyms**. The words are easier to understand than you might think. In any case, you can forget the names of the categories as long as you remember the problems which they represent.

HOMOPHONES

The word **homophone** comes from the Greek word *homophonos*, which means having the same sound. A homophone is a word that is **pronounced in the same way** as another but is **spelled in a different way** and has a **different meaning**. In other words they sound alike but have totally unrelated meanings.

Below are some examples of homophones. Sometimes only two words are involved, but sometimes there are three or four.

aisle/isle

Aisle is a noun meaning a passage between rows of seats in a church, theatre, cinema, etc:
  The bride walked down the aisle on her father's arm.

Isle is a noun meaning an island:
  I love to visit the Isle of Skye.

alter/altar

Alter is a verb meaning to change:
  They have had to alter their plans.

Altar is a noun meaning, in the Christian church, the table on which the bread and wine are consecrated for Communion and which is centre of worship, as in:
  The priest moved to the altar, from where he dispensed bread and wine for Communion.

Altar can also refer to a raised structure on which sacrifices are made in worship:
  The Mayans made sacrifices to their gods on an altar.

ail/ale

Ail is a rather old-fashioned verb meaning to be ill, as in:
  The old woman is ailing.

Ail can also mean to be the matter, to be wrong, as in:
  What ails you?

Ale is a noun meaning a kind of beer, as in:
  I drank a pint of foaming ale.

bare/bear

The verb forms of *bare* and *bear* are very frequently mixed up.

Bare is a verb meaning 'to uncover or reveal'.
 Bare your chest so that we can listen to your heart.

Bare is an adjective meaning uncovered or without decoration.
 She went out with bare legs since the weather was hot.

Bare, as an adjective, also means 'mere or just enough'.
 He did the bare minimum in terms of studying for the exam.

Bear is a verb meaning to endure:
 I can't bear this pain.

Bear, as a verb, also means to withstand the weight of something:
 That rotten floorboard couldn't bear my weight and my foot went through it.

Bear is also a noun referring to a large furry omnivorous mammal:
 The bear was hibernating in a cave.

blew/blue

Blew is a verb, the past tense of the verb to blow, as in:
 They blew the trumpets loudly.

Blue is a noun and adjective meaning a colour of the shade of a clear sky, as in:
 She wore a blue dress.

bated/baited

The expression *with bated breath* means 'to hold one's breath in fear or suspense', as in:
 We waited with bated breath for the judges to announce the winner.

Bait is a verb meaning to persistently harass or torment, *baited* is the past tense of *bait*.
 The boys baited the dog mercilessly until it tried to bite them.

boar/bore

Boar is a noun meaning a male pig, as in:
 Wild boar lived in the forest.

Bore is a verb meaning to make tired and uninterested, as in:
 I didn't mean to bore you, I just love talking about trains.

Bore is a verb, the past tense of the verb to bear, as in:
 They bore their troubles lightly.

CONFUSABLE WORDS

bridal/bridle
Bridal is an adjective meaning 'relating to a bride or to a wedding', as in:

The bridal car was decorated with white ribbons.

Bridle is a noun referring to a harness for a horse's head, as in:
He bought a new bridle for his horse.

brooch/broach
Brooch is the more common of these two words and is a noun referring to a piece of jewellery that is pinned to a garment, as in:
She wore a beautiful diamond brooch in the lapel of her jacket.

Broach is a verb meaning 'to introduce or mention a subject', as in:
He didn't like to broach the subject of the money she owed him.

canvas/canvass
Canvas is a noun that refers to a kind of heavy coarse cloth that is used to make tents, etc, and also used by artists to paint on.
It's fun to sleep outdoors under canvas.

The picture was acrylic paint on canvas.

Canvass is a verb meaning 'to try to get people's votes in an election':
Politicians canvass for votes.

cereal/serial
Cereal is a noun meaning a plant yielding grain suitable for food, as in:
Maize is a cereal crop.

Cereal is a prepared food made with grain, as in:
We often have cereal for breakfast.

Serial is a noun meaning a story or television play which appears in regular parts, as in:
The final instalment of the magazine serial I like is now out.

cheque/check
Cheque is the accepted form in British English of the meaning 'an order to a bank to pay money from a person's account', as in:
I don't have enough cash with me so I'll have to pay the bill with a cheque.

Check is the accepted American form of the above meaning.

Note the word in this meaning is being used less and less because payment by cheque has largely been replaced with credit or debit cards.

In American English *check* is a noun meaning *bill*, as in, the invoice presenting the amount you have to pay after a meal in a restaurant, as in:
Can we get the check, please?

Check is also a verb meaning to see if something is all right, as in:
> Please can you check if I locked the front door?

Check is also a noun meaning the act of seeing if something is all right, as in:
> Give the back of my head a check, please. Is my hair OK?

Check is also a noun referring to a pattern of small squares on material, as in:
> My bag is blue with a light-cream check to match my blouse.

As you can see, *check* has a few meanings and is itself a **homonym**, *see* page 275.

cite/sight/site

Cite is a verb meaning to quote or mention by way of example or proof, as in:
> The lawyer cited a previous case to try and get his client off.

Sight is a noun meaning the act of seeing, as in:
> They recognized him at first sight.

Site is a noun meaning a

complimentary/complementary

Complimentary and *complementary* are very frequently confused because although the meanings are different, they have similar kinds of positive themes. The very similar spellings confuses matters further.

Complimentary is an adjective expressing admiration or praise, as in:
> She was flattered by his complimentary remarks.

When connected with the giving of tickets, products, etc, *complimentary* is often used to mean 'given free', as in:
> Each copy of the magazine has a complimentary diary inside it.

Complementary is an adjective referring to things that form a useful or attractive combination, although they may be quite different, as in:
> She was careful to put together a team of people who had complementary skills.

In modern usage, *complementary* is commonly found in the term *complementary medicine*, which uses treatments that are not part of the usual scientific Western medical methods. The term emphasizes the fact that the treatments co-exist with scientific treatments, rather than replace them, as is the case with the term *alternative medicine*.

CONFUSABLE WORDS

location or place, as in:
> They have found a site for the factory.

cue/queue

These two words are pronounced to rhyme with *mew* and *dew*.

Cue in sport is a noun meaning a kind of stick used in billiards and snooker, as in:
> He chalked his snooker cue slowly and planned the next shot.

Cue in the theatre is a noun referring to a few words or an action that is a signal for another actor to do or say something:
> He was waiting for his cue to go on stage.

Queue is a noun referring to a line of people waiting in an orderly way to buy something, get into a building, etc, as in:
> There was a huge queue outside the shop for the opening day of their sale.

Queue can also act as a verb, as in:
> We had to queue for more than an hour to get into the pop concert.

currant/current

Currant is a noun meaning a small dried fruit, a grape, used in baking, as in:
> We need flour, butter, eggs, sugar and currants to make this cake.

Current has a much wider range of meanings. As a noun it can be found in such contexts as electric current, the current of a river and a current of cold air.
> The current of the river was very strong.

> An electric current ran through the wire.

Current is an adjective that means belonging to the present time, as in:
> Current affairs programmes on television discuss politics and contemporary events and issues.

> Chia seeds are the current fashion in food.

discreet/discrete

Discreet is an adjective. It is often misspelled as *discrete*. The word *discreet* is the more common of the two words and, when used of a person, means 'careful not to tell secrets' or 'careful not to offend or embarrass people', as in:
> You can safely confide in my mother because she's very discreet and won't tell anyone else about your problem.

Discreet, used of behaviour or actions means 'tactful' or 'careful to avoid attention', as in:

Thanks to her discreet handling of the situation, the affair was not made public.

Discrete is a much less common, often technical, adjective meaning 'separate' or 'distinct', as in:
Discrete particles of the mineral were found in the compound.

feat/feet

Feat is a noun meaning a notable act or deed, as in:
He received an award for his brave feat.

Feet is a noun, the plural form of foot, as in:
I got my feet wet in the puddle.

flu/flew

Flu is a noun. It's short for the illness *influenza*.
I had the flu for nearly two weeks; it was terrible.

Formerly *flu* was preceded by an apostrophe and spelled *'flu*. This was to show that the word is a shortened form of *influenza*, but the apostrophe is no longer commonly used. The long form, *influenza*, is only used in very formal or technical contexts.

Flew is the past tense of *fly*, as in:

The pigeon flew past.

I flew to Spain last year; that was my first time in a plane.

guerrilla/guerilla/gorilla

Guerrilla, which has the alternative spelling *guerilla*, means a member of a small unofficial group of fighters, as in:
The soldiers were set upon by a band of guerrillas in the mountain pass.

Gorilla is the name for the largest of the apes native to central Africa, as in:
The habitat of some gorilla species is being destroyed.

heal/heel

Heal is a verb meaning to become or make healthy again, as in:
The wound has started to heal.

Heel is a noun and is the back part of a foot below the ankle, as in:
Her shoes were too tight and she got a blister on her heel.

hear/here

Hear is a verb meaning to become aware of sounds by means of your ears, as in:
She didn't hear the door bell because she is deaf.

CONFUSABLE WORDS

its/it's

We will also mention these two little words in the following chapter on **Punctuation** but they are so commonly confused it is worth mentioning here too. They're **homophones**. They sound the same and look slightly different, and that **apostrophe** is the difference between one distinct meaning and another. It's crucial.

Its is the possessive form of *it* and so it is used in such contexts as:
> The dog has injured its paw.

> The holiday resort has lost its appeal for them.

Note that – confusingly – although an apostrophe is often used to show possession in the English language it is not used here. Sorry about that!

However, there is an apostrophe in *it's*, which is a contraction of *it is*, as in:
> It's (it is) difficult to find a decent restaurant around here.

> It's (it is) getting late and it's (it is) time I was getting home.

It is worth spending some time trying to memorize the difference here. Mixing up *its* and *it's* is a mistake that many, many native speakers make.

Here is an adverb meaning this place, as in:
> I'm not going anywhere. I'm staying right here.

hoard/horde

Hoard is a noun meaning 'a store or collection of something', as in:
> He has a hoard of rare comic books in the attic.

Horde is a disapproving word used to refer to a very large group of people, as in:
> The resort is restful in the winter but hordes of tourists flock to it in the summer.

know/no

Know is a verb meaning to have understanding or knowledge of, as in:
> He is the only one who knows the truth.

Know means to be acquainted with, as in:
> I met her once but I don't really know her.

No is an adjective meaning not any, as in:
> We have no food left.

passed/past

Passed and *past* are very commonly confused words.

Passed is the past tense and past participle of the verb *pass*, as in:
> We passed the school on our way here.

> I looked out of the window and saw them as they passed.

Past can be an adverb, and *passed* is most readily confused with this usage, as in:
> We walked past the school on our way here.

> I looked out of the window and saw them walking past.

Past can be a noun, as in:
> You must try to forget the past.

Past can be an adjective, as in:
> He seems to have forgotten all about his past crimes.

Past can also act as a preposition, as in:
> We must have driven past the church without noticing it.

> The garage is just past the cemetery.

No is a sentence substitute giving a negative response, as in:
> No, I will not go to the dance.

metre/meter

Metre, in British English, is the basic metric measurement of length, being also used in such derived forms as *kilometre* and *millimetre*.

Meter is a measuring instrument:
> It's time to pay the gas bill, better read the gas meter.

> Check my speed on the car's speedometer.

Note that in American English both the measurement and the measuring instruments are spelled *meter*.

none/nun

None is a pronoun meaning not any, as in:
> They are demanding money but we have none.

Nun is a noun meaning a woman who joins a religious order and takes vows of poverty, chastity and obedience, as in:
> She took holy orders and became a nun.

principal/principle

Principal as an adjective means 'chief or main', as in:

CONFUSABLE WORDS

Her principal source of income is child-minding.

Boredom was the principal reason for him leaving his job.

Principal as a noun refers to the head or leader, as in:
The principal of the school met with the parents.

Principle is a noun meaning 'a law', 'a basic truth' or 'a guiding rule', as in:
It was against her principles to eat meat.

The research must be proved to conform with scientific principles.

rain/reign/rein

Rain is water that falls from the sky, as in:
We got very wet in the heavy rain.

Reign refers to the period of time when a king or queen is ruling, as in:
The Second World War took place during the reign of George VI.

Rein is a noun meaning a long narrow band of leather used to control a horse and it is mostly found in the plural form, as in:
The rider let the reins fall from her hands as her horse came to a standstill.

rapt/wrapped

Rapt is an adjective meaning 'completely engrossed in something', as in:
The children watched with rapt attention while the magician performed his tricks.

Wrapped is the past tense of the verb *wrap* meaning 'to enfold' or 'to cover', as in:
She wrapped the gift in tissue paper.

It is the more figurative use of *wrapped* that is most likely to be confused with *rapt*, as in:
She was far too wrapped up in looking after her family to want to go out to work.

right/rite/write/wright

As an adjective *right* has several meanings. It can mean correct, as in:
He gave the right answer.

Right can also mean the opposite of left, as in:
He held it in his right hand.

Right is a noun that refers to something that you are legally or morally allowed to do or have, as in:
He works for an organization concerned with protecting human rights.

Rite is a noun meaning a ceremonial act or words, as in:

Homophones

their/they're/there

These **homophones** are frequently confused.

Their is a possessive pronoun meaning 'belonging to or connected with them'. Of the three words above *their* is the only one that shows possession, as in:
 They have parked their car at the station.

 Their clothes got wet in the rain.

 We thanked them for their kindness.

They're is a contraction of *they are*, a noun and a verb, as in:
 They're here now.

 They're too young to learn to drive.

There is a noun, an adverb, a pronoun, or an adjective. The words *there* and *their* are sometimes confused.

There can mean 'in that place', as in:
 My car is just over there.

There can mean 'in that respect', as in:
 I'm going to disagree with you there.

There can mean 'there exists', as in:
 There is an excellent library in the town.

There can be a dummy subject, as in:
 There's a good chance I'll be late.

 There's so much to do in the adventure park.

 The priest gave last rites to the dying man.

Write is a verb meaning to form readable characters, as in:
 We learn to write at school.

Write can also mean to set down words for others to read, as in:
 He writes regularly for the newspapers.

Wright is much less common than the other two words. Usually it comes as the second part of a compound word which indicates someone who works at particular trade or job, as in: *shipwright* and *playwright*.

stare/stair

Stare is a verb meaning to look fixedly and a fixed gaze, as in:
 She stared at him in disbelief when he told her the news

Stare is a noun meaning a fixed gaze:
 He gave me an angry stare.

Stair is a noun meaning a series of flights of stairs, as in:

CONFUSABLE WORDS

At the foot of the stair you'll find the umbrella stand.

stationery/stationary

Stationary is an adjective, meaning still, and not moving, as in:
The stationary train would soon be leaving the platform.

Stationery is a noun referring to materials you use for writing, like paper and pens, as in:
I've got some stationery with my address printed on it.

to/too/two

To is a preposition, as in:
I'm going to the supermarket.

To is also the infinitive of a verb:
They want to leave.

I'd like to play.

To be honest, I'm not sure.

Too is an adverb that means 'also' or 'as well', as in:
You can come too.

Too is an adverb that can mean 'excessively', as in:
This flat is far too expensive for us.

Two is a noun, it is the cardinal number represented by the numeral 2, as in:
One plus one equals two.

whose/who's

Whose means 'of whom' or 'of which', as in:
The employee whose wife has just had a baby has taken paternity leave.

Whose bike is this?

The word *who's* is short for *who is*, as in:
Who's giving the after-dinner speech?

Who's the woman in the red dress?

your/you're

You're and *your* are very commonly confused. Try to remember that the apostrophe is only used when you are shortening *you are*.

The word *your* is a possessive pronoun meaning 'belonging to or connected with you', as in:
I forgot to give you your pen back.

It was definitely your mistake.

The word *you're* is a contraction of *you are*, as in:
You're looking very cheerful today.

You're really too ill to go to work today.

HOMOGRAPHS

Homographs are words which have the **same spelling** but **different meanings**, and **different pronunciations** (these can also be called **heteronyms**).

bass/bass

Bass, pronounced to rhyme with *mass*, is a noun referring to a type of fish, as in:

> He caught a bass when he went fishing.

Bass, pronounced to rhyme with *face*, is an adjective meaning 'deep in tone':

> He has a beautiful bass voice.

> They pounded on the bass drum.

bow/bow

Bow, pronounced to rhyme with *how*, is a verb meaning to bend the head or body as a sign of respect or in greeting, etc, as in:

> The visitors bowed to the Queen.

> They bowed their heads in prayer.

Bow, pronounced to rhyme with *low*, is a noun meaning a looped knot or a ribbon tied in this way, as in:

> She wears blue bows in her hair.

Bow, pronounced to rhyme with *low*, is a noun meaning a wooden tool used to propel an arrow, as in:

> He shot the arrow from the bow.

close/close

Close, pronounced *cloze* (to rhyme with *hose*), is a verb meaning 'to shut', as in:

> Close the door, it's cold in here.

Close pronounced *cloass*, is an adjective meaning 'near', as in:

> The destination is very close now.

Close pronounced *cloass*, is an adjective meaning 'intimate', as in:

> She's a close friend, I trust her.

desert/desert

Desert is a noun, pronounced with the emphasis on the first syllable, **deh**-zert. It refers to an area of land that is very hot and dry, as in:

> The lizard lived in the desert.

Desert is also verb. In its pronunciation it has the stress on the second syllable, di-**zehrt**. It means 'to abandon someone or something', as in:

> Don't desert me here alone!

CONFUSABLE WORDS

lead/lead

Lead pronounced to rhyme with *feed*, is a verb and means to guide people somewhere by going in front of them, as in:
> The mountain guide will lead the party of climbers safely to the summit.

Lead pronounced to rhyme with *fed* is a noun that refers to a type of soft, heavy grey metal, as in:
> Lead was once used to make water pipes but this practice was stopped as lead is poisonous.

Note that the past participle of the verb *lead* is spelled *led* and it is pronounced like the metal.

refuse/refuse

Refuse, with the stress on the first syllable, pronounced **reff**-yoos, is a noun which refers to rubbish or waste, as in:
> Please put your refuse in the bin.

Refuse with the stress on the second syllable, pronounced re-**fyooz**, is a verb meaning to say no or reject, as in:
> I have to refuse your kind offer of dinner, but I must get to bed for an early rise tomorrow.

row/row

Row pronounced to rhyme with *low* and *mow*, is a noun that means a number of people or things arranged in a line, as in:
> There was a row of policemen blocking the entrance to the building.

Row, pronounced to rhyme with *cow* and *how*, is a noun meaning a quarrel or disagreement, as in:
> The boy and his father were always having rows.

minute/minute

Minute pronounced to rhyme with *min*-it, with the stress on the first syllable, is a noun referring to a unit of time, as in:
> There are 60 minutes in an hour.

Minute, pronounced as mine-*yoot*, the stress being on the second syllable, is an adjective. This means extremely small, as in:
> There were minute amounts of poison in the water.

sow/sow

Sow, pronounced to rhyme with *low* is a verb meaning to scatter seeds in the earth, as in:
> In the spring the gardener sowed some flower seeds in the front garden.

Sow, pronounced to rhyme with *how* is a noun meaning a female pig, as in:
> The sow is in the pigsty with her piglets.

HOMONYMS

Homonyms are words which have the **same spelling** and the **same pronunciation** but they have **different meanings**. They are sometimes referred to as *multiple meaning words*. Below are some examples.

bank/bank

Bank is a noun referring to a place where you receive financial services and where you can save your money:
  There was a big queue at the bank.

Bank is a noun referring to a mound of earth at the side of something, as in:
  A bank of silt had built up around the water.

Bank is a noun referring the slopes at the side of a river:
  I fell and slid down the river bank into the water.

bill/bill

Bill is a noun referring to a piece of paper which shows how much money you owe someone for goods or services, as in:
  I've just had a huge bill for repairs to the car.

Bill is a noun meaning a bird's beak, as in:
  The thrush had a small worm hanging from its bill.

Bill is a noun referring to a written or printed advertisement:
  We were asked to deliver handbills advertising the play.

calf/calf

Calf is a noun referring to a young cow, although it can also refer to the young of some other animals, such as elephants.
  The cow gave birth to a calf

Calf is a noun referring to the back part of the leg between the ankle and the back of the knee:
  She got cramp in her calf after exercising.

fair/fair

Fair is an adjective meaning light in colour, as in:
  She has fair hair.

Fair is an adjective meaning attractive. It is quite an old-fashioned usage:
  Fair young women.

Fair is an adjective meaning fine, not raining, as in:
  I hope it keeps fair.

CONFUSABLE WORDS

LEFT AND RIGHT

Left is an adjective meaning the side of a person or something that, if facing north, would be on the west side, as in:

Your heart is on the left side of your body.

Left is the past tense and past participle of the verb *leave* meaning to depart, as in:

He left early to catch his train.

Left is the past tense and past participle of the verb *leave* meaning to remain in a certain state, as in:

She left most of her dinner.

Right is an adjective meaning the side of a person or something that, if facing north, would be on the east side, as in:

Turn right at the traffic lights.

Right is an adjective meaning correct, as in:

You were right, I shouldn't have gone to that party.

Right is an adjective meaning appropriate, as in:

He is the right man to ask about plumbing.

Right is a noun meaning the permission to do something, as in:

I have the right to walk along this path if I want to, it is open to the public.

Fair is an adjective meaning just, free from prejudice, as in:

The referee came to a fair decision.

Fair is a noun meaning a market held regularly in the same place, often with stalls, entertainments and rides, as in:

He won a coconut at the fair.

Fair is a noun meaning a trade exhibition, as in:

We are going to the art fair.

foot/foot

Foot is a noun referring to the appendage at the end of the leg, as in:

Press your foot on the accelerator pedal.

Foot is a noun referring to a measurement of twelve inches, as in:

The golf ball was one foot from the bunker.

The plural of both words is *feet*.

grave/grave

Grave is an adjective meaning serious, as in:

I have grave concerns about this idea.

Grave is a noun meaning a place of rest for a dead person, as in:
We put flowers on Toby's grave.

lie/lie

Lie is a verb meaning to put yourself flat against something, as in:
Lie down on the examination table and I'll look at your injury.

Lie is a verb meaning to not tell the truth, as in:
She said that she was sorry but it was a lie.

pulse/pulse

Pulse is a noun meaning the throbbing caused by the contractions of the heart, as in:
The patient has a weak pulse.

Pulse is a noun meaning the edible seeds of any of various crops of the pea family, such as lentils, peas and beans, as in:
Lentils are a type of pulse.

row/row

Row is a verb meaning to propel a boat by means of oars, as in:
He plans to row across the Atlantic single-handed.

Row is a noun meaning a number of people or things arranged in a line, as in:
We tried to get into the front row to watch the procession.

spring/spring

Spring is a noun used to refer to a season of the year, as in:
Spring follows winter and comes before summer.

Spring is a noun meaning a wired coil, as in:
The springs in the mattress were very squeaky.

I've lost a spring from the mechanism of my antique clock.

Spring is a verb meaning to bounce upwards, as in:
The cat sprang after the shrew in the garden.

swallow/swallow

Swallow is a noun used to refer to a kind of bird, as in:
It was the end of summer and swallows were getting ready to fly to warmer lands for the winter.

Swallow is a verb meaning to cause food or drink to go down your throat into your stomach, as in:
He had a very sore throat and could only swallow very small pieces of food.

CONFUSABLE WORDS

WHICH WORD?

There are a huge number of English words that cause problems and they do not necessarily fall into a specific category. Sometimes confusion between words arises because they sound quite similar and this is further confused when the words are both associated with the same theme. Some of the most problematic are discussed below. Sometimes, over time, what is considered a misuse can be used so often that it becomes accepted Standard English, and we list some of these instances in this section. As global communication becomes easier, the distinctions in usage and spelling between American and British English start to blur too. You'll find a few examples of what used to be purely American English that are now starting to be used in the UK.

adopted/adoptive

Adopted and *adoptive* sound quite similar and they are both associated with the same theme, namely raising a child who is not your biological son or daughter.

Adopted is an adjective used to describe children who have been brought up by people other than their biological parents, as in:
 The couple have two sons, one biological, one adopted.

Adoptive is an adjective used to refer to adults who have done the adopting, as in:
 She would love to try and get in contact with her biological mother, but she does not want to upset her much-loved adoptive mother.

arbiter/arbitrator

Arbiter and *arbitrator* can cause confusion. The first part of *arbitrator* sounds like *arbiter* and they both refer to a similar theme, that of judging.

Arbiter is a noun. It refers to someone or something with the power or influence to make decisions or judgments, as in:
 The dress designer is very young but she is quickly becoming recognized as one of the leading arbiters of fashion.

Arbitrator is a noun. It refers to someone appointed to settle differences in a dispute, as in:
 Management and union leaders have called in an arbitrator to help try to avoid a strike.

Note that *arbiter* is one of those words that is in the process of changing. In modern usage it is occasionally used with the same meaning as *arbitrator*. This can only add to the confusion!

abuse/misuse

Abuse and *misuse* are nouns that refer to a wrong use or treatment, but they are used in different contexts.

Abuse is a noun referring to improper or wrong use or treatment; to something that is morally wrong, dangerous to health or illegal, as in: *alcohol abuse*; *drug abuse*; *solvent abuse*; *the abuse of political power*; *physical abuse* and *sexual abuse*.

Abuse is a verb with similar associations to that of the noun *abuse*, as in:
 The politician was being investigated for abusing his power.

Misuse usually refers to incorrect or inappropriate use, as in:
 Please do not misuse the gym equipment

 Having barbecues is misuse of the communal garden.

accept/except

Although not spelled exactly alike, nor sounding *exactly* alike, these words are enough alike to be often confused.

Accept is a verb meaning to take something that is offered.
 Please accept this gift

Except is a preposition. It can appear with the word *for*, and means with the exception of.
 He asked everyone except Mary.

 I like all the dishes except for the one with coriander.

adverse/averse

These words look and sound quite alike but they are used in quite different ways.

Adverse is an adjective that usually goes before the abstract noun to which it refers, and means 'unfavourable' or 'hostile', as in:
 The last thing we want is adverse publicity for our forthcoming exhibition.

Averse is an adjective. It is never placed next to the noun to which it refers and is followed by the preposition *to*. *Averse to* means having a strong dislike for, as in:
 They are not averse to the idea but they need more information before they make up their minds.

CONFUSABLE WORDS

advice/advise
These words look and sound quite alike and they both relate to telling someone what to do. They are regularly misused.

Advice is a noun referring to information that tells you the right thing to do, as in:
   You should seek medical advice.

Advise is a verb meaning the giving of *advice* as in:
   I would advise you to make an appointment with a doctor right away.

adviser/advisor
Adviser and *advisor* are acceptable spellings for a noun meaning 'someone who gives advice' in British English.

Advisor is the more usual form in American English.

Note that the adjective is always spelled *advisory*.

affect/effect
These words sound alike, especially when they are spoken quickly or carelessly, and they are frequently confused. In meaning they can both refer to influence or change.

Affect is a verb, used in such contexts as:
   How did the war affect the economy?

Effect is a noun, used in such contexts as:
   What was the effect of the war on the economy?

Effect can also be used as a verb in formal contexts meaning 'to bring about' or 'carry out', as in:
   The army effected a quick retreat.

afterwards/afterward
In British English, *afterwards* is the usual form of the adverb meaning 'later' or 'after something else has happened', as in:
   He thought that he had done well in the interview and he was told afterwards that he got the job.

Afterward is the usual form in American English.

alternate/alternative
Alternative, in British English, is an adjective which suggests the offer of a choice of a second possibility, as in:
   The road is closed but the police have suggested an alternative route.

Alternate, in American English, is often used in this context instead of *alternative*. To some extent the American use of *alternate* in this context is now found in British English also, although *alternative* remains the common British form.

The above use should not be confused with *alternate* meaning 'every other', as in:
> We meet for lunch on alternate Saturdays.

Nor should it be confused with *alternate* meaning 'happening in turns, one after the other', as in:
> The cake has alternate layers of cream and jam.

altogether/all together

Altogether can mean 'completely', as in:
> I can't say I'm altogether happy with the situation.

Altogether can also mean 'all in all', as in:
> The rooms were comfortable, the food was good, the staff were polite and altogether it was an excellent hotel.

All together means 'at the same time' or 'in the

all right/alright

All right is an adjective meaning 'acceptable' or 'satisfactory'.
> I worried about my test results but everything was all right.

All right is also a sentence substitute meaning 'very well' or 'OK'.
> It's all right, I can find my own way back.

There is a considerable dispute going on over the spelling of this word. On the one hand, we have many, many people who learned in childhood that *all right* is the correct form.

However, there are quite a few people, especially young people, who do not seem to think that there is anything wrong with using *alright*, and so that is the way they spell it.

Who is right? Well, at the moment the traditionalists are still in the majority. *All right* is the only spelling that is considered correct in the grammar books, but all that could change, particularly in informal contexts.

Why has the dispute occurred? Well, it probably has something to do with the spelling of words such as *already* and *altogether*.

All right is the accepted usage – at least for the time being!

CONFUSABLE WORDS

among/between

The prepositions *among* and *between* may be used interchangeably in most contexts.

Among used to be used when referring to three or more people or things, as in:
  We divided the remaining food among the five children.

Note that *amongst* means the same as *among*, but is now a rather old-fashioned usage.

Between used to be used only when referring to two people or things, as in:
  Sue's parents divided the money between her and her brother.

In modern usage, however, *between* is often used when referring to more than two things, as in:
  An agreement has been reached between all the states of America.

same place', as in:
  It is the first Christmas for many years that we have been all together as a family.

amiable/amicable

Both of these adjectives can mean 'friendly' but they are not interchangeable.

Amiable is usually used of people to mean friendly, pleasant and likeable, as in:
  He was an amiable young man and all his fellow workers got on with him.

Amicable is usually used to describe friendly relationships or dealings with other people, as in:
  The business partners have decided to part ways, thankfully it is an amicable agreement.

any more/anymore

Any more is an adverb meaning 'any longer'. It is usually spelled as two words in British English, as in:
  She's giving these clothes away because she doesn't wear them any more.

Anymore is the American English way of spelling the adverb and it is spreading to British English and becoming more and more common.

Expressions such as *any more*, *any place* and *any time* seem to be in the process of change in British English. In American English they are often spelled as one word.

As a determiner, *any more* is the correct usage in both British

English and American English. It means 'any additional' as in:
> I do not want any more pasta.
>
> She forgot to give me any more information on the new project, so I felt rather confused in the meeting.

anyone/any one

Anyone is spelled as one word when it means the same as *anybody*, as in:
> Anyone can succeed in this industry if they work hard enough.

Anyone is used with a singular verb. In modern usage it is sometimes followed by a plural personal pronoun or plural possessive adjective to avoid sexism, as in:
> Has anyone parked their car in the courtyard?

Any one is spelled as two words in contexts such as:
> Any one of those dresses would suit you.
>
> Any one of those college courses would be interesting.

any place/anyplace

Formerly in British English the term *any place* was always written as two words and it was considered to be less acceptable, especially in formal contexts, than *anywhere*, as in:
> We can't find any place to stay tonight.

The expression is much less common and more informal in British English than in American English. In American English the expression is often spelled as one word, *anyplace*, and this use is, to some extent, now spreading to British English.

any time/anytime

Formerly in British English the expression *any time* was always written as two words, as in:
> Please come and see us any time.

In American English, however, the expression is often spelled as one word, *anytime*, and this use is spreading to British English.

atheist/agnostic

These words do not mean the same but they both relate to the same theme, a belief, or rather a non-belief, in God.

Atheist is a noun referring to someone who does not believe in the existence of God, as in:
> My brother is marrying the daughter of a Church of England minister, although he himself is an atheist.

Agnostic is a noun referring to someone who believes that it is impossible to know whether God exists or not. However, the word is used in a more general sense to

refer to someone who doubts that God exists, as in:
> He says that scientists deal in facts and, as a result, many of them are agnostics.

backward/backwards

Backward, in British English, is normally used as an adjective, as in:
> She turned away and left without a backward glance.

Backwards is usually an adverb, as in:
> He stepped backwards to get away from the heat of the bonfire.

In American English *backward* is used as an adverb.

balk/baulk

Both spellings of this verb are acceptable. *Balk/baulk* means 'to stop short of' or 'to recoil from', as in:
> We balked/baulked at the idea of paying so much for theatre tickets.

bathroom

In British English a *bathroom* is usually a room containing a bath. In American English *bathroom* is often used as the word for a *toilet* or *lavatory* and this use is now sometimes found in British English. See also *toilet/loo/lavatory* on page 313.

can/may

Can is a verb used to indicate that someone or something is able to do something, as in:
> He can ski but not very well.

May is a verb that can be used to indicate what is likely or possible, as in:
> He may or may not attend the meeting – it depends on his other engagements.

In modern usage, both *may* and *can* are used to mean 'permitted or allowed to', as in:
> You may/can go to the party if you are back home by 11 pm.

In all but the most formal contexts *can* is now the usual word in this context, as in:
> Can I go now?

You will still find *may* being used when people are being exceptionally polite, as in:
> How may I help you, sir?

beat/beaten

These parts of the verb *beat* are liable to be confused.

Beat is the past tense of the verb

beat, as in:
> They beat the defending champions easily.

Beaten is the past participle of *beat*, as in:
> They have beaten last year's champions.

censor/censure

These words are closely related and liable to be confused as a result of their similarity in pronunciation and spelling.

Censor can be a verb meaning 'to examine letters, publications, films, etc, and remove any material that is thought to be unsuitable in the circumstances', as in:
> They censored the soldiers' letters in case they mentioned information that would be useful to the enemy.

Censor can also be a noun used to refer to someone who censors something, as in:
> He was employed as a censor of soldiers' letters.

Censure as a verb means 'to criticize or blame someone for something', as in:
> The young lawyer was censured for his poor handling of the case.

Censure as a noun means 'severe criticism or blame', as in:
> The government received censure for their unsuccessful economic policy.

centenary/centennial

Both of these words refer to a hundred-year anniversary.

Centenary is the usual British English word, as in:
> We are celebrating the centenary of the local school.

Centennial is used more frequently in American English.

continual/continuous

These two adjectives sound quite similar, look quite similar, and have very easily confused meanings.

Continual means 'frequently repeated', as in:
> Continual complaints from other residents were ignored by the students.

Continuous means 'without a break', as in:
> How do the factory workers put up with the continuous noise made by the machinery?

compulsory/compulsive

These two adjectives sound quite similar, and though they have quite different meanings, they both refer to something that must be done.

Compulsory describes a law or rule which must be done or carried out, as in:

> In that country it is compulsory to always carry identification documents.

Compulsive refers to behaviour or a habit that is very difficult or impossible to stop or control, as in:

> He is a compulsive gambler who has lost a fortune betting on horses.

chronic/acute

These words do not sound or look like each other at all. They have completely opposite meanings but they relate to the same theme. The confusion created by the adjectives *chronic* and *acute* arises from the fact they both refer to diseases or illnesses.

Chronic refers to a disease or illness that lasts a long time, frequently a period of several years, and often develops slowly, as in:

> Many elderly people suffer from chronic arthritis and need long-term drug treatment.

Acute refers to a disease that lasts a relatively short time and starts up quite suddenly, as in:

> She has acute earache and needs some strong painkillers immediately.

city/town

Nowadays a *city* is just a place that is larger and more important than a *town*, as in:

> Usually I just shop for new clothes here in the town, but if I want something special I go to one of the larger shops in the city.

In Britain the right for a town to be called a city is granted by the king or queen, although it is widely assumed that a town has to have a cathedral before it can be called a city. Many cities do have cathedrals, but this is not essential.

comprehensible/comprehensive

These two adjectives are both derived from the verb *comprehend*, but they are not derived from the same sense of that verb.

Comprehensible means 'able to be understood' as in:

> The child is just learning to speak and what she's saying is only comprehensible to her mother.

Incomprehensible is the negative

credible/credulous/incredible

These adjectives refer to belief but they are quite different in meaning.

Credible is an adjective meaning 'believable', as in:
> Both their accounts of what had happened sounded quite credible, but one of them must have been lying.

Credulous is used of someone who is too ready to believe that whatever they are told is true, as in:
> Only someone as credulous as Tom would believe that a car as cheap as that would be in good condition.

It is very common for people to use *credulous* when they really mean *credible*.

The opposite of *credible* is *incredible*, as in:
> It seems incredible that no one stopped to help the injured man.

form, as in:
> Why he suddenly decided to give up such a good job is completely incomprehensible.

Comprehensive means 'including all or most things', as in:
> You would be wise to take out fully comprehensive car insurance.

contagious/infectious

Both these words are adjectives referring to diseases that can be passed on from the sufferer to other people.

Contagious diseases are passed on by direct physical contact, as in:
> He has been told not to attend school as he is suffering from a skin disease that is highly contagious.

Infectious diseases are passed on by airborne microorganisms, as in:
> Some infectious diseases, such as measles and mumps, are now much rarer as a result of vaccination.

criteria/criterion

People often use *criteria* wrongly as a singular noun.

Criterion is the singular form, meaning a reference point against which things can be judged, as in:
> A good degree is not the only criterion for selecting someone for the job.

Criteria is the plural form, as in:
> He meets all the basic criteria for the job.

CONFUSABLE WORDS

decimate

The verb *decimate* literally means to kill or destroy one in ten of a set of people. It is derived from a Latin word meaning 'to kill one in ten of a unit of soldiers who took part in a mutiny'.

Nowadays there is not much call for a word meaning 'to kill one in ten people' and *decimate* has come to mean 'to kill a large proportion of', as in:
> The disease decimated the rabbit population of the island.

One tenth is not a huge proportion of a whole and so possibly there was a mix-up somewhere between one tenth being killed and one tenth surviving.

Decimate moved on even further and came to mean 'to inflict a great deal of damage on something or to destroy a large number or part of', as in:
> The event attracted a lot of adverse publicity to the area and decimated the tourist industry.

There was a great deal of opposition to the changes in the meaning of *decimate*. It seems that people did not want to let go of its connection with ten. It is advisable not to mention a specific amount when you are using the word.

cue/queue

These two nouns are pronounced in the same way but look different. They are **homophones**, *see* page 262.

data/datum

Data is the plural form of the word *datum* but the singular form *datum* is rarely used now. As a plural noun, *data* was formerly always used with a plural verb, as in:
> The data released by the bank were carefully studied by financial journalists.

In modern usage *data* is often accompanied by a singular verb, as in:
> The data on which the research was based has been found to be inaccurate.

Formerly *data* was used mainly in a scientific or technical context, but it is now frequently used with reference to computer information, and so is in more general use.

deceitful/deceptive

Both of these adjectives

are connected with deceiving or misleading someone.

Deceitful is used of people or their words or actions when these are intended to deceive or mislead someone, as in:
> She's a deceitful person; she pretended the money was hers.

Deceptive is used to describe things that are likely to mislead people, although there may be no dishonest intention involved, as in:
> The cottage looks deceptively small on the outside – it's actually very spacious inside.

delusion/illusion

These two words are liable to be confused because they are very close in meaning as well as sounding a little alike.

Delusion refers to a false or mistaken belief or idea that someone holds about themselves or their situation, as in:
> He is under the delusion that she has fallen in love with him.

Sometimes such an idea or belief can be part of a mental disorder, as in:
> She suffers from the delusion that she is Joan of Arc.

Illusion refers to something that appears to be the case, but is not, as in:
> The mountains seemed to be very close but it was an optical illusion.

dependant/dependent

The noun *dependant* refers to a person who depends on someone else to supply their means of living, as in:
> He said that he would resign from his job tomorrow if he could but he has dependants.

Dependent is an adjective meaning 'relying on' or 'unable to do without', as in:
> She can't drive any more and she is dependent on her neighbour taking her for her hospital appointments.

Dependent often means 'relying on someone for financial support', as in:
> He has no dependent relatives.

Note that in American English both the noun and adjective are spelled *dependent*.

derisory/derisive

The adjective *derisory* is normally used in the sense of 'ridiculously small' or 'inadequate', as in:
> The workers say that they have been

CONFUSABLE WORDS

deprecate/depreciate

These words look quite alike and they are liable to be confused.

The verb *deprecate* means 'to feel or express deep disapproval of', 'to deplore' or 'to condemn', as in:
> The speaker deprecated the company's decision to lay off more workers.

The verb *depreciate* can mean 'to decrease in value', as in:
> Shares in the company have depreciated to an all-time low.

The verb *depreciate* can also mean 'to belittle or treat as insignificant', as in:
> He was doing his best to speak French, but the teacher depreciated his efforts in front of the rest of the class.

It is this second meaning of *depreciate* that has become confused with that of *deprecate* and the two are now often used interchangeably, although language purists remain opposed to this. The change began with the adjective *self-deprecating*, which means 'modest or playing down your own achievements', as in:
> Jeremy is very clever but very self-deprecating.

offered a derisory pay rise and they are planning to go on strike.

The adjective *derisive* means 'mocking', as in:
> The comedian's act was not at all funny and was greeted with derisive comments from members of the audience.

desert/dessert

Desert has the emphasis on the first syllable and, as a noun, it refers to an area of land that is very hot and dry, as in:
> We had a trip of a lifetime to the Sahara Desert.

As a verb *desert* has the stress on the second syllable and means 'to abandon someone or something', as in:
> She deserted me when we were out together so I had to go home alone.

Desert the noun and *desert* the verb are *homographs*, see page 273.

The noun *dessert* has the emphasis on the second syllable and it means the last, sweet course of a meal, as in:
> The children all want ice cream for dessert.

device/devise

Device is a noun pronounced to rhyme with *advice* and means a tool or gadget, as in:
> Do you have one of those devices for taking the corks out of wine bottles?

Devise is a verb pronounced to rhyme with *advise* and means 'to invent or put together', as in:
> The prisoners of war devised a clever escape plan.

disc/disk

In British English the correct spelling is *disc*, as in:
> He is suffering from a slipped disc and his back is very sore.

But when the word is associated with computers it becomes *disk*, as in:
> I need a new disk drive.

In American English the word is spelled *disk* whatever the meaning and many British English users are beginning to follow suit.

downward/downwards

In British English *downward* is normally used as an adjective, as in:
> The downward escalator is at the back of the store.

Downwards is used as an adverb in British English, as in:
> He took a few steps downwards from the summit and slipped.

In American English *downward* is frequently used as an adverb.

drunk/drunken

The words *drunk* and *drunken* are

disinterested/uninterested

Until very recently, *disinterested* meant the same as *impartial* or *unbiased*. It was often confused with *uninterested*, meaning 'not having any interest in something', and now it has come to share this meaning. This has been a gradual change and many young people are not aware that the distinction between the meanings of the two words ever existed.

This change has not been universally welcomed by any means. However, this particular example of a language change is actually a reversion to a previous definition. According to historical dictionaries from the 17th century *disinterested* could mean the same as *uninterested*.

connected with alcoholic intoxication, but they are not used interchangeably.

The adjective *drunk* is often used after a verb and refers to a temporary state of intoxication:
   The friends got very drunk in a bar.

Drunk can also be used as a noun to describe someone who drinks a lot of alcohol and is often drunk, as in:
   The old drunk stopped me and asked for money.

The adjective *drunken* is used before a noun, as in:
   He was suffering from a hangover after a drunken party.

Drunken is often used to describe someone who is in the habit of drinking too much and becoming intoxicated, as in:
   The shop had to close because the owner had the reputation of being a drunken lush.

economic/economical

Economic is an adjective referring to the economy or to economics, as in:
   I wouldn't open a new business in the present economic climate.

Economical is an adjective meaning 'concerned with using the minimum of resources and avoiding waste', as in:
   He's looking for a small car that's economical to run.

e.g./i.e.

These abbreviations refer to quite different things but they are frequently confused, perhaps because not very many people learn Latin at school any more.

The abbreviation *e.g.* means 'for example' and is short for the Latin expression *exempli gratia*. The abbreviation *e.g.* is used in such contexts as:
   There are many historical places to visit in London, e.g. the Tower of London and the Natural History Museum.

The abbreviation *i.e.* is short for the Latin expression *id est* and means 'that is'. It is used to introduce a brief explanation or amplification of what has just been said, as in:
   Before we set up business in here we need to get some office equipment, i.e. a computer, a printer and some desks.

Originally both of these abbreviations were spelled with full stops, but they are now frequently spelled without them in British English, as in:
   eg and *ie*.

elder/older

Elder and *older* are both adjectives relating to age comparison and are sometimes confused. The word *elder* is used only in comparing the ages of people within a group, often a family group, as in:
> John was Anne's elder brother.

> Aunt Jane was my mother's elder sister.

You can also say:
> She was the elder of my mother's two sisters.

Elder cannot be followed by *than*. *Older* can be used instead of *elder* but it can also be used of things as well as people, as in:
> I prefer older houses.

Older can be followed by *than*, as in:
> Their car is even older than mine.

enquiry/inquiry

The words *enquiry* and *inquiry* can be used interchangeably in British English, although *inquiry* is the standard form in American English. Some people, however, prefer to use *enquiry* in British English to refer to an ordinary request for information, as in:
> One of the library staff will deal with your enquiry.

Inquiry is used for a formal investigation of some kind, as in:
> Police are interviewing him as part of a murder inquiry.

envelope/envelop

These words look quite alike but they are pronounced differently and they have different meanings. The emphasis is on the first syllable of the noun *envelope*, which is a folded paper container in which you send a letter or card, as in:
> I need an envelope for this birthday card.

The emphasis is on the second syllable of *envelop*, which is a verb meaning 'to enclose or surround', as in:
> The grandmother enveloped her grandson in a big hug.

Note that the past tense and present participle of the verb *envelop* are spelled with a single *p*, as in:

enveloped and *enveloping*.

extant/extinct

The adjectives *extant* and *extinct* are opposites. *Extant* means 'still in existence', as in:
> These are some of the traditions extant in the area around here.

Extinct means 'no longer in existence', as in:

CONFUSABLE WORDS

every day/everyday
Every day is used to mean 'daily', it is spelled as two words, as in:
> She goes to the gym at least once every day.

Everyday, as one word, has the meaning 'completely ordinary', as in:
> It's a nice enough everyday dress but I want something special to wear for the wedding.

Perhaps under the influence of such expressions as *any more/anymore*, the distinction between *every day* and *everyday* is beginning to fade slightly and *everyday* is beginning to be used for both meanings. However, there is quite a long way to go before this is declared correct and acceptable and it will meet many protests along the way.

There are quite a few theories about why dinosaurs became extinct.

extrovert/extravert/introvert
Extravert is the original spelling but *extrovert* is now the more common spelling.

Extrovert refers to someone who is more concerned with what is going on around them than with their own thoughts and feelings, and more particularly someone who is lively, confident and sociable, as in:
> Our first two guests are both extroverts so they should get the party off to a good start.

The opposite is *introvert* which refers to someone who is preoccupied with their own thoughts and feelings, particularly someone who is withdrawn and unsociable, as in:
> He's an introvert who prefers his own company to that of other people.

farther/further
Both *farther* and *further* can be used to refer to physical distance, as in:
> The hotel is much farther from the city centre than we were told.

> My house is a bit further down this road.

However, only *further* is used in other senses, as in:
> The police officer said that he would take no further questions from members of the press.

The verb form is also always *further*:
> The rebels vowed to further the cause of freedom.

first/firstly

When mentioning items in a list the first item may be preceded by either *firstly* or *first*, as in:
> There are several reasons for my refusal to go: firstly/first, I am much too busy to attend …

Formerly *firstly* was considered unacceptable in this context.

forbear/forebear

The verb *forbear* is pronounced with the stress on the second syllable and it means 'to refrain from doing something'. It is mostly used in formal contexts, as in:
> I shall forbear from punishing the students in the circumstances.

The noun *forebear* is pronounced with the stress on the first syllable and can also be spelled *forbear*. It is used to refer to an ancestor, as in:
> Some of our forebears probably lived in these ruins.

for ever/forever

For ever is often used to emphasize that something is for all time, as in:
> He said he would love her for ever.

Forever in the sense of 'continually or without stopping' is usually written as one word, as in:
> The child is forever asking for sweets.

fortuitous/fortunate

Signs of change are particularly likely to go unspotted for a while where the word affected is not very commonly used.

Fortuitous is such a word. Originally, and in line with its derivation, *fortuitous* meant 'happening by chance' or 'accidental', as in:

fewer/less

Fewer, the comparative form of *few*, means 'a smaller number of', as in:
> Fewer students than usual have signed up for this course.

> This cash register is for baskets containing nine items or fewer.

Less, the comparative form of *little*, means 'a smaller amount than', as in:
> Tell the children to make less noise.

> Give me less sugar than that in my tea, please.

It is becoming common, especially in informal contexts, to use *less* in many cases where *fewer* is correct, although this use is ungrammatical and should be avoided in formal contexts.

CONFUSABLE WORDS

She bumped into her old friend in a completely fortuitous meeting. They hadn't seen each other since they were at school together.

Because the words sound quite similar, *fortuitous* began to become confused with *fortunate*, meaning lucky, as in:

Meeting her father's old friend was fortuitous for her because he offered her a job in his company.

And in time *fortuitous* began to be used to describe an event that was not only accidental but also lucky.

forward/forwards

In British English *forward* is used as an adjective, it means 'facing towards the front' as in:

She gave a forward motion.

Forward is an adjective that also means 'looking into the future' as in:

Some forward planning is required.

Forward and *forwards* can be used as adverbs, meaning 'towards the front', as in:

Please step forward if you are next in line.

Let's move forwards.

However, in sentences using idiomatic phrasal verbs the word *forwards* is not used:

Put forward a motion at our next meeting.

The police are asking witnesses to come forward.

gipsy/gypsy

Both these spellings are acceptable, although many regard this word, regardless of spelling, to be **offensive**. It is accepted by some when spelled with a capital as in *Gypsy*. An alternative word is *Traveller*, although this is often used to refer to a wider range of people than Gypsies who are Romany in origin, including, for example, *Irish Travellers*. The approved modern alternative preferred by many in Europe is *Roma*.

gourmet/gourmand

These two words are sometimes confused. They are both connected with food.

Gourmet is a complimentary term used to describe someone who likes the best quality food and who is knowledgeable about it.

Francis is real gourmet who is an expert at cooking.

A *gourmand* also likes food, but is concerned with the amount of it that can be eaten, as well as the quality of it. *Gourmand* means much the same as *glutton*, but does not sound so insulting!

> Bernard loves eating in the best restaurants. He admits he is a total gourmand.

hire/rent

Hire and *rent* are another two words that get confused, although they do not resemble each other at all in appearance or sound. However, they both relate to the temporary use of something in exchange for payment. Sometimes whether you use *hire* or *rent* depends on how long the temporary use is likely to last.

Hire is more likely to be associated with short-term use, as in:

> She thinks she might hire a wedding dress rather than buy one.

Rent suggests a more long-term use, as in:

> Their plan is to rent a flat for the two years that their college courses last.

historic/historical

It looks as though a change is affecting these two adjectives which are derived from the word *history*. The adjectives are *historic* and *historical*, and traditionally they have different meanings.

Historic refers to an event that is important enough or memorable enough to be recorded in history, as in:

> The Battle of Waterloo was a historic victory for the British.

It is now often used exaggeratedly of an event, often a sporting event, that is not nearly as important as that description suggests, as in:

> The cup final ended in a historic victory for the Spanish team.

According to traditional usage, *historical* simply refers to something that took place in the past or means 'based on the study of history', as in:

> Most of the country's historical records are held in the national archive.

Probably because these words sound so alike and are so frequently confused, the distinction between them is beginning to disappear. This is bound to arouse some protest. Change always does.

However, there is a problem. In American English *rent* is used in connection with short-term use as well as longer-term use. The American use is having some influence on British English, so that you will now find both *hire a car for the weekend* and *rent a car for the weekend* being commonly used.

Note that the verb *charter*, rather than *hire* or *rent*, is used in connection with boats or planes, as in:

Let's charter a yacht for the holidays.

hyper-/hypo-

These prefixes are liable to be confused. Although they sound similar they are opposite in meaning.

Hyper- means 'above', 'over,' or 'in excess', as in:

The child was said to be hyperactive.

Hypo- means 'under', 'beneath', as in:

She has to inject insulin with a hypodermic syringe.

Hypothermia is a medical condition in which the body temperature is much lower than normal.

illegible/eligible

These two words are liable to be confused, mainly because they sound similar, but they have entirely different meanings.

Illegible means 'impossible to read', as in:

I hope he types the information I asked for because his handwriting is virtually illegible.

Eligible means 'suitable' or 'having the right qualifications', as in:

She was pleased to find out that she was eligible for a scholarship.

immigrant/emigrant

These words are liable to be confused. This is quite understandable as the two words can refer to the same person, looked at from two different viewpoints.

The word *immigrant* concentrates on people arriving in a new land, as in:

There were many Irish immigrants in America following the potato famine in Ireland.

The word *emigrant* concentrates on people leaving their native land, as in:

Many of the Irish people who left their native shore were reluctant emigrants, but they travelled to Britain and America to avoid starvation.

Immigrant and *emigrant* are liable to

imply/infer

Imply means 'to suggest something in an indirect way', as in:
> He didn't actually accuse the student of cheating outright, but he implied it.

Infer means 'to deduce something' or 'to conclude that something is true', as in:
> We inferred from the report that the hospital was almost certain to close.

Nowadays *infer* is often used when the correct word is *imply*, as in:
> He inferred that he would be leaving the job shortly.

This is incorrect and should read:
> He implied that he would be leaving the job shortly.

be confused with *migrant*, see pages 305–6.

impracticable/impractical/practicable/practical

The words *impracticable* and *impractical* are similar in meaning, but they are not interchangeable. *Impracticable* means 'not able to be put into practice' or 'unworkable', as in:
> He persuaded several people that the scheme was a good idea but it was so expensive that it was completely impracticable.

Impractical means 'not sensible' or 'unrealistic', as in:
> He has come up with various money-making ideas but all of them are impractical.

Practicable and *practical* are the positive forms of these words, as in:
> Do you think it is practicable to build a house halfway up a mountain?

> A two-seater car like that's not very practical when you have two children.

indexes/indices

The noun *index* has two possible plural forms, *indexes* and *indices*. The word *indexes* is the usual plural form in most contexts, as in:
> Her job is to compile indexes for reference books.

The word *indices* is mostly restricted to technical or mathematical contexts.

individual

The word *individual* means 'a person', but it can only be used in certain contexts.

Individual is often used in a context in which a single person is contrasted with a group, as in:
> We must give some thought to the rights of the individual as well as concerning ourselves with the nation as a whole.

The word *individual* is sometimes used in a derogatory or insulting way, as in:
> She was very nice but I always thought her husband was a most unpleasant individual.

industrial/industrious

The words *industrial* and *industrious* are both adjectives. They look and sound like each other, apart from their endings, and are liable to be confused. They both refer to work, but not the same meaning of work.

Industrial has to do with industry in the sense of the business of making or producing goods, usually on a large scale, as in:
> The land on which the houses were built was formerly an industrial site.

Industrious is an adjective based on a much less common and more formal meaning of industry meaning 'hard work' or 'diligence', as in:
> He was not as intelligent as some of the other students but he was very industrious and usually managed to do well in exams.

immoral/immortal

Some words which get confused because they resemble each other quite closely and because they have a reasonably similar pronunciation do not belong to the same theme. They are actually unrelated. Two such words are *immoral* and *immortal*. These two adjectives would be the same word but for the letter *t*, and this gives rise to confusion. What a difference one letter can make!

Immoral means 'morally wrong'. In other words, wrong according to the principles of what is considered to be right and wrong behaviour, as in:
> It is immoral to make people work long hours for very little pay in order to be able to export cheap goods.

Immortal literally means 'living or existing forever', as in:
> No one is immortal, although some people behave as though they think they are.

Immortal can also be used to refer to something, such as a line of prose, poetry or song, that has

become very famous and has lasted a very long time, as in:
> Just think of the immortal line 'Tomorrow is another day'.

inflammable/flammable/non-flammable

The two words *inflammable* and *flammable* both mean 'capable of burning' or 'easily set on fire', as in:
> Children's nightclothes should not be made of inflammable/flammable material.

It is a common error to think that *inflammable* means the opposite, i.e. 'not capable of burning', because *in–* words, are often negative, as in *incredible*, but the word for this is *non-flammable*.

its/it's

These two little words can cause a lot of bother! See the entry under *homophones see* page 268.

–ize/–ise

Either of these verb endings is correct in British English, with a few exceptions.

In American English the *–ize* ending is the standard spelling and many British English dictionaries and reference books also use this spelling.

ingenious/ingenuous

These words are frequently confused although they are neither spelled the same way nor pronounced the same way and their meanings are entirely different.

The e of the word *ingenious* is pronounced like the double e in the word *seen*, while the e of the word *ingenuous* is pronounced like the e in the word *egg*.

Ingenious means 'clever, especially in an inventive or unusual way', as in:
> She's a brilliant cook and finds a great many ingenious ways to use up left-over food.

Ingenuous means naïve or innocent, as in:
> His latest girlfriend is very young and too ingenuous to realize that he is dishonest.

However, as long as British English users are consistent in their use of *–ize* or *–ise* it usually does not matter which they use. Note that there are some words in British English where the *–ize* spelling should not

CONFUSABLE WORDS

be used. These include *advertise*, *advise*, *chastise*, *comprise*, *compromise*, *exercise*, *improvise*, *revise*, *supervise*, *surmise*, *surprise* and *televise*. It is best to check a dictionary to be sure.

jail/gaol

Both of these are acceptable spellings of the word for *prison*, although *jail* is the more common spelling, with *gaol* seeming a bit old fashioned.

jewellery/jewelry

Jewellery/jewelry is a noun which refers to decorations made of precious stones and metals that are worn on the body, as in:
> I keep my diamond jewellery in the safe.

Both *jewellery* and *jewelry* are acceptable spellings in British English, although *jewellery* is the more common spelling. In American English *jewelry* is the standard spelling.

lay/lie

These words can cause confusion. Not only are their meanings related, but the **past tense** of the word *lie* is *lay*. This is, indeed, a recipe for confusion.

The verb *lay* takes a **direct object** and means 'to put or place something down', as in:
> The doctor asked them to lay the injured man on the stretcher.

The verb *lie*, which gets confused with the verb *lay*, does not take a **direct object** and means 'to rest on something in a horizontal position', as in:
> I feel faint and need to lie on the sofa.

The **past tense** of *lay* is *laid*, as in:
> We laid the baby on the bed.

The **past tense** of *lie* in this context is *lay*, as in:
> He lay on the bed and tried to sleep.

The **past participle** of *lay* is *laid*, as in:
> We had laid the baby on the bed.

The **past participle** of *lie* is *lain*, as in:
> The tiger had lain in wait, unnoticed by its prey.

Just to add more confusion, there is another verb *to lie* which means 'to tell untruths'. Fortunately, neither its **past tense** nor its **past participle** causes any problems, both being formed regularly as *lied*.

judgment/judgement

Both of the spellings of this word are considered acceptable.

Judgment/judgement is a noun and one of its meanings is a decision:
 I can't make a judgment/judgement based on that information.

As a noun, another of its meanings is the capability of making a decision:
 I trust his judgment/judgement on this subject.

Judgement with an **e** after **g** is common in British English, while this is often considered a misspelling in American English.

Judgment with no **e** after **g** is being increasingly used in British English, probably because of the American influence.

In Britain, in a legal context, *judgment* has traditionally been a preferred spelling.

More and more, it is becoming a style preference, rather than a spelling choice based on the use of the word.

learn/teach

The word *learn* is sometimes used wrongly instead of *teach*. If you are giving information or instruction about something to someone you *teach* them, as in:
 She teaches English to Spanish students.

When you are gaining information or knowledge or getting instruction about something you *learn* something, as in:
 The French student has gone to live with a family in London in order to learn English.

lend/loan

The word *lend* is used as a verb and means 'to give someone the temporary use of', as in:
 I'm sure he'll lend you the book which you need for your homework assignment.

The verb *loan* is commonly used in American English in the above context, but in British English *loan* is mostly used with reference to the lending of reasonably large sums of money, etc, as in:
 The bank has agreed to loan us the money to start our new business.

Lend is also commonly used in this context.

The word *loan* is also used as a noun, as in:
 We have to repay the bank loan by the end of the year.

CONFUSABLE WORDS

lose/loose and lose/looser

Lose is spelled with only one *o* and is pronounced to rhyme with *whose*. *Loose* has a double *o* and is pronounced to rhyme with *goose*.

Lose is a verb meaning 'to be unable to find something', as in:
> If you lose your credit card you should ring your bank right away.

It can also mean 'to fail to win', as in:
> If you lose this match you'll be out of the competition.

Loser is a noun referring to someone who fails to win, as in:
> How did such a successful businesswoman come to marry such a loser?

Loose is an adjective meaning 'not tight', as in:
> There is a loose wire and the food mixer isn't working.

If something is *looser* than it was before it is not so tight or close-fitting.
> She's lost some weight and her clothes are now looser.

> I'd like a loan of your pencil, please.

It is not correct English to use *lend* as a noun, although some people do so in informal contexts.

libel/slander

Both *libel* and *slander* are nouns that refer to untrue statements intended to give people a bad opinion of someone.

In *libel* such statements are *written down* or *printed*, as in:
> She is suing the newspaper on the grounds of libel.

In *slander* the statements are *spoken*, as in:
> She is guilty of slander if she told you that he deserted his wife and children. He's not even married.

Both *libel* and *slander* can also be used as verbs.

licence/license

These words are often wrongly used.

In British English *licence* is a noun, as in:
> The police officer asked to see his driving licence.

> The shopkeeper has applied for a licence to sell alcohol.

Note the spelling of *off-licence*, which is a noun referring to premises in the UK where you can buy bottles or cans of alcoholic drinks to take away.

License is a verb, as in:
The organizers of the event are not licensed to sell alcohol.

The past participle form *licensed* is often used as an adjective, as in: *licensed grocer* and *licensed restaurant* and this is often wrongly written as *licenced*.

In American English things are simpler because both the noun and the verb are spelled *license*.

masterly/masterful

These adjectives are both derived from the noun *master* but they have different meanings.

Masterly means 'very skilful', as in:
The audience applauded a masterly performance by the orchestra.

Masterful means 'showing strength or dominance', as in:
He thought he was being masterful, but she thought he was being a bully.

migrant/emigrant

A *migrant* is someone who travels from one place or country to another, often in order to try to find work, as in:

media/medium

Media is the plural form of *medium* when this refers to a means of transmitting information, as in:
Television is certainly a useful educational medium for children.

The most popular forms of news media were found to be radio and television.

The media is the term used to refer to our means of mass communication, i.e. newspapers, radio, television, and online news services.

The use of *media* as a singular noun is disliked by some people, but this use is very common, as in:
The media is often blamed for making young people body-conscious.

Many people now do not know that *media* is the plural form of the Latin word *medium*, and see no reason why it should not be used in the singular.

CONFUSABLE WORDS

The farmer employed several migrants from eastern Europe.

Migrant can also be used as an adjective, as in:
The farm used migrant workers.

Migrant is also used frequently to refer to birds travelling from place to place according to the season of the year, as in:
Swallows are migrants to Britain during the summer months.

Migrant is liable to be confused with *immigrant* and *emigrant*. See *immigrant/emigrant* on page 298.

momentary/momentous

These two adjectives are both derived from the noun *moment*, but they are connected with different meanings of *moment*. The stress on *momentary* is on the first syllable and the stress on *momentous* is on the second syllable.

Momentary comes from the common 'time' meaning of *moment*, i.e. 'a very short time', and it means 'lasting a very short time', as in:
The chess player had a momentary failure of concentration, but then he began to play better than ever.

Momentous comes from a less common meaning of *moment*, i.e. 'importance' or 'significance', and means 'very significant or having far-reaching consequences', as in:
It was a momentous decision to invade another country, and one that the president was to regret.

moral/morale

Although these words are pronounced in different ways and have totally different meanings the fact that they look quite alike makes them easily confused.

Moral is most commonly an adjective and means 'referring to the principles of right and wrong', as in:
Their mother is a very moral person and yet both her sons are criminals.

He had a moral responsibility to look after the children in his care.

Moral as a noun is used to refer to a lesson on how to behave or act, often one which you learn from reading a story, as in:
There is often a moral in the stories from Aesop's Fables.

Morale refers to how members of a group are feeling and the extent of their confidence and optimism, as in:
After their election victory, morale in the political party is at an all-time high.

nauseous/nauseated

Nauseous is another word that appears to be undergoing a change, but it is not exactly a word in everyday use and the change may not yet be very obvious. The adjective *nauseous* in British English traditionally means 'nauseating' or 'causing nausea'.

In other words, it is a formal way of saying something makes you feel sick or want to vomit, as in:

   There was a nauseous smell of rotten meat coming from the fridge.

In American English *nauseous* means 'nauseated' or 'feeling sick' or 'about to vomit', as in:

   Going on a boat trip always makes me feel nauseous, even when the sea is calm.

The British English equivalent of American English *nauseous* is *nauseated*, but users of British English have begun to adopt the American usage, as in:

   She says that she felt nauseous for most of her pregnancy.

next/this

The adjective *next* in one of its senses is used to refer to the day of the week, the month of the year, etc, that will follow, as in:

   I'll see you next Wednesday.

The adjective *this* can also be used in this way and this can give rise to ambiguity. For example, some people use *this* to refer to the very next Wednesday, reserving *next* for the Wednesday after that. Others use *next* for both.

Note: the best policy, in order to avoid this ambiguity, is to specify exactly what day or date you are referring to!

of/have

Of is sometimes used wrongly instead of the verb *have* in certain contexts, perhaps because they sound rather alike when not emphasized or pronounced clearly. To write or say *should of come* instead of *should have come* or *must of done* instead of *must have done* is becoming more and more common but it is considered wrong. See page 192.

off/from

The word *off* is used by some people instead of *from* in certain contexts, for example when they wish to

CONFUSABLE WORDS

indicate where they acquired something, as in:

> I certainly wouldn't buy a second-hand car off him. [Wrong]

This use is *incorrect* and should be avoided, especially in formal contexts.

off + of

Some people wrongly use *off* followed by *of* when only *off* is necessary, as in:

> The cat jumped off of the table and ran out the door. [Wrong]

oral/aural

These words are liable to be confused. This is not surprising because they sound the same and they both refer to parts of the body involved in communication.

Aural means 'relating to the sense of hearing'. The word *aural* can also refer to the ear, but usually only in technical or formal contexts.

> In an aural comprehension test, the test is read out to the students so that they have to understand it through hearing before answering the questions in writing.

Oral means 'referring to speech'. In an *oral test* the questions and answers are all spoken. *Oral* is also used to mean 'referring to the mouth', as in:

> Good oral hygiene is very important so that you can avoid gum disease and tooth decay.

orientate/orient

Both of these forms are considered acceptable in British English in the sense of 'to get your bearings', although *orientate* is the more commonly used, as in:

> The mist was coming down and it was becoming increasingly difficult to orientate themselves on the mountain slopes.

In American English the standard form is *orient*.

outdoor/outdoors

These words refer to the same thing, but they are different parts of speech.

Outdoor is used as an adjective, as in:

> They try to persuade their children to get involved in outdoor sports at the weekend and during the holidays.

Outdoors is used as an adverb, as in:

> It's not often warm enough to eat outdoors in this climate.

outward/outwards

These words both mean 'towards the outside', but they are not generally considered to be interchangeable in British English.

Outward is used as an adjective, as in:
> The train on the outward journey was very late, but it was on time on the way back.

Outwards is used as an adverb, as in:
> The dancers stood with their toes pointing outwards.

In American English *outward* can be used both as an adjective and an adverb.

passed/past

These words sound alike and are **homophones** which are liable to be confused, see page 269.

persecute/prosecute

The verbs *persecute* and *prosecute* are frequently confused These words look quite like each other and, there is a degree of

practice/practise

This is an interesting example of two words from the same source but in British English the verb and the noun forms are spelled differently. These words are liable to be confused and used wrongly.

Practice is a noun, meaning the repetition of something until you improve, as in:
> He goes to football practice after school on Tuesdays.

Practice as a noun can also refer to the place of work of a doctor, as in:
> Unfortunately our doctor has moved to a new practice in another town.

Practice as a noun can also refer to actions, as in:
> Some members of the company were involved in illegal practices.

Practise is the verb form, meaning to repeatedly do something until you improve; or to carry out something, as in:
> They practise playing the piano every day.

> He is not qualified to practise medicine in this country.

Note that *practise* is not one of those verbs in English that can end in **-ize**. **Note** also that in American English both the noun and verb forms are spelled *practise*.

CONFUSABLE WORDS

similarity in their pronunciation. There is also a degree of similarity in their theme but they are at opposite ends of the scale. The theme is fairness or justice.

Persecute comes under the heading of 'unfairness' or 'lack of justice' in that it means 'to treat someone very unfairly and unjustly, and usually with great cruelty, over a long period of time'. This treatment often takes place on the grounds of political or religious beliefs, as in:
> Many people were persecuted for their opposition to racial discrimination.

Prosecute, on the other hand, is mostly on the side of fairness and justice, or at least we hope so. It means 'to charge someone with committing a crime and to try to show that they are guilty of it', as in:
> There was a sign on the shop door saying 'Shoplifters will be prosecuted'.

phenomenon/phenomena

People often use *phenomena* wrongly as a singular noun when it is *phenomenon* that is the singular form, as in:
> There have been many reports of the phenomenon that appeared in the sky last night but astronomers are still baffled by it.

precede/proceed

These words are commonly confused.

Precede is a verb meaning 'to go or come in front of someone or something', as in:
> The staff and sixth-year students preceded the rest of the school into the assembly hall.

> The main text of the book was preceded by a short but informative introduction.

Proceed is a verb meaning 'to go on' or 'to continue', as in:
> They did not proceed with the changes.

> You should proceed to Gate 4.

prescribe/proscribe

Prescribe is the more common of these two words and means 'to advise' or 'order the use of', often in a medical context, as in:
> The doctor prescribed a mild sleeping pill for the patient.

> He prescribed a few days of complete bed rest for my child.

Proscribe is used in formal contexts to mean 'to forbid', as in:
> The law proscribed the carrying of knives.

prostrate/prostate

These two words are often confused. *Prostrate* as an adjective means 'lying on the ground facing downwards', as in:

> The victim of the attack was lying prostrate at the entrance to the park.

It can also mean 'overcome' or 'shocked', as in:

> She was prostrate with grief when she heard of her brother's sudden death.

Prostrate can also be a verb meaning 'to throw yourself on the ground, as in submission', as in:

> They had to prostrate themselves on the ground to avoid the gunfire.

Prostate is a noun which refers to the gland round the neck of a man's bladder, as in:

> He is being treated for prostate cancer.

Scottish/Scots/Scotch

These adjectives all mean 'of or relating to Scotland'. However, they are not interchangeable.

Scottish is the most general of these adjectives and it can be used in a wide range of contexts, as in:

> She is very interested in Scottish culture.

> He paints watercolours of the Scottish landscape.

Scots is an adjective. It tends to be restricted to describing people, language or the law, as in:

> I own a dictionary of the Scots language.

> He studies Scots law.

Scots is also a noun used to refer to a person who comes from Scotland, as in:

> Many Scots emigrated to Canada.

The noun *Scots* is also used to refer to the Scots language, as in:

> The poetry was written in Scots.

Scotch is the least general of the three adjectives, being restricted to a few contexts such as *Scotch broth*, *Scotch mist* and, the most famous of all, *Scotch whisky*.

Scotch can also be used as a noun to mean 'Scotch whisky', although this is not a common use in Scotland where whisky is simply *whisky*.

It is wrong to refer to the Scottish people as '*the Scotch*'.

seasonal/seasonable

These words are both adjectives formed from the noun *season*.

Seasonal means 'relating to a particular season', 'occurring during a particular season' or 'varying with the seasons', as in:

CONFUSABLE WORDS

supposedly (NOT supposably)

It's possible that you may have heard 'supposably' and 'supposively', or even 'supposingly', used instead of *supposedly*.

It can be assumed that these misuses occur because *supposedly* has been repeatedly misheard. The *–ably* ending of 'supposably' sort of makes sense though, when you think of the words *believably*, *considerably*, *dependably*, etc. While 'supposively' could only exist if the word 'supposive' existed, and there is no such word.

Supposedly is the only accepted standard usage and means 'seemingly, according to what is believed to be true'. It is used to convey doubt, as in:

> He supposedly does his own tax returns but I have my doubts.

You might be surprised to hear that 'supposably' *is* a recorded word, however it is not modern Standard English, and it has a slightly different meaning to *supposedly* (it means capable of being supposed). Its use is widely considered to be wrong so it should be avoided.

> The steak is served with seasonal vegetables.

> Farm work is usually seasonal in that area.

Seasonable means 'suitable for or appropriate to a particular season', as in:

> The weather this summer has not been very seasonable.

systematic/systemic

Both these adjectives are connected with the noun *system*. *Systematic* means 'well-organized and orderly', as in:

> The police conducted a systematic search of the house and grounds.

> You need to establish a more systematic process for selecting new staff.

Systemic refers to a system and is a much less common word sometimes used in error for *systematic*. *Systemic* is used mainly in scientific or medical contexts, as in:

> Her illness began with an infected finger but it has developed into a serious systemic disease of the blood.

their/they're/there

These words are **homophones**, which means they have the same

that/which

That and *which* are both relative pronouns. *That* can be used to refer to people or things, as in:

There is the man that I was talking about.

That pen was very expensive.

Whereas *which* can only be used to refer to things or animals and not people, as in:

The cat, which I see every day, lives with John.

That and *which* are often used interchangeably as in:

This is the cake that Mary made.

This is the cake which Mary made.

This is not necessarily considered wrong, however, there is a distinction to be made: *that* defines (it appears in a restrictive relative clause), and *which* gives extra information (it appears in a non-restrictive relative clause) and is usually preceded by a comma.

The cake, which Mary made for me, is damaged.

The boy told me that he was Spanish, which is what I thought originally.

The relative pronoun *who* can be used instead of *that* to refer to people:

That is the boy who told me he was Spanish.

pronunciations even though they are spelled differently. They are frequently confused. See page 271.

to/too/two

The words *to* and *too* are sometimes confused. *Two* also sounds the same, although it is not confused with the others quite as much. The three words are all **homophones**, see page 272.

toilet/loo/lavatory

There are lots of words to name the place where we go to pee! There are lots of slang words and euphemisms for the *lavatory* because it is something we are mildly embarrassed about. These include *john*, *bog*, *WC*, *rest room*, *smallest room*, *little boys'/little girls' room*, etc.

Toilet is the most widely used word for *lavatory* in British English, although *loo* is becoming more and more widely used, especially in less formal situations. The word *lavatory* is more formal but not often used

CONFUSABLE WORDS

nowadays. *Toilet* is usually found on relevant signs in public places. In American English, *bathroom* and *rest room* are commonly used for a public toilet. *See* **bathroom** on page 284.

toward/towards

These two forms of the preposition meaning 'in the direction of something or someone', 'close or closer to a point in time' or 'in relation to someone or something' are interchangeable except that in British English *towards* is the more common form, as in *walk towards them* and *towards the end of the week.*

try to/try and

These two expressions are often interchangeable in modern usage, as in:

Let's try to get this finished today.

Let's try and get this finished today.

Formerly *try and* was considered to be unacceptable in all but very informal or colloquial contexts, with *try to* being the acceptable form. Now *try and* is acceptable in all but the most formal written contexts.

In American English *toward* is the more common form, as in:

There was a horse coming toward us

Toward the end of the week.

until/till

These words mean the same. *Till* is a shorter form of *until*.

Until is a conjunction meaning 'up to a time that', as in:

I walked until I got blisters on both my feet.

Until is a preposition sometimes preceded by *up*, meaning 'in the period before something', as in:

I only have the car up until 10pm when my dad needs it.

Till can be used instead of either of these forms and is suitable in formal and informal language. *Until* is usually more formal and just used in written language.

up/upon

Up is a preposition and means in a direction going above, or at a higher level, as in:

The goat was up the mountain side.

The squirrel was up the tree.

Up can be an adverb meaning in an upwards direction, as in:

His goal was to go up the mountain.

Look up at the fluffy clouds.

Upon is also a preposition. It is another word for *on*, but *upon* tends to be used in more formal contexts.
  The ornate carvings upon the table were in the Tudor style.

upward/upwards

Upward is used as an adjective, as in:
  Go on the upward escalator.

Upwards is an adverb, as in:
  pointing upwards.

In American English *upward* is frequently used as an adverb.

verbal/oral

There is a certain amount of ambiguity associated with the use of the word *verbal*. It can mean 'expressed in words' in writing or in speech, as in:
  There was no verbal reaction from the palace about the allegations.

However, *verbal* is often used to refer to something that is spoken and not written down, as in:
  Although we had a verbal agreement, we didn't put anything in writing.

If you are referring to something that is spoken rather than written, and if there is any possibility of ambiguity from the context, it is best to use the word *oral*, which can mean 'expressed in speech'.
  It was an oral agreement.

  The librarian had recorded an oral history of the wartime experiences of the older people in the village.

Oral also means relating to the mouth.
  The surgeon specialized in oral surgery.

See also **oral/aural**.

whom/who

The word *whom* is used as the object of a verb or preposition, as in:
  Whom did he choose as his assistant?

  To whom did he leave his house?

  To whom did he give his old car?

Whereas the word *who* is used as the subject, as in:
  Who said that?

  Who is the new teacher?

However, in modern usage *who* is increasingly being used instead of *whom* (except in very formal contexts) in situations where this is technically ungrammatical, as in:
  Who did he choose as his assistant?

CONFUSABLE WORDS

Who did he leave the house to?

Who did he give his old car to?

See also page 123.

whose/who's
These words are **homophones**, see page 272.

will/shall
The future tense of verbs is formed by using *will* or *shall*, or a contracted form of these, with the infinitive form of the main verb, as in:
  The new shop will open for business next week.

  We'll start work tomorrow.

Formerly, the verb *shall* was always used with *I* and *we;* and *will* with *you*, *he/she/it* and *they*.

In modern usage a change has occurred. The verb *will* is now commonly used in most contexts.

The word *shall* is still used when questions are being asked or suggestions being made when these relate to the immediate situation, as in:
  Shall I proceed?

  Shall we get going?

There's also a contracted form:

Who'll go first?

What'll you have?

See also **Future Tense** page 180.

you/one
Both of the pronouns *you* and *one* can be used to refer to an indefinite person or people in general. *You* is the pronoun you would use most often for this purpose, as in:
  You need to book a seat when you buy your train ticket.

  You learn a foreign language more quickly if you spend some time in the country where it is spoken.

  You must buy a ticket before you board the train.

The pronoun *one* was used formerly in these and other contexts, as in:
  One must guard against pickpockets in the market.

Now, however, *one* is usually restricted to very formal contexts, as in:
  Etiquette demands that one must curtsy when being introduced to the Queen.

your/you're
Your and *you're* are **homophones**, see page 272.

PUNCTUATING PROPERLY

When you said you ate like a bird every day ...
I didn't realize you meant you ate, like, a bird every day.

WHAT USE is punctuation? Punctuation helps make sense of language and gives it structure. It breaks up what might be a rambling, fairly meaningless piece of writing and makes it into a meaningful unit.

PRESERVING MEANING

If you've ever had to try to decipher meaning from a piece of text where the writer hasn't bothered to use any punctuation (probably on social media!) then you'll realize how important good (or any!) punctuation is. If good punctuation is not observed, meaning can be lost or changed – and you are giving your reader a lot of unnecessary hard work. It means you are not communicating at your best, and it might even mean, at worst, that your writing is so annoying that people don't bother to read it.

APOSTROPHE

The apostrophe (written as ') has two main uses: to indicate **possession**, i.e. that something belongs to someone; and to show that there are **missing letters or spaces in a contracted word**, as in *can't*, *haven't* and *isn't*.

Correct use of the apostrophe can be difficult, we can't deny it. It is one of the most misused pieces of punctuation. To use the apostrophe correctly you need to know quite a lot about the formation of plurals in English, which is itself a difficult subject because of the number of plurals that are irregularly formed. *See* page 135 which provides information on **irregular plural nouns**.

Possession

When indicating **possession** an **s** is added after the apostrophe for singular words and for plurals that don't already end in an **s**. For example:

>a girl's bike
>a person's right
>John's car
>the company's premises
>the children's school
>women's rights.

If a plural word ends in an **s**, the apostrophe follows the **s** and no extra **s** is added, as in:

>students' dictionary
>employees' contracts.

Apostrophe

If a person's name ends in an **s, x** or **z** sound or the silent French **s** in words like *Descartes*, then the accepted modern usage to show **possession** is, most of the time, to add **'s** as in:

> Descartes's *Meditations*
> Charles's wife
> Camus's novel
> Francis's birthday.

It is slightly old fashioned to use the apostrophe alone. However, in **biblical** or **classical texts** it might seem more appropriate as in:

> in Jesus' name
> Herodotus' works.

Use the **sound of the end of the word** as a guide, too. If adding **'s** makes the pronunciation of longer words harder then it's acceptable to just use an apostrophe as in:

> Williams' latest singles victory.

Whether you use an apostrophe alone or apostrophe and s – both are acceptable – just remember to do it consistently.

Common errors when the apostrophe indicates possession

1. It is wrong to insert an apostrophe when there is no suggestion that possession is involved, and no contracted forms are involved

    This is a particularly common error and there are examples of it all over the place, particularly in shop windows, informal advertisements and menus. For example, you might see the following on a sign outside a fruit and vegetable sign:

    > fresh local leek's **[Wrong]**
    > new potatoes' for sale **[Wrong]**
    > try these juicy tomatoes' **[Wrong]**

    The vegetables do not own anything and the apostrophes are

PUNCTUATING PROPERLY

completely wrong. They should be omitted.

2   It is a common mistake to insert an apostrophe where none should be when this relates to such expressions as *sports coach* and *games teacher.*

Again, there is no suggestion of possession being involved

> sports' coach **[Wrong]**
> sport's coach **[Wrong]**
> games' teacher **[Wrong]**
> game's teacher **[Wrong]**

3   It is a common mistake to insert an apostrophe in the wrong place in *plural* and *singular words*.

For example, when we are only talking about one boy, the following example is **wrong**:

> The *boys'* favourite hobby was football. **[Wrong]**

When we are only talking about one boy, the following example is **correct**:

> The *boy's* favourite hobby was football. **[Correct]**

When several workers are involved the following is wrong:

> The *worker's* living quarters can be found a mile from here. **[Wrong]**

When we are talking about several workers, the following example is **correct**:

> The *workers'* living quarters can be found a mile from here. **[Correct]**

The above error is all the more common with regard to irregular plural forms that do not end in the letter *s*. Consider the following:

> *women's* athletics **[Correct]**
> *children's* literature **[Correct]**
> *womens'* athletics **[Wrong]**
> *childrens'* literature **[Wrong]**

4 It is a common mistake to insert an apostrophe on such **personal possessive pronouns** as *hers*, *its* or *theirs*.

They show **possession** and so you could be forgiven for thinking that they might need an apostrophe. Well, they may end in **s** but they NEVER contain an apostrophe.

Do not write:
These books are *theirs'*. **[Wrong]**
These books are *their's*. **[Wrong]**

The correct form is:
These books are *theirs*. **[Correct]**

5 One of the most common errors involving an apostrophe is to use *it's* instead of *its* to indicate possession, as in:

The dog has lost *its* ball. **[Correct]**
The dog has lost *it's* ball. **[Wrong,** *it's* only ever means *it is*]
The cinema had put *its* prices up. **[Correct]**
The cinema had put *it's* prices up. **[Wrong,** *it's* only ever means *it is*]

The word *it's* is only used as a contracted form of *it is*, as in:

It's unusual to find a very stylish car that is economical to drive too.
It's my pleasure to introduce our new sales manager.

See also **The apostrophe in contracted forms** on the next pages.

6 Another very common mistake is to use *you're* instead of *your* to indicate possession:

Does that answer *you're* question? **[Wrong,** *you're* means *you are*]
Does that answer *your* question? **[Correct]**

You're is a contracted form of *you are* and should only be used in such sentences as:

I'm sure *you're* next. **[Correct,** *you're* means *you are*]
I'm sure *your* next. **[Wrong]**

See also **The apostrophe in contracted forms** on the next pages.

PUNCTUATING PROPERLY

7   Omitting the apostrophe for the sake of appearance when one should be inserted is quite common in advertising and product design. They want to omit the apostrophe because they feel that a word looks cleaner and less cluttered without it. You'll also see it in street signs and place names. It maybe doesn't need to be said, but don't follow this example in your own written English.

The apostrophe in contracted forms

The apostrophe is also used to show the **omission of letters** in **contracted forms**, as in the blue box below:

can't	for	cannot	won't	for	will not
isn't	for	is not	he'll	for	he will
haven't	for	have not	she's	for	she is or she has
you'll	for	you will	you've	for	you have
couldn't	for	could not			

Common errors when the apostrophe is used in contracted forms

1   It is a common error to **omit the apostrophe** where there should be one. Punctuation may be becoming more informal and relaxed and you may not bother with apostrophes if you are dashing off a text to a friend, but you must put them in if you are writing a formal letter. The use of the apostrophe in this context is one that may well fade over the years, but, for the moment, it is still very much alive.

2   It is a common error to omit the apostrophe in **it's**, the contracted form of **it is**, as in:

> It's not my fault that the car got damaged. [Correct]
> Its not my fault that the car got damaged. [Wrong]

This use should not be confused with the use of **its** to show possession when there should be no apostrophe, as in:

The hamster is sleeping in *its* cage. **[Correct]**
The hamster is sleeping in *it's* cage. **[Wrong]**

3   It is a common error to omit the apostrophe in **you're**, the contracted form of **you are**, as in:

You're going to get into trouble if you're late again. **[Correct]**
Your going to get into trouble if you're late again. **[Wrong]**

This use should not be confused with the use of **your** to show possession as in:

It was *your* fault that we were late. **[Correct]**
It was *you're* fault that we were late. **[Wrong]**

See the apostrophe showing **possession** on pages 318–22.

4   There is no need to use an apostrophe when indicating the end of a decade. Since it's simply a plural:

We've lived here since the *1990s*. **[Correct]**
We've lived here since the *1990's*. **[Wrong]**

BRACKETS

Brackets, especially round brackets, occur in pairs and are used to enclose information that is additional to a main statement. They can often be removed without altering the basic meaning of the statement, as in:

The student was very rich (richer than anyone his age had any right to be) and that alone made him very popular.

Common errors involving brackets

1   Don't forget to insert the second one of a pair of brackets. They come as a pair and you never just use one, though it is sometimes easy to forget, especially in a long sentence.

2   Avoid overusing brackets. Too many of pairs of brackets really interrupt the flow of what you are writing. Take time to

PUNCTUATING PROPERLY

reorganize what you want to say rather than relying on a lot of brackets to add extra information as you go along.

CAPITAL LETTERS

The capital letter has suffered a decline because of the rise in electronic communication. If you are sending someone an email or using your mobile phone to text them it is much easier and quicker to type lower-case letters than capital letters.

We are not witnessing the general collapse of the capital letter though. It is still very much alive in more formal contexts, whether these take the form of electronic communication or snail mail.

Tips regarding capital letters

Initial letter of the first word of sentence

Do not forget to put a capital letter as the initial letter of the first word in a sentence, question or exclamation, as in:

> Tourists only go there in the summer.
> Did you buy tickets for the concert?
> Don't do that!

Initial letter of a name or proper noun

Do not forget to put a capital letter as the initial letter of a name or proper noun, as in:

> His younger brother's called Michael.
> Stockholm is the capital of Sweden.
> When did the Ice Age begin?
> His birthday is in October.
> What date is Easter Sunday this year?
> She has converted to Buddhism.

The seasons

Although the **months of the year** and the **days of the week** are spelled with an initial capital letter, the **seasons** of the year are usually spelled with an initial lower-case letter, as in:

Capital letters

> It's too hot for us there in the summer.
> His favourite season of the year is spring.
> It was a cold and wet autumn day.

Some people prefer to use an initial capital letter in this context, and it is not wrong to do so, just a style decision.

Nouns and adjectives which refer to nationalities or ethnic groups

Nouns and adjectives which refer to **nationalities** or **ethnic groups** are spelled with an initial capital letter, as in:

> She speaks Spanish fluently.
> It was a conference of French economists.

However, there is an exception to this. Where an adjective referring to a nationality is **not used literally**, it is usually spelled with a lower-case letter, as in:

> The brussels sprouts were overcooked.
> She walked through the french windows into the garden.

Dogs breeds such as *labrador* and *chihuahua* don't have to have initial capitals.

The names of languages are spelled with an initial capital letter:

> She has gone to London to study English.

But other academic subjects are spelled with an initial lower-case letter, as in:

> He is studying psychology.

Pronouns

Although the pronoun **I** is always spelled with a capital letter, the other pronouns are spelled with a lower-case letter, as in *you*, *he*, *she*, *they*, etc, unless they are the first word in a sentence.

Trade names

Do not forget to put a capital letter as the initial letter of a trade name, as in:

> He has just bought a Toyota.
> I need to buy a roll of Sellotape to wrap my Christmas presents.
> We used to play Scrabble in the evenings.

For emphasis

In formal writing do not use capital letters simply to emphasize a word, as in:

> Their new house is HUGE.

In your informal writing it's fine occasionally, just don't overdo it.

COLON
Introducing a list

Using the colon in formal contexts will save you from using the already overused dash. Use it, for example when you are introducing a list of some kind, as in:

> You will need the following ingredients: eggs, milk, flour, sugar, cocoa powder and vanilla essence.

Leading on

The **colon** is used to separate two parts of a sentence when the first part leads on to the second part, as in:

> This area has been significantly upgraded during the last few years: property prices have soared.

SEMICOLON
Between clauses

The **semicolon** (;) is considered a rather formal type of punctuation. It is mainly used between clauses that are not joined by any form of conjunction, as in:

> We had a wonderful holiday; sadly they did not.
> He was a marvellous friend; he is much missed.

The part before the semicolon and the part after could both be sentences in their own right. The semicolon is used to show a closer link between the two parts of the sentence. It has the force of a strong comma. A dash (*see* page 334) is sometimes used instead.

In lists

The semicolon is also used to separate the items in a long list or a series of things. Functioning like a particularly strong comma, the semicolon is often used in more complicated lists to make them easier to understand, as in this rather long sentence:

> While we are in Edinburgh we plan to visit Edinburgh Castle; the Canongate area, including the Palace of Holyroodhouse, Holyrood Park and the Scottish Parliament; the shops, of course, if we have any money left from all the sightseeing; the National Gallery of Scotland and the National Portrait Gallery.

COMMA
Common errors involving the comma in lists

Be aware of the following. Commas are often used to separate the various items in lists. Formerly, in British English, it was considered wrong to put a comma before the *and* which follows the second-last item in a list, as in:

> I bought bread, butter, cheese, grapes and wine.

Nowadays it is becoming increasingly common in British English – and it's the norm in American English – to insert a comma in that position, as in:

> I bought bread, butter, cheese, grapes, and wine.

This comma is known as 'the Oxford comma' or 'the serial comma'. In British English it is only used if the sentence is going to be ambiguous without it. Confusion may arise if the last item in a list of items itself contains the word *and* used in its own right as

PUNCTUATING PROPERLY

part of the sentence, as in:

> For the children there was a choice of pizza, chicken nuggets, macaroni cheese and fish and chips.

For the sake of clarity it is as well to put a comma after the word *cheese*, as in:

> For the children there was a choice of pizza, chicken nuggets, macaroni cheese, and fish and chips.

Some examples are likely to be found even more ambiguous, as in:

> We had a film marathon and watched *The Hobbit*, *Spider-Man*, *Avatar* and *Harry Potter and the Deathly Hallows*.

To avoid ambiguity put a comma after *Avatar*, as in:

> *Avatar*, and *Harry Potter and the Deathly Hallows*.

If you are dealing with an exceptionally long list of items or with a list in which the items each consist of several words, you should consider using **semicolons** instead of **commas**.

LAST ITEM IN A LIST

Confusion may arise if the last item in the list contains the word *and* used in its own right as an essential part of the sentence, as in:

> In the pub they served ham salad, shepherd's pie, omelette, and pie and chips.

In such cases it is advisable to put a comma before the final connecting *and* to avoid confusion.

If the list of items is a very long one or the items in the list consist of several words a **semicolon** is sometimes used instead of a comma (*see* page 326–7).

Adjective lists and commas

It was formerly absolutely standard practice to separate with a comma the individual adjectives in a list of adjectives placed before a noun, as in:

> She wore a long, black, low-necked, evening dress.

It was considered wrong not to do so. It is now becoming very common for people not to insert these commas. Although this is a relatively new broken rule, it is one that is spreading fast. The practice of not inserting commas may become standard usage before too long.

A word of warning if you decide to carry on separating adjectives with commas: do not insert a comma before the adjective which comes immediately before the relevant noun when this adjective has an exceptionally close relationship with the noun and, indeed, may help to define it, as shown in the following examples:

> We bought some large, glossy, red peppers to stuff for dinner.

> She was delighted with her shiny, tough, hardwood flooring.

Even if you decide to insert commas between the other adjectives, as above, do not separate *peppers* from *red*, or *hardwood* from *flooring*. The words belong together.

See the box on page 150 about **coordinate adjectives**.

Common errors involving the comma and clauses
Relative clauses

Where what is known as a **non-defining relative clause** divides the parts of a **main clause**, this clause is placed within commas. For example, in the sentence

> Buenos Aires, whose name means 'fair winds', is the capital of Argentina. **[Correct]**

The clause *whose name means 'fair winds'* is a **non-defining relative clause**; it doesn't identify the city, it just gives a bit more

PUNCTUATING PROPERLY

information, so it could be taken out without altering the essential meaning of the sentence. It is a common error not to insert these commas, as in:

> Buenos Aires whose name means 'fair winds' is the capital of Argentina. **[Wrong]**

When the **relative clause** is an integral part of the sentence and not just an extra piece of information, it is called a **defining relative clause** and there is no need for commas, as in:

> The restaurant that you mentioned has closed now. **[Correct]**
> The restaurant, that you mentioned, has closed now. **[Wrong]**

The clause *that you mentioned* identifies the restaurant, so is essential to understanding the sentence and does not need commas.

Subordinate clauses

Do not use a comma to separate a **main clause** from **a subordinate clause**, as in:

> She was leaving as he arrived. **[Correct]**
> She was leaving, as he arrived. **[Wrong]**

Even when the subordinate clause is placed before the main clause you do not usually need a comma to separate them (although it is not wrong to use one), as in:

> If it rains we'll have the party indoors.

However, if the **subordinate clause** is quite long you should use a comma to separate the different actions for the sake of clarity, as in:

> When we had cleaned the windows, vacuumed the carpets, polished the furniture and filled some vases with flowers, the room was ready for the party.

Where there is any risk of confusion you should insert a comma between the **subordinate clause** and the **main clause**, especially when the subordinate clause ends with a **verb** and the following main clause begins with a **noun**, as in:

> If you do not return, the books will be put back on the shelves.
> When the students finished painting, their pictures were displayed on the walls.

It is wrong to insert a comma between a **main clause** and a **subordinate clause** beginning with *that*, as in:

> I suspected, that she was dishonest.

Main clauses

Where main clauses are joined by **and**, are quite long and have different subjects, it is a good idea to insert a comma before the **and** for the sake of clarity, as in:

> The Olympic stadium has a capacity of 80,000 and houses a nine-lane athletic track, and it will continue to be used as a sports venue for years to come.

TO AVOID CONFUSION

It is important to insert a **comma** between a **subordinate clause** and a main clause if doing so prevents any possibility of confusion.

For example, confusion can arise when a subordinate clause ends with a verb and the following clause begins with a noun, as in:

> After the pupils had finished reading, the books were returned to the school library.

Here the use of the comma is an aid to clarity. Otherwise you could read the first part of the sentence as:

> After the pupils had finished reading the books ...

PUNCTUATING PROPERLY

When main clauses are joined by **but** users may choose either to use a comma or not to mark off the main clause, but a comma is helpful when both clauses are quite long.

Common errors involving commas with adverbs or adverbial phrases

It was formerly standard practice to use a comma to separate **adverbs** or **adverbial phrases** at the beginning of a sentence, such as *however*, *of course*, *in the meantime*, *for example*, from the rest of the sentence, as in:

> It's been a pleasant evening. However, it's late and I must go home now.

Nowadays, the comma in this situation is considered optional, but you should insert a comma after the adverb or adverbial phrase if there is any possibility of confusion, as in:

> Normally, intelligent adults will appreciate the advantages of the savings scheme.

It is also a good idea to insert a comma if the adverbial phrase is very long, as in:

> After a great deal of careful consideration, I agreed.

Common errors involving commas in parenthesis

A pair of commas is often used to separate off a piece of information that is not central to the meaning of a sentence, but is additional to it in the way that bracketed information is. The length of such pieces of additional information can vary from very short to quite long. Do not forget to enclose such information in commas in such situations, as in:

> Mark Taylor, the club treasurer, has asked me to address the meeting in his place as he has been unexpectedly called away.
> It is quite clear, as you have probably all realized, that the market is not likely to improve in the near future.

Do not forget to include a pair of commas in such situations. One will not be enough.

Common errors involving commas in various other situations

1. Do not forget to insert a comma between the last word in a piece of direct speech and the closing quotation mark and before the word *say*, etc, as in:

    'You're late,' she said accusingly.
    'The bus is coming,' he called out.

2. Do not forget to use a comma to separate a person's name, or the name of a group, from the rest of the sentence when you are addressing them, as in:

    Jim, welcome home!
    I'm over here, Peter.
    I'm sorry, Ms Park, but you have not got the job.
    Gentlemen, let me show you the way.

3. Do not forget to insert a comma after an interjection at the start of a sentence, as in:

    Heavens, it's hot!
    See, the display has started.

4. Do not forget to use a comma to separate a question tag from the rest of the sentence, as in:

    It was a lovely evening, wasn't it?
    You do still want to go, don't you?

5. Remember to insert a comma in numbers that are made up of more than four figures, as in *86,350* and *150,600*. A comma is also sometimes used in numbers consisting of four digits, as in *3,000*, but there is a growing tendency to omit this comma.

    Do not use commas to separate the numbers in dates, as in the years *1941* and *2013* (not *1,941* or *2,013*).

DASH

The dash can be used as part of a pair in much the same way as brackets, although dashes are generally much more popular than brackets and used in less formal contexts as in:

> My parents' next-door neighbour – I can't remember his name – has opened a wine bar on the high street.

The single dash used on its own has several uses, often at the end of sentences, as in:

> I never saw him again – and I wasn't sorry.
> You can keep the book – I've finished with it.

Common errors involving dashes

1. Do not forget to insert the second one of a pair of dashes.
2. Do not overuse pairs of dashes. This is a common thing to do as dashes are very popular with a great many writers. Using a lot of dashes is fine if you're just writing a chatty email to a friend, but use them very sparingly in any kind of formal communication. Too many of them really interrupt the flow of what you are writing and can look messy.
3. Do not overuse the single dash. As is the case with pairs of dashes, it should be avoided in formal communication.

EXCLAMATION MARK

The exclamation mark is used at the end of a sentence instead of a full stop when the sentence is expressing someone's strong reaction to something, e.g. anger, shock, surprise, as in:

> I absolutely hate him!

The exclamation mark often follows a single word or a group of words without a verb that also express a strong reaction, as in:

> How amazing! Wow!

REMARKS ON EXCLAMATION MARKS

Be careful not to overuse the **exclamation mark**. One is enough at the close of a sentence.

Overuse of such sentences within any piece of writing can detract from the potential dramatic effect of the occasional use of the mark.

It is common for people to overuse exclamation marks in emails, because we are often trying to convey points of view and emotions that we would not normally be doing in a formal piece of writing. Beware of this too. It's not very professional to make a statement and to follow it with lots of exclamation marks, no matter how annoyed you are.

Exclamation marks may also function as markers of friendly interaction, for example, by making *Good luck!* seem friendlier than simply *Good luck*.

FULL STOP

The main function of the full stop is to mark the end of sentence where this does not end in a question mark or exclamation mark.

Omission

Full stops are often omitted in error. It is very common for writers to simply forget to put the full stop at the end of the sentence or to mistype and just not notice its omission. If the text is typed, sometimes it can be hard to spot onscreen that a full stop is missing:

> I don't know why he left He went away very suddenly without saying anything

A more serious error is omission of the full stop because you have failed to recognize the end of a sentence, resulting in failure to use the appropriate punctuation, as in:

PUNCTUATING PROPERLY

> ## LOOK AT YOUR SENTENCE ...
> If you find that you have just written a very long sentence, have a careful look at it. Is it correctly punctuated? Should you have broken your piece of writing into more than one sentence and inserted full stops and capital letters where appropriate?

> He knew he wasn't likely to win the match he hadn't been training as much as usual.

There should be a full stop after the word *match* and the *he* that follows should have a capital letter. Alternatively, there should be a conjunction after *match*, as in:

> He knew he wasn't likely to win the match because he hadn't been training as much as usual.

Dialogue

In dialogue, a common error is to put the full stop in the wrong place when it is used with quotation marks. It should go before the closing quotation mark not after, as in:

> 'I'm afraid I can't come with you.'

Abbreviations

The full stop is also sometimes used in connection with abbreviations.

> Inc., etc., e.g., a.m., p.m., c.m.

The modern tendency is to use full stops far less frequently in abbreviations than was formerly the case. It is now quite likely you'll see see the above examples without full points and, in fact, it would be quite rare to see titles using a full stop, as in:

> Mr., Mrs., Dr., Rev.

Whether you use them or not is a matter of style, as long as you are consistent within any one piece of writing.

Putting a full stop in abbreviations which involve initial capital letters is not in keeping with modern usage, but it's not wrong, simply a style choice:

> BBC, TUC, USA, DIY, MP
> B.B.C, T.U.C., U.S.A., D.I.Y., M.P.

Acronyms – pronounceable words made up of initial caps – should not have full stops in them. It is also a matter of a style choice whether you choose to use allcaps or lowercase letters to present the acronym. If it's an organization it's best to follow what they do on their official websites and publications. If it's a brand name or a trademark it may require an initial capital, as in:

> AIDS, HIV, radar, scuba, laser, NASA, NATO sonar, taser, GIF

You also wouldn't tend to put a full stop in abbreviations if one or some of the initial letters do not relate to a full word, such as *TV*.

If an abbreviation comes at the end of a sentence and you are using full stops, you do not need an extra full stop to end the sentence.

> I had an uncle who worked at the B.B.C.

HYPHEN

The hyphen is used in various situations but it is now used much less frequently than formerly. It was once common practice to join two words together as a compound using a hyphen, as in *boat-hook*, *boat-house*, *bake-house*, *boot-guard*, *boot-brush*, *dog-house*, *dog-walker*, *door-handle*, *gun-rack*, *tree-house*.

Now the tendency is to remove the hyphen, making the compound either one word or two. Often this is a matter of taste, although longer words are more likely to become two words than one word. If in doubt consult a dictionary – style will even vary from dictionary to dictionary – and try to use hyphens consistently within one piece of writing.

PUNCTUATING PROPERLY

Common errors involving hyphens

1. Having made your choice about whether to make a **compound noun** one word or two, remember to stick with this system throughout any one piece of writing and be consistent.

2. Remember that there are some fixed compounds of two or three or more words which still usually retain the hyphen, as in:

    brother-in-law
    mother-in-law
    good-for-nothing.

3. Remember that the hyphen is normally used in **compound adjectives** before **nouns**, as in:

    the wine-producing areas of France
    a ten-year lease
    a three-bedroom house.

4. Remember that the hyphen is normally used in **compound adjectives** where the second element of the compound ends in *–ed*, as in *fair-minded judges*.

5. Remember that the hyphen is normally used in certain **adverbs**, sometimes to avoid ambiguity, as in

    a well-established method
    a half-organized scheme
    the best-known writer of travel books about that area.

6. Do not use a hyphen to separate an **adverb** from an **adjective** or **participle** if the adverb ends in *–ly*, as in:

    a highly successful fashion designer
    an immaculately dressed young man.

7. Some **compound numbers** are not hyphenated such as:

    two hundred
    seven thousand

    But compound numbers from **21** to **99** when written in full are often hyphenated, as in:

seventy-five years ago
forty-five miles

8 Be careful when you are using **two or more hyphenated compound adjectives** which have the same second element and which qualify the same noun. You do not need to repeat the second element, but you do need to repeat the hyphen, as in

four- and five-storey buildings.
low- and full-fat yoghurt

QUESTION MARK

The question mark is used, as you might expect, at the end of a sentence that asks a **direct question**, as in:

Why did you do that?
Have you seen him lately?

Do not forget to insert a question mark at the end of a question, as in:

Why are you here?

Do not use a question mark when the question is part of **reported** or **indirect speech** instead of a question in direct speech, as in:

She asked me where he was.
I wondered who told him that.

Rhetorical questions, *see* page 126, require a question mark.

QUOTATION MARKS

Quotation marks are used in pairs and have several uses. They are used to enclose **direct speech**, i.e. the actual words that someone has spoken, as in:

'Why on earth did she marry him?' I asked.

They are also used in a piece of writing to enclose a direct quotation from another piece of writing or speech, as in:

PUNCTUATING PROPERLY

> It was a bit of an exaggeration when she referred in her report to 'record-breaking sales'.

They are also sometimes used to indicate titles of books, plays, etc, as in 'Jane Eyre', though italics, *Jane Eyre*, is more usual.

Quotation marks in all cases can either be double or single according to taste, as long as this is consistent in any one piece of writing. It is clearer for readers if a different style is used for anything quoted within a quote, so either single quotation marks within double quotation marks or double quotation marks within single quotation marks, as in:

> 'It's "business as usual" even though we've got scaffolding up,' the shop manager told us.

Common errors involving quotation marks

Do not omit the second set of quotation marks, as in:

> 'We are leaving tomorrow, she said. **[Wrong]**

Do not use a single quotation mark followed by a closing double one, as in:

> 'Let's meet for lunch next week," he suggested. **[Wrong]**

THREE-DOT ELLIPSIS

The **three-dot ellipsis (...)** is used to indicate missing material. This missing material may be one word, as in the sentence:

> I told you to get the ... out of here

where the missing word is the swear word *hell*.

The missing material may be several words or a longer piece of text. For example, the *three-dot ellipsis* may be used to replace part of a quotation, proverb, etc, as in:

> You know what they say. A stitch in time ... (*saves nine* is omitted).

It can also be used to indicate an unfinished thought or statement, as in:

> We might win handsomely; on the other hand ...

340

WRITING

*Sorry I haven't fed you in two days ... I've been rewriting.
It is very important to revise your work.*

IN EVERYDAY writing it is important to be clear, unambiguous, easily understood, relevant and appropriate. There is a place for poetical language and creative turns of phrase, for jargon and technical terms – but there is also a place for what we refer to as **plain English**. While you have to use the appropriate style for the appropriate context, there is *always* an argument for trying to be as clearly understood as possible.

PLAIN ENGLISH

What is plain English and why it is so important? It really does make a huge difference when you can read and understand

WRITING

something easily the first time round. Plain English writing always keeps the reader in mind, so it is clear and concise and uses the appropriate tone.

Think about why we write in the first place. We write to communicate a message to our reader – not to show how clever or educated or well-read we are. If we can't communicate our message to the reader in a way that they understand then what's the point? We are excluding them, rather than including them.

And apart from anything else, plain English is faster to write and faster to read. People understand your message more easily and respond more positively if it is written using a straightforward and friendly tone, rather than a stuffy and formal one.

Here are some plain English principles that you can apply to your writing. Apply these to your writing and notice the difference. It can take a while to retrain yourself to write this way, but it's well worth the effort.

Think ahead – plan and structure your writing

Ask yourself the following questions before you start to write. If you do this, then you are more likely to produce a well-structured and effective piece of work. If you don't, then your writing is more likely to ramble on, go off at a tangent and not make sense because you don't really know what you want to say.

- What do I want this piece of writing to do?
- What are its aims and outcomes?
- Who are my readers?
- What do I want them to learn/know?
- What do they need/want to learn/know?
- What is the simplest and most effective way of passing on this information?

Make a plan of the structure of your work. How you do this is up to you. Some people think of their piece of writing as a story,

ALTERNATIVE WORDS AND PHRASES

If you want accessible, readable text, try to avoid using words that most people wouldn't know. For example, *you* might know what 'egregious' means but it's not a common word, so you're probably safer to use 'shocking' or 'extremely bad' instead.

There are also a number of words and phrases that are overused. They don't add anything to your text, but they do give it a vague and 'woolly' feel. Here are some examples – try to avoid them where possible or use the suggested alternatives.

word/phrase	suggested alternative
as mentioned previously	as we have already said
a number of	some
as regards to/with regards to	about
by means of	by
commence	start
consequently	so
for the purposes of	for
in excess of	more than
in order to	to
in relation to (for example, 'my thoughts in relation to')	on or about (or just leave out)
in the event of	if
inform	tell
necessitate	cause
prior to	before
until such time as	until
utilize	use
whilst	while
with reference to	about

WRITING

and write out main headings and subheadings. Some people make out a list of points, in a logical order. Some people use mind maps. Use a method that you feel comfortable with.

Talk directly to your reader – use 'you' and 'we'

Writing doesn't have to be formal and intimidating. You wouldn't speak to your reader that way, so you don't need to write that way. Try to address your reader personally, and call them 'you' – it will make your writing seem less intimidating.

Here's an example. If you were applying for a job, which of the following would you prefer to read?

> It is suggested that job applicants submit a handwritten form and hand it in prior to the interview. Applicants will be notified by telephone of their success or otherwise.

or

> Please fill in your job application form and hand it in before the interview. We will phone you to let you know if you have been successful.

In the same way, you should also use 'we' or 'I' if you are talking about your business or organization. It gives a much more direct and positive tone to your writing.

Use simple, straightforward words

People sometimes make the mistake of thinking that by using simple, straightforward words, you are patronizing your reader. Quite the opposite – if we're honest, we all prefer to read clear and straightforward text rather than difficult, convoluted text.

In general, always imagine that you are talking to your reader, and stick to straightforward English where possible.

Keep sentences short and concise

Sentences containing lots of clauses (not to mention parentheses – and this is an example) are difficult to read. Readers might give up before they get to the end of long, multi-clause sentences.

Plain English

Experts on plain English think that an average sentence should be between 15 to 20 words long, although not every sentence has to be the same length. In fact, you can vary them to great effect. Be creative. (Like this!) Try to stick to one idea in each sentence, or, at the most, one idea and one related point.

It can be quite difficult to keep to short sentences when you are trying to explain something that is complicated. In that case, write your long sentence, then look at ways you can break it up.

Keep paragraphs short

The same principles apply to paragraphs. There's nothing more daunting than a long paragraph that deals with so many points that you're lost by the time you reach the end.

Like a sentence, a paragraph is a small, self-contained unit. You state your idea, develop it and then link it to the idea in the next paragraph. If you have planned your writing carefully, your reader will be able to understand each paragraph quickly and easily because they are clear, concise and logical.

Be active, not passive

An **active clause** is where **A does something to B**. In other words, the order is **subject**, **verb**, **object**. The **verb** is **active**.

For example:

> The candidate completed the job application.

A **passive clause** is where **B is done by A**. In other words, the order is **object**, **verb**, **subject**. The **verb** is **passive**.

For example:

> The job application was completed by the candidate.

You'll notice that when you use the **passive voice**, you have to introduce the words *was* and *by*, and this can make text more clumsy and long-winded. Passives also de-personalize the text and can sometimes be confusing.

WRITING

And finally, because you are not talking directly to your reader, you lose your friendly and approachable tone.

Try to use **active verbs** in the majority of your writing. The **passive voice** isn't wrong. You need to use it sometimes, but it can be a wordy and unclear way of expressing yourself. *See also* pages 187–8 about **active** and **passive voice**.

Here are some examples of how to turn passive sentences into active ones:

> The land was farmed by student workers. [Passive]
> Student workers farmed the land. [Active]
>
> The screenplay was written by a famous author. [Passive]
> A famous author wrote the screenplay. [Active]
>
> The criminals were chased by the police. [Passive]
> The police chased the criminals. [Active]

When passive can be useful

There are times when using the passive can be useful.

It can sound softer and more polite:

> The cup has been broken. [Passive]
> You broke the cup. [Active]

You might not know who or what the 'doer' of the sentence is:

> The soldier was awarded a medal for bravery. [Passive]
> The corner shop has been robbed. [Passive]

If it is unclear who or what did something, or if you want to deliberately make it unclear for effect, then you use the passive voice.

> Where are all the sweets that I bought?
> Erm, all those sweets have been eaten. [Passive]
> You ate all the sweets, didn't you? [Active]

The passive voice can give an air of objectivity to a text. For example, in a piece of technical text it is not usually acceptable to insert 'I' or 'we' into your conclusions.

> The findings suggest that the vitamin, administered in quantity, does help to prevent the illness. **[Passive]**

The above sounds better than:

> We believe that the vitamin, administered in quantity, does help to prevent the illness. **[Active]**

Tell it like it is!

People can feel uncomfortable about giving commands or instructions (or **imperatives**, as they are called) because they can sound a bit harsh. But then you can take forever to say what you want and your writing comes across as boring and longwinded. You can still use clear and concise commands without sounding like you are barking out an order.

For example:

> Customers are advised that they should report to reception on arrival at the building.
> *Visitors please report to reception.*

> I would be grateful if you could send the parcel to me.
> *Please send me the parcel.*

> The packaging should be removed and the contents of the box should be checked before assembling the furniture.
> *Remove the packaging and check the contents of the box. Then assemble the furniture.*

Examples of plain English

The **Plain English Campaign** website has some excellent 'before' and 'after' examples of not-so-plain English. If you can, have a look at the website: www.plainenglish.co.uk.

EDITING YOUR WRITING

No matter what you are writing – whether it's an email or a thesis – it's essential to revise and edit it. There will always be mistakes to correct or things you could improve. Even top writers either edit their own work or use professional editors to do this.

Here is a process for editing your work effectively.

Think before you write.

Before you even write a word, let alone edit anything, make a plan. If you rush straight in without thinking about what you want to say, you might ramble. Do some planning before you start to write and you will have less editing to do later.

Making a plan and keeping notes can help you to gather your thoughts and remind you, if at any point you forget, of the important points that you want to bring up. This is as true for writing a short, but important, email as it is a for long essay or a dissertation.

Leave it and go back to it

Once you have finished writing, leave it for a while – even if it's an email and you only leave it for one or two minutes. This will help you to come back to the writing fresh and spot what's right – and what's not.

Have you ever written an angry email and pressed send … and then regretted it? Giving yourself a bit of time between writing the first draft of any piece of text and going back to revise it can give you a bit more perspective on whether it is good or bad.

Revise the big picture

Read your first draft and concentrate on the big picture, and the overall flow of what you have written. Does it make sense? Is the order logical, or does it need changed?

Does anything need cut or added? What is your overall impression? Ask someone else to read it for you if you're not sure yourself.

Make notes regarding any general observations made about your writing style and bear them in mind the next time you write something.

Check spelling, punctuation, and look for word mix-ups

Read it over. Make sure that you have spelled all the words correctly. Remember that you cannot always rely on your computer's spell-checker. It might indicate that *there* was correct in a situation when you meant *their*. Some people find it easier to read words on paper than on a computer screen, so consider printing off and revising that way.

Check consistency

Be consistent with your spelling and hyphenation. For example, if you choose to use the *–ise* ending in verbs instead of the *–ize* ending, be sure to use it in all relevant verbs throughout your piece of writing.

Do not mix up British English spelling and American English spelling or British and American vocabulary in one piece of writing. You need to opt for one and stick to it.

Is the piece formal or informal? Use styles appropriately

For example, in a formal piece of writing do not use contracted forms such as *don't*, *isn't*, *you're* and *he'll*. Use the full forms, as in *do not*, *is not*, *you are* and *he will*.

Avoid using colloquialisms and slang in formal pieces of writing.

Avoid using jargon unless you happen to be writing to a work colleague who is familiar with the jargon used.

Check for clichés

Avoid using clichés (*see* pages 72–84) in a formal piece of writing. They have their place in spoken English and in informal written English, but, even there, they should not be overused.

Avoid using words, such as *epic* and *iconic*, that are already so over-used that they have become virtually meaningless.

WRITING

Use plain English

As we've already discussed (*see* pages 341–7) use plain English to make your text as comprehensible as possible.

Pay attention to paragraph and sentence length

Look critically at sentence and paragraph length. If you are aiming to produce a piece of writing that is more stylish and interesting than something that just conveys information, try adding some variety. Vary the length of your sentences and introduce a range of conjunctions. Do not stick solely to the use of *and* and *but*. Do not always begin your sentences with a main clause.

Are the idioms used correct and appropriate?

If you choose to use an idiom, make sure you have got the wording right (*see* pages 50–84). Because idioms are more often used in spoken English than written English, it is common not to know how to spell some of their key words. Also, make sure you have the meaning correct. Some idioms develop more than one meaning and this can cause confusion.

Cut!

Avoid redundant words. Do all the words need to be there? Are they relevant? Are you showing off knowledge that is irrelevant for the sake of it? Cut away anything that does not build your argument or add similar worth to the text.

Read over again

Most people can only process one thing at a time. So after looking for spelling, punctuation and grammar mistakes in the text and carrying out corrections, read it over again to see if your corrections make sense and if the structure and arguments are OK.

Get feedback and act on it

If someone reads your work and finds difficulty in understanding it, or thinks it needs improvement, listen to them. Look again at the passages that gave them a problem and see if you can improve them. You don't necessarily have to take their particular advice on how to change it, but take on board that there is a problem with how someone else is understanding it, and work on a solution.

Spellcheckers – use with caution

These features can all be useful for editing your own work, if you use them with care, but they can't differentiate between a context that makes sense and one that doesn't. There are pages of hilarious 'AutoCorrect' mistakes on the internet that show what the problems can be.

WRITING YOUR OWN NON-FICTION COMPOSITION

A non-fiction composition might be a biography, a cookery book, a travel article, a political manifesto or a computer manual. It could be in the form of an essay, a report, a news feature, a leaflet, a website, a blog or a book. There are different styles of non-fiction writing – they are not all serious. Compositions can be informative, creative, funny, serious, formal, informal, balanced, opinionated, instructional or just for fun.

Accuracy

Accuracy is essential in most types of non-fiction writing though. You must get your facts straight if you are writing a recipe, or telling somebody how to assemble a wardrobe. And if there is a health and safety aspect to what you are writing, you must be particularly careful about accuracy because people's safety could be put at risk. If in doubt, ask somebody else to check what you've written and actually try it out.

Research

Research is essential in any sort of non-fiction writing – and in some fiction writing too. You need to know your subject or topic thoroughly before you write about it. Here are some points to help you.

WRITING

What information are you looking for?

It sounds obvious, but it's worth saying: you need to know what you're looking for before you start looking for it. What is your subject or topic? Who is the person you are writing a biography about? Which phone are you writing a manual for? Which aspects does your travel article have to cover? Once you know this, you can start looking for appropriate research material.

Where can you find that information?

There are many different types and sources of information, but the main ones for non-fiction writing are:

Primary sources – such as people, interview transcripts, diaries, letters, original artefacts, data and photographs.
Secondary sources – reference materials, books, journals and the internet.

Looking for information can be daunting, so use all the help you can get.

When you are researching and using **primary sources**, make sure you do the following:

- Check that they are authentic.
- Ensure that you have permission to use them – is Mrs Brown happy for you to use her grandmother's shortbread recipe in your charity cookery book? Don't just assume it's OK.
- Check that you have all the information you need from your interview before you leave – you probably won't be able to go back and ask further questions.

When you are looking for **secondary sources** try the following:

- Look through the contents page and index of reference material – this will tell you quickly whether the information you are looking for is there.
- Ask the librarian for help if you are having problems

Writing your own non-fiction composition

using the library cataloguing system.
- Stay focussed! Don't go wandering off onto websites that have nothing to do with your project.
- Stick to two or three sources on the internet at one time. You can come back for more.
- Don't go past the first page of your search engine.
- Don't believe everything you read on the internet – stick to reputable sites.

And remember, you can't beat **first-hand experience** as a form of research. If you are writing about a place to spend the night, then you won't get the information you need from the internet – you have to go there yourself and check it out.

Organizing your information

Now that you have researched your information, don't let it overwhelm you. Organize it and you'll be able to use it effectively:

- Keep going back to your subject or topic. What information are you looking for?
- Plan your writing, so you know what your structure is going to be.
- Ignore any information that is too detailed or not relevant.
- Remember to write down the author, title, place of publication, publisher, date of publication, page numbers and web addresses for articles from books, journals, periodicals, encyclopedias and the internet. Make sure that web links are current at the time of writing, and convert them to working hyperlinks. This way, you will build a bibliography as you go along.

Acknowledging sources/copyright

This last point is very important. You must identify all the material in your biography, article, manual, instruction leaflet or scientific paper that is not your own – no matter where it

WRITING

comes from or what it is. Make a list of all the references to books, journals, periodicals and websites you have used in your work. You should also acknowledge **primary sources** (*see* page 352) that you have used, and actually make sure that you are allowed to use them.

Beware cut and paste and plagiarism!

Copying and pasting text into your own work without using quotation marks or citing it appropriately is a form of plagiarism. Plagiarism is when you take somebody else's ideas or writing and present them as your own. It's easy to do this accidentally.

When you are taking notes, decide what information you need from your source, and then write or summarize it in your own words. That way, you won't be tempted – consciously or subconsciously – to copy the source, word for word.

Don't cut and paste from the internet. You can easily forget that you have taken somebody else's work and put it into your own.

Style and tone

The style and tone of your writing will very much depend on what it is and what its purpose is. For example, a travel article will be informal and chatty, while a scientific paper will be objective and factual.

Planning your composition

Once you have researched and gathered your information for your non-fiction composition, you will need to plan it. Here are some tips to help you do this:

- Write down all your ideas. Don't worry about perfect writing at this point – just get the content down.
- Get a clean piece of paper. Put the topic box in the middle of the page.
- Now think about your main ideas – what are they?
- Draw lines from the topic box to these main ideas.
- Now add information where you think it sits within

these main ideas.
- Make links between the main ideas.

Structuring your composition

Once you've got your plan worked out, it's time to structure your composition. Again, this will vary according to what you are writing. What are your paragraph and chapter headings likely to be?

Biography

The structure of a biography might look like this:

Contents
Prologue
The early years and influences
The middle years
The later years
Bibliography
List of illustrations
Index

Recipe collection

The structure of a recipe collection or cookery book might look like this:

Foreword
Acknowledgements
Introduction
Starters
Main courses
Salads and vegetables
Desserts
Equipment
Index

Staying relevant, objective and factual

Structuring your non-fiction composition will help you to stay relevant, objective and factual. If you wander off subject, your reader will lose interest and give up reading.

WRITING

We've already covered the need for accuracy and facts – but it's worth saying again that you need to get your facts right!

The writing process

Like all types of writing, there is a process for writing non-fiction. Aspects of this process will vary slightly, depending on the genre, or type of non-fiction you are writing. But it will help you to focus your thoughts and give you somewhere to start on your biography, manual, recipe book, travel article, scientific paper – or whatever!

Here's the suggested process:

Define the purpose of this piece of writing

Why are you writing it and who are your readers? If you are writing a short biography, who is it about and who wants to know about them? If you are writing a manual, who will be using it? If you are writing an engineering paper, who and what is it for?

Research the information you need

This will obviously depend on what you are writing. You might need to interview people, use the internet or look in an archive or museum to get the information you need. If you are compiling a recipe book, you will probably have to get into the kitchen and try some of the recipes out yourself.

Plan and structure

Again, this will depend on what you are writing. The structure of a biography will be based on the sequence of events in a person's life. A recipe book will probably be divided into categories like starters, main courses and desserts. An instruction leaflet to set up a DVD will go through a strict sequential process from opening up the box to pressing the 'on' button. Whatever the subject or topic, a clear plan and structure will help you to make sense of all the information you have gathered, and this will help you to produce an organized, clear and concise piece of writing.

Write your first draft
> Do a rough draft – don't worry too much about how it looks at this stage – just get the information down on paper.

Revise and edit
> Follow the guidelines for editing on pages 348–51.

Identify any missing information
> Revising and editing your writing usually reveals any gaps that need to be filled.

Cut out what you don't need
> The editing process also reveals what you don't need!

Write the final draft
> Give this version to a 'critical friend' to look over.

ESSAYS

An essay is a short piece of writing, and it can be on any subject. An essay takes a subject and analyses it in detail. It's one of the most common ways of assessing learners. Essays are usually written in response to a question and the essay must answer that question properly and in depth. Whether you are at school, college, university or any other type of learning institution, you will have to write essays at some point. In the workplace, too, you may have to write concise reports that also use the skills needed to write a good essay. George Orwell, Oscar Wilde and Leo Tolstoy were notable for their essays as well as their fiction. It is an art form where a writer can discuss and justify his or her opinions and ideals in great detail. A good essay will be balanced and well researched as well as well argued.

The process of writing an essay

There is a process involved in writing an essay. This doesn't have to be linear, where each stage is only done once. You can repeat different parts of the process and revise your work until

WRITING

you are happy with it. Here's an example of a process you could use:

Analyse the question or title of your essay

What is it asking for? How are you going to answer it? Many teachers and tutors say that this is where many students fall down – they don't stay relevant to their theme because they don't keep looking back at what the question is asking for.

Brainstorm your ideas

People often find it very stressful when they are faced with writing an essay because they don't know where to start. Don't panic. Instead, get some paper and write down all your ideas about the title, what your structure might be and where you might look for evidence. If it helps, do this with a friend or colleague. Don't try to sort anything out at this stage. That can come later.

Research. Read around the question/title and make relevant notes

Don't waste time on irrelevant reading or too much detail. Keep the length of the essay in mind. Focus. Take notes (in your own words) and keep full reference details (including page numbers of direct quotes) of all the material you have looked at and think you will use.

Plan your structure

You need to do this to help you answer the question and develop a clear argument, so keep referring back to the question to make sure that your structure is relevant.

Write the first draft and then revise

Once you have your first draft written you can revise and edit as much as required. Use the tips we suggested on pages 348–51.

Identify any missing information

Editing usually reveals where there are gaps in your writing.

Cut out anything you don't need
> Editing also reveals repetition and unnecessary detail.

Write the final draft
> At this point having someone else read it and give feedback is very useful.

Include full references and a bibliography
> Which books and journals did you use? Record the edition, year of print, publisher, and place of publication as well as title and author details.

Time and length limits

You need to bear in mind that, at least in the case of essays written under exam or test conditions, there will be a time factor. You need to get all you want to say written down within the limits of the time set for the essay. There is no point in having written an interesting first half if you do not have time to write the second half.

Then you must take into consideration the length required. Whether you are writing an essay as part of an assignment to be written in class or as homework, or writing it under exam conditions, you are almost certain to be allocated a certain number of words for the project. It is important that you pay due attention to this.

You should be careful not to write far more material than you have been asked for, while it is equally important that you do not write far too little.

Writing the correct length of material is an important skill that is required in some work situations too – and not just in jobs like journalism. In the workplace it is vital that a report is readable and relevant. Getting people to understand and act upon the requests it contains might depend on this. It can be a difficult skill to acquire but practice helps you to get it right.

WRITING

Structure

The simplest structure to think of for an essay is an **introduction**, a **middle** (where you develop your argument and write critically on the subject) and a **conclusion**.

In an essay, the first paragraph should introduce the subject, while the last paragraph should act as a summing-up of what has been said in the rest of the essay.

Introduction

The introduction should set the question or title in its wider context by giving background information about the central issue. It should also explain the main ideas of your argument and how you are going to answer the question.

You can then make a link from the introduction to the first point in the 'middle' or 'development' section.

THESAURUS

A thesaurus is a writer's best friend. A thesaurus is a reference book that presents you with alternative words to help keep your writing varied and interesting. Some have their words listed by theme, but others give lists of synonyms for particular words that are listed alphabetically. The latter is a little easier to use, but the former is a great tool for leading from one theme to another.

With the help of a thesaurus you will be able to be a bit more adventurous about the words you use in your writing. This will be particularly true if it is used together with a dictionary where you can check meanings, and perhaps be given an example of how the word is used. Be cautious though. Make sure the words you choose are used in the correct context.

Developing the argument

The middle part of your essay must develop the arguments you set out in your introduction, and it must support your final conclusions. This is where a good structure is really useful. This will help you to stay relevant to your theme while you expand on and explain your ideas and provide relevant references and examples to support them.

You should write clearly and concisely. You can still write in plain English, although an academic style is more likely to use the third person (he, she or it) instead of the second person (you and we), and some institutions may insist upon third person.

Remember to write critically, not descriptively. One of the biggest criticisms that teachers and tutors have of their students is that they are just regurgitating the facts, rather than analysing and evaluating those facts. Don't just say that something happened – say why or how it happened and back it up with evidence.

Make sure that you link each idea or point to the next one, so that your argument flows logically and smoothly.

Writing the conclusion

The conclusion should recap on and answer the essay title; summarize and evaluate the main arguments; and highlight the most important aspect or aspects covered.

Style

An essay should be interesting, accurate and well-constructed, but you should also give some thought to the style of your essay.

Adding some variety to the style of your writing will add interest to your essay. For example, you should try to vary the lengths of your paragraphs. Doing so will prevent your style of writing from becoming monotonous and is likely to retain your reader's attention. You should avoid paragraphs consisting of only one sentence unless you are doing so to achieve a dramatic effect.

It is also important to make the sentence structure of the essay as varied as you can. A lot of very short sentences can make a

VOCABULARY

In order to improve the quality of your writing you should think carefully about the actual words you use as well as the structure and style. Try to make sure that the vocabulary used in your writing is varied. In the course of your research make a note of any interesting vocabulary you come across that you think might be appropriate, or fun, to use.

Some words will be relevant to your subject. For example, if you are writing about healthy eating you will probably want to include expressions such as:

> additive, balanced diet, convenience food, junk food, nutritious, obesity, vitamins

Should you be writing on some aspect of the media you might want to make a note of such terms as:

> tabloid, investigative journalism, foreign correspondent, paparazzi, online edition, breaking news

Even if you are not undertaking specific vocabulary research, simply trying to familiarize yourself with a few new words may well spark off some new ideas as well as improving the content of the writing.

Consideration should be given to ordinary general words as well as to specialist words. Some words in English, such as the word *nice*, are much overused. Try to find alternatives and avoid repeating the same word over and over again.

Over time, the best way you can improve your vocabulary is by reading as much as possible, in many varied subjects. You could also regularly consult a **thesaurus**, *see* box on page 360.

piece of prose sound staccato and rather boring, while a lot of very long sentences can be over-complicated and confusing.

You should avoid using only the **coordinating conjunctions** *and* or *but*, in longer sentences. This can make a piece of prose sound very rambling and difficult to follow. Try to make use of sentences which include clauses beginning with other **conjunctions**, so as to introduce variation and increase interest. There is a wide range of such conjunctions to choose from, such as:

> since, because, if, while, as, when, before, after

To improve the style of your essay it is a good idea to vary the position of the clauses in your sentences. Do not always begin sentences with the **main** or **principal clause**. For the sake of variety and interest begin some of them with a **subordinate clause**, starting with a conjunction of the kind mentioned above, as in:

> As the volume of traffic increased in the town the atmosphere became more and more polluted.
>
> Wherever the celebrity goes, photographers rush to follow.

LETTERS, EMAILS AND TEXTING

Communication by email, SMS text, and instant messaging has had an important effect on the use of language in various ways. It has made some people more careless about spelling, grammar and punctuation. They rely on spelling and grammar checkers on their devices to alert them to any errors, and these have their own failings that we have mentioned previously.

Emails have increased the informality of all aspects of writing. There is a pressure to get emails written as quickly as possible in the expectation that you will also get a very rapid reply. This need for speed has resulted in an increase of informality, and sometimes carelessness. Though if there are mistakes in emails we also tend to be a lot more forgiving than we would have been of a printed letter, knowing of the pressures we are all under.

WRITING

Omitted punctuation

Writers of emails, in a rush, tend to miss out commas, full stops and capitalization. These are potentially bad things to miss out – they can alter the meaning of what you want to say and make you harder to understand – which are things you really should avoid in a business context.

Too much punctuation

Many senders of emails are particularly fond of dashes and ellipses, which many of them overuse. The exclamation mark is also particularly popular, and in the absence of being able to convey tone of voice and emotion, etc, it can be used too much. See **Punctuating Properly** on pages 317–40.

Contracted forms

People tend to use contracted forms even in relatively formal emails. So we find a much higher occurrence of words such as *I'll*, *he'll*, *you'll*, *work'll*, *John'll* and *Mary'll* than was formerly the case. Likewise, we find the contracted forms *don't*, *didn't*, *won't*, *haven't*, *hadn't*, *could've* and *should've* used with increasing frequency. Not only that, but the apostrophe is often omitted.

Greetings and sign-offs

Hi John is probably more common at the start of an email than *Dear John*. If this seems too informal, the slightly more abrupt *John* or *Mr Smith* might be an alternative.

Alternatively, you can omit a greeting altogether and simply begin the email.

Formal letters often used to end with *Yours faithfully*. The alternative to this was *Yours sincerely*. Nowadays both are fading fast in all but the most formal letters. In emails you can opt for a greeting such as *Regards* or *Kind regards* instead. Some people prefer to opt for *Best regards*, *Best wishes* or reduce this just to *Best* and *All best*. If you want to choose something much more informal I am sure that you will have some ideas of your own. If you run out of inspiration there is always *Cheers!*

HOW TO WRITE A CV (RÉSUMÉ)

When applying for a job, a *curriculum vitae* – or résumé – needs to be concise, clear, organized and well presented.

Personal details

Provide your name, address, day and evening telephone numbers, email address and age.

Education and qualifications

Put these in reverse chronological order – most recent first, and oldest last.

Work experience

Put this information in reverse chronological order (most recent first). Provide: the starting and finishing date for each job, your work title, who you worked for, where you worked and a description of what you did.

Further information

In this section, include other skills, qualifications or information that you think will make a good impression. Include things that show you can apply yourself and learn, and include things that show you can show initiative, lead a team or work in a team.

Interests

Use this section to give a glimpse of your personality, but only include those which will put you in a positive light. Those which show you to be friendly, sociable, good at organizing etc are particularly good. Include clubs, societies, choirs and sports clubs.

Referees

Choose two professional references. Your referees must not be related to you. Remember to ask their permission and check their details before you include them.

READING COMPREHENSION

You have one hour to read a story and then give me an impressive theory about it that the writer never had in the first place.

AT EVERY stage of your time learning about the English language you will be given tests of **reading comprehension**. These texts will probably be a mixture of extracts from works of **fiction** and **non-fiction**. As you progress, these tests might increase in difficulty, and the questions will go from being straightforward ones asking about vocabulary and what the passage is describing, to questions that discuss the aims of the **narrative** and language style as well as the author's writing technique.

APPROACHING A READING INTERPRETATION

In an exam or classroom situation you may be presented with a text to read and accompanying questions to answer. It often helps to read through the questions before you even begin reading the text. Then, as you read through for the first time you can highlight any areas that you think were related to the questions. Then read the questions again. Can you answer some? Make notes and then read the text again. Now, working from your notes, go ahead and answer all the questions. Use examples from the text to show how you got your answers.

WHAT KIND OF QUESTIONS?

The questions asked may depend on the stage you are at in your studies, and so will your answers. More advanced students will probably be expected to explain their answers using evidence from the text. Less advanced students may only be required to give short or one-word answers just to show they have understood the passage. Discuss what the expectations are with your tutor or teacher.

The simplest questions will be about what is being described by the passage.

You might be asked direct questions about what happens in the story: who goes where, or does what, with whom and why. The 'why' might not be obvious and require more interpretation. 'Why' requires you to work out things about characters' motivation.

Some questions might talk about the meanings of words used in certain contexts. As we've discussed, sometimes English words have different meanings depending on where and when they are used. You might be asked what other words could have been chosen instead. A *dictionary* and, especially, a *thesaurus* will help you understand.

You might be asked what kind of mood or emotion is being created by the use of some words. For example, a *beautiful room* (which could be any style of room as long as it is found to be beautiful) could be very different to an *opulent room* (which is, more specifically, a room with expensive furnishings; it might well be beautiful, but an opulent room could potentially be a bit overdone and tasteless!). A *delicious meal* might be very different to a *carefully prepared meal*. A *wise person* is subtly different to a *sophisticated person* though they both might be worldly. Knowledge of **synonyms** is important here.

What is the author's purpose and how does he or she achieve it?

The questions will most likely not ask you things that cannot be found from reading the extract, so do not just guess or make it up, the clues will be there, though there may be more than one acceptable answer.

PREPARING FOR A BOOK REPORT OR ESSAY

A book report is usually an **essay** on a book that you have been given to study in class. You will probably have discussed the themes, context and characters as a class. You may then be given a question, or a selection of questions to choose from, on which to base your report. Always keep this question in mind while writing your essay (*see* pages 357–63 for tips on essay writing).

As you read the book on which you will make the report, make notes as you go. Use sticky notes to highlight pages and make a note of paragraphs that you think are significant and might merit closer interpretation later on.

The first and most obvious question you might ask is: what is the story about? This is not as simple a question as it sounds. Another way of putting it is: what is the author trying to convey? If this is a long **novel** you might not know this immediately. You might change your mind by the time it gets to the end. You might realize that the story is an **allegory** (*see* page 370). You might discover that the **narrator** (*see* page 369) is not as reliable as you first thought.

If there are characters in the book you might think about psychology, and following on from this, why the author has decided to present the characters in this way. Does their motivation seem realistic? Do they behave this way to enable the writer specifically to tell the story in a certain way?

When was this story written? Would the historical context have affected the way it was written or the subject matter? How does the language represent emotion? How does the language help you decide what kind of person the narrator is?

A WRITER'S STYLE

As you are reading, think a little about the writer's style and what effect it has on you as a reader, and what, if anything, makes it unique to them.

Look for repetitions and patterns. Look at sentence and paragraph length. Look for similarities and differences. Does the writer use simple English or more elaborate words? Are any descriptive passages in **poetical** language, showing **metaphors** or **symbolic imagery**?

WHAT ARE THE THEMES INVOLVED?

A theme is different to plot, subject matter or the historical context in which a story is set. For example *Pride and Prejudice* (the title gives you a big clue) by Jane Austen is a story about a group of sisters, and their mother's wish to get them all married off. That is the **plot**, however the **themes** are pride and prejudice: the assumptions we make about people based on wrong first impressions, and how their class and appearance also play into those prejudices.

NARRATIVE

A narrator or storyteller, is the voice telling the story (the narrative). Sometimes the narrative is written in the **first-person** using 'I' or 'we' (as in an autobiography or when the main character in the book tells the story from their point of view).

A **second-person narrative** will use 'you' (where the narrator is addressing the reader as if they are part of the story). This is a rarer type of narrative.

A **third-person narrative** is when each and every character is referred to by the narrator as 'he', 'she', 'it' or 'they'. This can be an **omniscient narrative** is where the narrator knows everything that is going on, including what all the characters are thinking. A third-person narrative can still tell a story from a certain character's point of view

A narrative can be told in the **past tense**, **present tense** or, more rarely, the **future tense**. Most works of fiction will be in the past tense.

CLOSE READING

A **close reading** is the careful study of a piece of text. If you are reading a novel for fun, at normal speed, you tend to skim and may not pick up on particular subtleties of language. By contrast, in a close reading careful attention is given to individual word choices, the **syntax** (that is, the way sentences are formed and structured), how sentences are ordered, and any other patterns that might have a significance in how the text is interpreted. Close reading analyses are often studies of short extracts, poems and short stories. If you are specifically studying English language as it is used in literature, at college or university level, you will have a lot of close reading to do!

LITERARY TERMS

act a division of a play, the acts often being divided into **scenes**.

allegory a form of narrative in which the characters and events represent a hidden meaning beneath the literal one.

alliteration the repetition of, or a sequence of, the same sound in a piece of writing.

analogy a figure of speech, rather like the **simile**, in which there is an inference of a resemblance between two items that are being compared.

assonance a figure of speech in which vowel sounds are repeated to give a half-rhyme effect, as in 'with gun, drum, trumpet, blunderbuss and thunder'.

Literary terms

autobiography the story of one's own life.

ballad a narrative poem or song in brief stanzas, often with a repeated refrain, and frequently featuring a dramatic incident.

bathos a **figure of speech** consisting of a sudden descent from the lofty or noble to the ridiculous or trivial.

biography the story of someone's life.

context the circumstances surrounding a piece of writing.

comedy a form of drama, usually of a light and humorous kind and frequently involving misunderstandings that are resolved in a happy ending.

couplet a pair of rhymed lines of verse of equal length.

elegy a serious and reflective poem, especially one written as a lament for someone who has died.

epic a word that originally referred to a very long narrative poem dealing with heroic deeds and adventures on a grand scale, as Homer's *Iliad*.

euphemism is a term given to an expression that is a milder, more pleasant, less direct way of saying something that might be thought to be too harsh or direct.

fable a story that is intended to convey a moral lesson. Fables frequently feature animals that speak and act like human beings. Most famous are the fables of Aesop.

figure of speech a form of expression used to heighten the effect of a statement. The most commonly known are **similes** and **metaphors**, but there are many more, such as **personification**.

genre a style of something.

hyperbole a figure of speech consisting of exaggeration or over-statement, used for emphasis, as in 'I could eat a horse' and in 'I am boiling in this heat'.

imagery writing that evokes visual things.

irony the use of a word or words to convey something that is completely different from the literal meaning.

READING COMPREHENSION

lyric in ancient Greece the name given to a verse sung to a lyre. In modern English the word is used to refer to most forms of short poetry, especially to those poems which are personal in tone and theme or those which are of a non-narrative kind.

metaphor a figure of speech that compares two things by saying that one thing is another, as in 'He was a lion in the fight' (meaning that he was as brave as a lion). By extension, metaphor refers to a word or phrase used in a sentence where it does not have a literal meaning, as in 'a butter mountain'.

metonym a figure of speech in which a word or expression is used as a substitute for something with which it has a close relationship, as in 'The White House has yet to comment' (meaning that the President of the United States has yet to comment).

meter the measure of the rhythm of a line of verse when the line can be divided into units of metrical feet.

mixed metaphor the situation that occurs when unrelated **metaphors** are put in the same sentence. Examples include 'She sailed into the room with both guns blazing'.

novel a sustained fictional prose narrative, with complex characterization and multi-layered strands of plot and character development.

novella a short version of the **novel**.

ode in ancient Greece, originally a poem intended to be sung, a lyric poem written in an elaborate form. The word is now applied to any elaborate lyric poem.

onomatopoeia a figure of speech that uses words whose sound suggests their meaning, as in 'The sausages sizzled in the pan'.

oxymoron a figure of speech that is based on the linking of contradictory words, as in 'the wisest fool in Christendom'.

pathos poignancy; writing that evokes sadness.

personification a form of **metaphor** that represents an inanimate object or abstract notion as possessing the attributes of a person. For example, Uncle Sam is a personification of the United States of America, and John Barleycorn is a personification of whisky.

plot what happens in a novel, play or short story.

poetry writing with a distinct structure and rhythm and rhyme, which may also feature **assonance** and **alliteration**.

pun a play on words based on the use of a word with more than one meaning, or of two words which sound the same. Examples include 'Whether life is worth living or not depends on the liver.'

realism in literature, a true and faithful representation of reality in works of fiction.

rhyme the effect produced by using words that end with the same or similar sounds.

simile a figure of speech in which something is compared with another and said to be like it.

sonnet a short poem consisting of 14 lines and a rhyme scheme which conforms to one or other of a variety of patterns. Originally, the subject matter was usually love, although it became more varied after the 16th century.

symbolism a French poetry movement of the late 19th century; a means by which one thing can represent another.

tragedy a form of drama in which a hero or heroine comes to a bad end. The cause of this unfortunate state of affairs can either be a personal flaw in the hero or heroine, circumstances beyond his or her control, or a combination of these two factors.

MAKING A SPEECH

You're doing great. They're probably just throwing fruit because you look hungry.

PUBLIC SPEAKING is the process of addressing a group of people in a structured, deliberate way, whether the intention is to inform, influence, or simply entertain.

BOTH WORLDS

In the previous chapters we've discussed structures of spontaneous speech, and more formal speech, and in the last chapter we've discussed ways to improve your writing. Making a speech is going to draw on your knowledge of both. If you are required to make a speech, you may be content to rehearse, and possibly read verbatim, words you have written beforehand. However, it is better to make your speech seem 'off the cuff'. It is a great accomplishment to be able to say just the right thing at the right time in public, and preparation is everything.

YOUR AUDIENCE

You must be able to communicate your enthusiasm about your subject to your **audience**. You must also appear to be interested in your audience. If you don't, they won't be interested in listening to you.

You must think carefully about the style of language you use – it must be appropriate for the audience. Don't use jargon and abbreviations in front of an audience that may be unfamiliar with their meaning.

Speakers often overestimate their audience's ability to keep up – don't expect your audience to absorb information fast. If you are an expert in your subject remember that you can never make your subject too simple. Repeating information with different words increases the chance of the information being absorbed.

MIND MAP

Build a **structure** into your speech. A **mind map** will help you structure and organize what you want to say. It is key to helping you arrange the importance of a series of steps with branches and connections to other themes and groups.

A mind map is a picture or diagram which represents key words and ideas that are provoked by a central theme. It is a pictorial brainstorm, on one piece of paper, which is in fact a far better starting point than just to set out with a preconceived order and structure. Keep your mind map handy – you can add to it over a period of time. A mind map really helps in getting balance to a speech. It highlights the key points and those which are perhaps less important. It is particularly useful in sorting out the timeline if you have a set time slot and can't over-run.

Keep your mind map in your pocket. Remember – keep it to just one sheet of paper.

MAKING A SPEECH

THE SPEECH

The best basic template for a speech is:

1. Tell your audience what you are going to tell them.
2. Deliver.
3. Sum up and remind them what you have just said.

Looks a little similar to the plan for writing an essay, doesn't it? To an extent you can draw on the guidelines for the structure of an essay but bear in mind the other important elements of a speech that are listed below.

The opening

The opening is key. Make it punchy – grab their attention. Maybe you are one of several speakers and the audience's attention is already starting to diminish. Tell them why what you are saying is important to them.

Try to engage them immediately. Take them with you by conjuring up a picture that they can create in their minds – 'Picture this' or 'Imagine that you are …'. Your audience will find themselves wanting to listen to you.

Watch how others do this. One of the best online resources for talks in front of an audience is www.ted.com.

Timing

Time your speech and rehearse it over and over again (out loud if possible). If you have been allotted a specific time slot and what you have to say will invite questions – then make sure you leave enough time at the end for a Q & A exchange. If there is no clock within sight, take your wristwatch off and put it beside you and glance at it from time to time.

Quite often if a speaker says 'any questions' there is absolute silence, with no-one putting their hand up. This is perhaps due to embarrassment on the audience's behalf. Perhaps they are a group of people who have never met each other before or they have widely different experience or interest in the subject.

Be ready for this. Have something in reserve that might provoke a question, or have a question of your own ready to pose to the audience which might be answered with a show of hands. If there are still no questions, fill the silence with a further few minutes reflecting upon what you have said.

The ending

Structure your ending, don't just fade away. The ending is what your audience is left with and that's what they will be discussing when they file out for their coffee or lunch.

When you are ready to close make sure no-one is in any doubt that you have finished. Something like: '... and thank you for coming today. If anyone would like to get in touch or seek clarification on anything I have said, please feel free to contact me.' Give the audience a few seconds at the end to take in the fact that you have finished.

The subject

Beware of consulting authoritative works on the internet or in libraries, and then serving chunks up to your audience as it stands. The key thing is to make the subject your own. If you do, your presentation of it will be fresh, and original, and you will not be delivering someone else's words.

Read your research material carefully, digest it, then make brief notes. When you have done this, close the reference sources and prepare your own case.

Talk the subject over with friends and colleagues. This will generally bring out ideas for additional material and highlight other points of view. The whole process will help you get a clear picture of the subject and allow you to gauge the level of common understanding and knowledge that others already have.

Organize your material and discard what is irrelevant.

Rehearse with your notes but if you want your speech to seem impromptu, don't attempt to memorize them. An impromptu

MAKING A SPEECH

speech takes on much of the nature of conversation, and this is the most effective style for a speech. Practise out loud.

Notes

Try condensing the final draft of your speech to the dimensions of a postcard, but if you feel more comfortable with a full script make sure you prepare your script in a type size large enough to read, with short lines, plenty of line spaces. Punctuate the script with pauses.

Have your **mind map** close at hand in case you lose your place (or worse still find that your script is out of order) and you will have the confidence that you need.

MAKING THE SPEECH

Find out in advance where you will be speaking. Is there a microphone? Will you be on a platform? Get there early – check out the room, the seating arrangement and any equipment you will need, such as a computer or screen projector.

On the day itself you need to **warm up** your face and your voice and relax. Humming or singing before you set off to the event – or in the car on the way – will warm your voice up. Tongue twisters are a great warm-up. Give yourself a shake-down. Shake out your hands and loosen your arms. Waken up your whole body. Run up and down some stairs.

When your moment comes walk slowly and confidently to the podium or lectern and take in your audience as you move forward. You need to have a good posture and a balanced comfortable stance. Take your time. Before you speak, look at your audience and smile – unless of course you are delivering some extremely sad or serious news, where smiling may be inappropriate.

Only start when you are absolutely ready. If there is some chattering within the audience or a latecomer is trying to find a seat, wait until the disruption ceases.

Don't rush your delivery. Let your audience know that you are in command and that you are interested in them. Make sure that you vary the intonation of your voice – imagine that your speech is a poem or a song.

Slow down, speed up, and use pauses. You yourself need to keep in control of your thoughts as you move on to the next point.

Troubleshooting

Be prepared for every eventuality. Perhaps you are one of several speakers who are all contributing to a theme. Imagine your horror if, one by one, all of the speakers who have gone before you in the programme have mentioned everything you have in your prepared speech. What do you do? Give your speech anyway? Best not to do that!

Go to your **mind map**. You can quickly look at it and you will see among the branches and pictograms, ideas and tangents that you can introduce and add to or change what you had planned to say.

If you are new to public speaking, take every opportunity to challenge yourself in as many situations as you can. Whether this is speaking at dinner parties, or to school groups or clubs, the more opportunities you embrace, the more confident you will become.

> We hope the tips in this book will arm you with enough knowledge of the intricacies of English usage to enable you to improve your familiarity and fluency.

INDEX

abbreviations 336
accent 48
acronyms 337
act 370
active voice 186, 187, 188, 346, 347
  active clause 345
  active verbs 346
adjective 143–54
  adjective or adverb 152
  attributive 146, 147
  classifying 145
  colour 148, 149, 152
  comparative 145, 152, 153, 154
    irregular 153
    syllables 152
  compound 151
  coordinate 150
    commas 150
  cumulative 150
  emphatic 148, 167
  gradable 144–5, 170
  interrogative 151
  non-gradable 144–5, 170
  order of adjectives 149
  phrase 131
  possessive 159
  postnominal 146
  post-positive 146
  predicative 147
  qualitative 144, 152
  qualities 149
  size 149
  superlative 145, 154
    irregular 154
  used as nouns 152
adverb 152, 163–71
  adjective or adverb 165
  clause 173–5
  degree 144–5, 167, 169, 170
  duration 166
  emphasis 167, 169
  frequency 165
  gradable 169
  interrogative 169
  irregular 165
  manner 167
  modifying adjectives 163
  modifying conjunctions 163
  modifying other adverbs 163
  modifying prepositions 163
  non-grading 170
  phrase 132
  place 166
  time 165
allegory 370
alliteration 370
alveolar 48
an 158
analogy 370
and 172
answer 14–16, 23, 25, 47, 91, 93, 103, 121–8, 226, 270, 308, 321, 357–8, 360–1, 366–8
  echo answer 128
  emphatic response 128
apologizing 19, 37, 100, 129
apostrophe 268, 318–23

apostrophe (ctd)
  common errors 319, 322
  contracted form 321–3
  personal possessive pronouns 321
  plural 320
  possession 318–9
article. *see determiner*
assonance 370
audience 375
'augh' words 41
autobiography 371
ballad 371
bathos 371
biography 355, 371
body language 14, 18
book report 368
brackets 323
  common errors 323
brainstorm 358
but 172
call centre 29
capital letters 324
  initial letter of the first word of sentence 324
  pronouns 325
  proper noun 324
  seasons 324
  tips 324
  trade names 325
classification 149
clause 115, 116, 129
  main clause 117–8, 129–30, 171–3, 175, 329–32, 350
  relative clause 130, 173, 329, 330
  subordinate clause 114–116, 118, 129, 130, 173, 175, 330, 331, 363
close reading 370
closing a conversation 26, 27
  closing a telephone conversation 29
colon 326, 326
comedy 371
comma 125, 150, 327–34
  adjective lists 329
  adverbial phrases 332
  clarity 331
  common errors 327, 329, 332-3
  coordinate adjectives 150
  lists 327
    last item in a list 328
  main clauses 331
  non-defining relative clause 329
  parenthesis 332
  subordinate clauses 330
command 113, 120, 125, 347, 378
comment clause 130
common noun 136
comparative adjectives 152–3
complex sentences 118
composition 351–7
compound sentences 117, 129
concrete noun 136
confidence 7, 16

confusable words
abuse/misuse 279
accept/except 279
adopted/adoptive 278
adverse/averse 279
advice/advise 280
adviser/advisor 280
affect/effect 280
afterwards/afterward 280
ail/ale 262
aisle/isle 262
all right/alright 281
alter/altar 262
alternate/alternative 280
altogether/all together 281
amiable/amicable 282
among/between 282
any more/anymore 282
anyone/any one 283
any place/anyplace 283
any time/anytime 283
arbiter/arbitrator 278
atheist/agnostic 283
backward/backwards 284
balk/baulk 284
bank/bank 275
bare/bear 263
bass/bass 273
bated/baited 263
bathroom 284
beat/beaten 284
bill/bill 275
blew/blue 263
boar/bore 263
bow/bow 273
bridal/bridle 264
brooch/broach 264
calf/calf 275
can/may 284
canvas/canvass 264
censor/censure 285
centenary/centennial 285
cereal/serial 264
cheque/check 264
chronic/acute 285
cite/sight/site 265
city/town 286
close/close 273
comprehensible/comprehensive 286
compulsory/compulsive 286
contagious/infectious 287
continual/continuous 285
credible/credulous/incredible 287
criteria/criterion 287
cue/queue 266, 288
currant/current 266
data/datum 288
deceitful/deceptive 288
decimate 288
delusion/illusion 289
dependant/dependent 289
deprecate/depreciate 290
derisory/derisive 289
desert/desert 273
desert/dessert 290
device/devise 291
disc/disk 291
discreet/discrete 266

confusable words (ctd)
disinterested/uninterested 291
downward/downwards 291
drunk/drunken 291
economic/economical 292
e.g./i.e. 292
either or/neither nor 199
elder/older 293
enquiry/inquiry 293
envelope/envelop 293
every day/everyday 294
extant/extinct 293
extrovert/extravert/introvert 294
fair/fair 275
farther/further 294
feat/feet 267
fewer/less 295
first/firstly 295
flu/flew 267
foot/foot 276
forbear/forebear 295
for ever/forever 295
fortuitous/fortunate 295
forward/forwards 296
gipsy/gypsy 296
gourmet, gourmand 296
grave/grave 276
guerrilla/guerilla/gorilla 267
heal/heel 267
hear/here 267
hire/rent 297
historic/historical 297
hoard/horde 268
hyper-/hypo- 298
illegible/eligible 298
immigrant/emigrant 298
immoral/immortal 300
imply/infer 299
impracticable/impractical/ practicable/practical 299
indexes/indices 299
individual 299
industrial/industrious 300
inflammable/flammable/ non-flammable 301
ingenious/ingenuous 301
its/it's 268, 301
-ize/-ise 301
jail/gaol 302
jewellery/jewelry 302
judgment/judgement 303
know/no 268
lay/lie 302
lead/lead 274
learn/teach 303
left and right 276
lend/loan 303
libel/slander 304
licence/license 304
lie/lie 277
lose/loose and lose/looser 304
masterly/masterful 305
media/medium 305
metre/meter 269
migrant/emigrant 305
minute/minute 274
momentary/momentous 306
moral/morale 306
nauseous/nauseated 307

380

Index

confusable words (ctd)
next/this 307
none/nun 269
off/from 307
off + of 308
of/have 307
oral/aural 308
orientate/orient 308
outdoor/outdoors 308
outward/outwards 309
passed/past 269, 309
persecute/prosecute 309
phenomenon/phenomena 310
practice/practise 309
precede/proceed 310
prescribe/proscribe 310
principal/principle 269
prostrate/prostate 311
pulse/pulse 277
rain/reign/rein 270
rapt/wrapped 270
refuse/refuse 274
right/rite/write/wright 270
row/row 274, 277
Scottish/Scots/Scotch 311
seasonal/seasonable 311
sow/sow 274
spring/spring 277
stare/stair 271
stationery/stationary 272
supposedly 312
swallow/swallow 277
systematic/systemic 312
that/which 313
their/they're/there 271, 312
toilet/loo/lavatory 313
to/too/two 272, 313
toward/towards 314
try to/try and 314
until/till 314
up/upon 314
upward/upwards 315
verbal/oral 315
which/that 313
which/what 151
whom/who 315
whose/who's 272, 316
will/shall 316
you/one 316
your/you're 272, 316
conjunction 171–5, 363
adverbial clauses 173–5
coordinating conjunction 117, 171–2, 363
subordinating conjunction 118, 173–5
consonant 36, 38–41, 158, 194–5
consonant sounds 36, 158
context 371
contracted forms 124, 318, 364
conversation 6, 8, 9, 10, 11, 13–33, 76, 83, 85, 127, 140, 253, 377
conversation endings 26, 28–31
telephone 29
conversation openings 21–3, 26
telephone 25
formal conversation 15, 19, 26
overlaps 15, 18–19
repair 19–20, 107, 275
telephone conversations 9, 16, 18, 21, 25–26, 30, 96, 197, 208, 324, 344, 352

conversation (ctd)
turn-taking 13, 15, 18
winding down 18, 26, 27, 29, 30
coordinate adjectives 150
coordinating conjunction 117, 129
copyright 353
coronal 48
could of 192
couplet 371
CV writing 365
dangling participles. *See* participle
dash 334
common errors 334
declarations 113
declarative sentences 119
definite article. *See* determiner
dental 48
determiner 141, 155, 155–161
and nouns 161, 162
definite article 151, 156, 157
demonstrative 159
indefinite article 151, 156–9
indefinite or general 160
numbers 161
cardinal numbers 161
ordinal numbers 161
possessive 155, 159
quantifying 155, 160
referring 155, 160
dialogue 8, 9, 10, 13–30, 336
informal 9, 14
dictionary 33, 360, 367
digraph 48
diphthong 48–9
directions 24
directive 120
direct object 116, 189, 302
direct speech 339
disyllabic 48
editing 348–51, 357
check consistency 349
check spelling 349
cutting 350
formal or informal 349
revise 348
either or 199
elegy 371
elision 48
ellipsis 340
email 363–5
greetings and sign-offs 364
epic 371
essays 357–63, 368
argument 361
conclusion 361
introduction 360
structure 360
style 361
time and length limits 359
euphemism 371
everyone 142
exclamation mark 85, 119–21, 334, 335, 364
exclamatory questions 121
exclamatory sentences 119
fable 371
facial expressions 14, 18, 29
fiction 366
figure of speech 371
filler phrases 8, 10, 83–4, 130
fricative 48
full stop 335–7
future tense. *See* verb, tense
genre 371
gerunds 184

gestures 14, 17–18, 29
gliding vowel 48
goodbye 28
grapheme 48–9
Great Vowel Shift 35
greetings 21–2, 364
hello 22
he or she 141
heteronyms 273
homographs 262, 273
homonyms 262
homophones 262, 268, 271
hopefully 164
hyperbole 371
hyphen 337
common errors 338
hypothetical statements 185
idioms 10, 50–83, 349, 350
accident waiting to happen 76
achilles' heel 51
acid test 52
at the end of the day 83
at this moment in time 83
axe to grind 52
back of beyond 52
beat about the bush 53
bee in your bonnet 53
between a rock and a hard place 73
big fish in a small pond 53
blow off steam 60
bow to the inevitable 81
buck stops here 54
burn your boats 54
by the board 58
by the same token 81
carry the can 54
catch someone red-handed 55
catch someone with their hand in the till 55
cat got your tongue? 50, 51
chalk and cheese 55
cross that bridge when you come to it 55
daggers drawn 56
daunting prospect 81
diamond in the rough 56
dog eat dog 56
dulcet tones 81
Dutch courage 57
end of an era 76
end of your tether 57
fall on your sword 73
flavour of the month 73
flog a dead horse 57
flying colours 58
goes with the territory 77
green fingers 58
green thumbs 58
hidden agenda 77
hit the ground running 58
hit the sack 59
if you ask me 83
in all honesty 84
in point of fact 84
jewel in the crown 59
jump on the bandwagon 59
jump the gun 51
jury's still out 74
keep the wolf from the door 74
kill two birds with one stone 60
last but not least 78
leave no stone unturned 74
left holding the baby 60
let off steam 60
level playing field 74

idioms (ctd)
lock, stock and barrel 60
loose cannon 75
make a mountain out of a molehill 61
mark my words 84
merciful release 78
moment of truth 61
moot point 82
move the goalposts 75
nail in someone's coffin 61
needs no introduction 78
once in a blue moon 61
one hundred and ten per cent 78
only time will tell 79
open the floodgates 75
over the moon 61
paint the town red 62
pale into insignificance 82
par for the course 62
pass the buck 62
pie in the sky 62
race against time 79
rat race 63
red herring 63
rest is history 79
rest on your laurels 63
rough diamond 56
score an own goal 64
shoot yourself in the foot 64
smell a rat 64
spanner in the works 65
speculation is rife 82
stab someone in the back 64
stick to your guns 65
storm in a teacup 65
these things happen 80
the thing is 84
thought that counts 77
tighten your belt 65
too big for your boots 66
too numerous to mention 80
turn over a new leaf 66
twist someone's arm 66
up in arms 67
up in the air 66
usual suspects 80
wash your hands of someone/something 67
when all is said and done 84
imagery 369, 371
imperative mood. *See* verb, mood
imperative sentences. *See* sentences
indefinite article. *See* determiner
Indicative mood. *See* verb, mood
indirect object 116
indirect speech 339
infinitive. *See* verb
inflection 48
instructions 347
interjections
about time too 86
ah 86
ahem 86
alas 86
all right 87
as a matter of fact 87
believe it or not 88
believe you me 88
by all means 89
by the way 89
come on! 89
come to think of it 89
don't bank on it 90
don't say that! 90
dream on! 90

INDEX

interjections (ctd)
  for goodness' sake 90
  good! 91
  good grief! 91
  good heavens! 91
  good question! 91
  great! 92
  hang on! 92
  hardly! 92
  having said that 93
  heaven knows! 93
  how's it going? 93
  I can't tell you 93
  I can't think why 93
  I could do without 94
  I dare say 94
  If you don't mind my saying so 94
  I hate to think 95
  I'm afraid 95
  I must say 95
  I suppose so 95
  I thought as much 96
  I thought I'd 96
  I told you so 96
  it's beyond me 96
  it's just that 97
  it's no big deal 97
  I've no idea 97
  I was wondering if/whether? 97
  let me see 98
  listen 98
  look! 98
  look out! 98
  me too 99
  never mind 99
  no chance! 99
  no fear! 99
  not on your life! 100
  not to worry/don't worry 100
  no way! 100
  no wonder 100
  oh dear! 101
  oops! 101
  ouch! 101
  ow! 101
  phew! 102
  quite right too! 102
  rather you than me! 102
  really? 102
  right you are 103
  roll on! 103
  same here 103
  search me! 103
  shh! 104
  shoo! 104
  some hope! 104
  so what? 104
  so what's new? 104
  speaking of 105
  suit yourself! 105
  sure! 105
  talk about 105
  that's all I need! 106
  that's fine by me 106
  that's news to me 106
  that's OK with me 106
  that's too bad 107
  there's no doubt about it 107
  there you go/are 107
  though 107
  too true! 108
  tut!/tut, tut! 108
  ugh! 108
  uh-huh 109
  what about? 109
  what about it?/how about it? 109

interjections (ctd)
  what did I tell you? 109
  what if? 110
  what's more 110
  what's the use? 110
  what's up? 110
  why don't ...? 111
  wonders will never cease! 111
  wouldn't you know it? 111
  you could always 111
  you'll never guess! 112
  you never know 112
  yuck! 112
interrogative pronouns. *See* pronoun
interrogative sentences. *See* sentences
interruptions 14–17, 18–20, 30, 98, 323, 334
interview for a job 15
intrusive R 40
IPA (International Phonetic Alphabet) 35, 36, 37, 38, 48, 49
irony 371
it's 322
its 322
labial 48
labiodental 48
length mark 49
letter writing 363
linking r 40
listening skills 9
lyric 372
macron 49
metaphor 369, 371–3
meter 372
metonym 372
mind map 375, 378, 379
mixed metaphor 372
monosyllabic 49
mood. *See* Verb
narrative 369
  first-person narrative 369
  omniscient narrative 370
  second-person narrative 369
  third-person narrative 369
narrator 369
nationality 149
neither nor 199
nice 32
non-fiction
  comprehension 366–7
  composition 351
non-verbal communication 16, 17, 18
noun 116, 133–142, 149, 184
  abstract 136
  already plural in form 135
  clause 116
  collective 200
  compound 138, 338
    plural forms 138
  count/countable 134, 138, 161, 162
  foreign plurals 137
  group 200
  irregular plurals 135
  phrase 114, 116, 131, 133, 138
  proper noun 136, 324
  regular plurals 134
  singular genderless 142
  subject 114
noun (ctd)
  uncount/uncountable 134, 161, 162
novel 372

novella 372
numbers
  cardinal numbers. *See* determiners
  ordinal numbers. *See* determiners
object 116, 123, 189
ode 372
omniscient. *See* narrative
onomatopoeia 372
'ough' words 41
oxymoron 372
paragraphs 345
participle
  dangling participle 183
  misrelated participle 183
  past participle 132, 179, 181–3, 190, 193–98, 201–6, 269, 302
  present participle 132, 178, 182–4, 193–96
  participles used as adjectives 149
passive voice 30, 186–8, 190, 345–7
  clause 345
past tense. *See* verb, tense
pathos 373
personification 371, 373
phoneme 49
phonemic orthography 34
phonemic transcription 49
phonetics 49
phrasal verb 207–19
  adverb and a preposition 209
  and adverb 208
  and preposition 208
  phrasal verbs figurative or literal meaning 212
  position of the object 209
  pronoun objects 210
phrasal verb examples
  come down on 215
  come down with 215
  come up with 215
  cut back on 215
  cut down on 215
  do away with 215
  do out of 216
  get along with 216
  get away with 216
  get behind with 216
  get down to 216
  get out of 216
  get round to 216
  get through to 216
  get up to 216
  go along with 217
  go back on 217
  go in for 217
  go off 217
  go off with 217
  go through with 217
  keep in with 217
  keep on at 218
  keep out of 218
  keep up with 218
  make off with/make away with 218
  make up for 218
  make up with 218
  pull out of 218
  put down to 218
  put in for 218
  put up to 218
  put up with 219
  stand up for 219
  stand up to 219

phrasal verb examples (ctd)
  take up on 219
  walk away from 219
  walk in on 219
  walk off with 219
phrase 6, 114, 116, 131–32, 168, 199, 207, 212–3, 233, 343
  adverbial phrase 132
  nominal phrase 131
  noun phrase 114, 116, 131, 133, 138
  participial phrase 132, 183
  preposition phrase 132
  verb phrase 131
plagiarism 354
plain English 341–347, 350
  word/phrase suggested alternative 343
plosive 39, 49
plot 369, 373
poetry 369, 373
politeness 15–20, 24, 29, 97, 125, 139, 153, 207, 260, 281, 346
possession. *See* apostrophe
possessive case. *See* verbs, gerunds
predicate 113, 115–6, 147
preposition 123, 147, 148, 192, 209, 220-260
  common errors 221
  complex 221
  sentences ending in a preposition 222
  simple 220
preposition word pairs
  absent from 224
  absolve from 224
  absolve of 224
  accuse of 224
  accustomed to 224
  adhere to 225
  afraid of 225
  agree on 225
  agree to 225
  agree with 225
  alternative to 226
  answer for 226
  answer to 226
  anxious about 226
  anxious for 226
  anxious to 226
  apart from 227
  appeal against 227
  appeal to 227
  apply for 227
  apply to 227
  approve of 227
  arrive at 228
  arrive in 228
  ashamed of 228
  ask after 228
  attached to 228
  aware of 228
  bank on 229
  because of 229
  become of 230
  begin by 230
  begin with 230
  believe in 230
  belong to 230
  benefit from 231
  blame for 231
  blame on 231
  bored of 231
  bored with 231
  capable of 231

Index

preposition word pairs (ctd)
care about 232
care for 232
centre around/round 232
centre on 232
charge with 224
close to 249
commitment to 232
committed to 232
communicate to 233
communicate with 233
compare to 233, 234
compare with 233
compatible with 234
complain about 234
complain of 234
complain to 234
compliment on 234
composed of 235
concentrate on 236
concerned about 235
concerned about/for 235
concerned with 235
conditional on 235
conducive to 235
confidence in 235
confident of 236
conform to 236
connect with 236
connect with/to 236
conscious of 229
consent to 236
consist of 236
content to 237
content with 237
contrast with 237
convinced of 237
cope with 237
correspond to 237
correspond with 237
critical of 238
culminate in 238
deal with 238
decide on 238
decide upon 238
delighted with 238
delight in 238
dependent on 239
depend on 238
deprive of 239
deter from 239
detract from 239
devoid of 239
devoted to 239
different from 239
different than 240
different to 239
disagree with 226
disloyal to 248
dispose of 240
distract from 240
dressed in 240
due to 229, 230
end in 240
end with 240
engaged in 240
engaged to 241
engrossed in 241
envious of 241
escape from 241
except for 241
faithful to 242
faith in 241
familiar to 242
familiar with 242
fond of 242
free from 242
free of 242

preposition word pairs (ctd)
friendly with 243
friends with 243
frightened of 225
full of 243
glad about 243
glad for 243
glad of 243
glad to 243
graduate from 243
grateful for 243
grateful to 244
guilty about 244
guilty of 244
half/half of 244
harmful to 245
heard of 245
hear of/hear about 245
hope for 245
hope of 245
incapable of 231
incompatible with 234
inferior to 245
in need of 249
inquire into 245
insist on 246
intention of 246
interfere in 246
interfere with 246
in the habit of 224
involved in 246
involved with 246
irrespective of 247
lack of 247
lean on 247
liable for 247
liable to 247
loyal to 248
masquerade as 248
meet with 248
merge into 248
merge with 248
mindful of 248
model on 249
native to 249
near to 249
need for 249
next to 249
object to 249
oblivious of/to 249
obsessed by 250
obsessed with 250
opportunity for/to 250
opposed to 250
opposite of 250
opt for 251
owing to 230
pleased about 251
pleased with 251
pore over 251
preferable to 251
prefer to 251
present at 224
press charges against 225
prevent from 251
prior to 251
prohibit from 252
protest against 252
protest at 252
proud of 252
provide for 252
react to 252
recover from 253
refer to 253
reflect on 253
reflect upon 253
refrain from 253
regardless of 247

preposition word pairs (ctd)
rely on/upon 253
remind of 253
renege on 254
resistant to 254
responsible for 254
restrict to/limit to 254
result from 254
result in 254
retire from 255
revert to 255
rich in 255
rob of 255
satisfied with 255
sceptical about 255
sceptical of 255
sensitive to 255
separate from 256
share out 256
share with 256
sick of 256
similarity between 257
similar to 256
smell of 257
sorry about 257
sorry for 257
strive for 257
subject to 257
substitute for 258
succeed in 258
suffer from 258
superior to 245
susceptible to 258
suspicious of 258
sympathize with 258
take pleasure in 251
tamper with 259
tendency to 259
think over 259
think through 259
think up 259
together with 259
true to 259
unaware of 229
unconscious of 229
unfaithful to 242
wait for 260
wait on 260
with the exception of 241
present continuous tense.
    See verb, tense
present perfect tense. See verb,
    tense
present tense. See verb, tense
primary sources 352, 354
principal clause 363
pronoun 114–6, 125, 129, 130,
    133, 138–42, 155, 178, 184,
    210, 220, 271, 313, 325
always post-modified 147
indefinite pronouns 200
interrogative pronouns 127
personal pronoun 125, 139,
    141
relative pronoun 129, 130,
    313
sexist language 141
subject-pronoun dropped
    140
pronunciation 10, 34–49, 275,
    285, 300, 310, 319
proper noun. See noun
proverbs
absence makes the heart grow
    fonder 69
agile as a monkey 68
alike as (like) two peas in a
    pod 68

proverbs (ctd)
apple a day keeps the doctor
    away 69
better late than never 70
better safe than sorry 71
bird in the hand is worth two
    in the bush 69
blind as a bat 68
bold as brass 68
brave as a lion 68
brown as a berry 68
cheerful as the day is long 68
clear as daylight 68
curiosity killed the cat 69
darkest hour is that before the
    dawn 70
don't bite the hand that feeds
    you 69
don't count your chickens until
    they are hatched 70
early bird catches the worm 69
every cloud has a silver lining 70
fools rush in where angels fear
    to tread 70
friend in need is a friend
    indeed 70
leopard cannot change its
    spots 70
let sleeping dogs lie 70
live and let live 70
look before you leap 70
love is blind 70
never look a gift horse in the
    mouth 70
once bitten 69
one good turn deserves
    another 71
practise what you preach 70
slow and steady wins the
    race 71
stitch in time saves nine 71
too many cooks spoil the
    broth 71
variety is the spice of life 71
when in Rome 70
when the cat's away the mice
    will play 70
you cannot have your cake and
    eat it 69
you can't judge a book by its
    cover 69
you can't teach an old dog new
    tricks 70
public speaking 374
pun 373
punctuation 11, 268, 317–39,
    364
apostrophe 318, 322
brackets 323
capital letters 324
colon 326
comma 327, 331
dialogue 336
ellipsis 340
exclamation mark 334
full stop 335
hyphen 337
possession 318
question mark 339
quotation marks 339
semicolon 326
question mark 339
questions 9, 14–15, 23–24,
    102, 112–13, 121–7, 130,
    140, 151, 169, 190–91, 294,
    308, 339, 342, 352, 366–8,
    376–7

INDEX

questions (ctd)
  alternative questions 122
  intonation 126
  question tag 124–5, 333
    comma 125
  tag question 125
  wh-questions 123
  yes/no questions 121
quotation mark 339
  common errors 340
R
  intrusive R 40
  linking R 40
  rhotic R 40
  silent R 40
reading comprehension 366, 366–73
  questions 367
realism 373
received pronunciation. *See* RP
relative clauses. *See* clause
relative pronoun. *See* pronoun
repair. *See* conversation
reported speech 339
research 356, 358
résumé writing 365
revision 358
rhetorical question 126, 339
rhotic R 40, 49
rhyme 373
RP (received pronunciation) 40, 48–9
schwa 40
secondary sources 352
semicolon 326–8
  clarity 328
  defining relative clause 330
  lists 327
    last item in a list 328
    long list 327
  main clauses 331
sentences 113–132, 344
  complex sentences 118
  compound sentences 117
  imperative sentences 113, 120, 185
  interrogative sentences 121
  irregular 113
  length 344, 350
  minor sentence 113, 114
  negative sentences 190
  questions. *See* questions
  sentence-statements 119
  simple sentences 115–17
  statements 119
sexist language 141
shall 180
sibilant 49
silent letters 42–7
similes 68, 371, 373
  clear as mud 68
  common as muck 68

similes (ctd)
  cool as a cucumber 68
  cunning as a fox 68
  dead as a doornail 68
  deaf as a post 68
  drunk as a lord 68
  dry as a bone 68
  easy as pie 68
  fit as a fiddle 68
  flat as a pancake 68
  good as gold 68
  hard as nails 68
  hot as hell 68
  keen as mustard 68
  light as a feather 68
  mad as a hatter 68
  neat as a pin 68
  old as the hills 68
  playful as a kitten 68
  pleased as Punch 68
  poor as a church mouse 68
  pretty as a picture 68
  proud as a peacock 68
  quick as a flash 68
  quiet as a mouse 68
  rare as hen's teeth 68
  safe as houses 68
  sharp as a razor 68
  sick as a dog 68
  sick as a parrot 68
  silent as the grave 68
  sly/wily as a fox 68
  smooth as silk 68
  sober as a judge 68
  straight as a die 68
  stubborn as a mule 68
  swift as an arrow 68
  tall as a steeple 68
  thick as thieves 68
  thick as two short planks 68
  tough as old boots 68
  uncertain as the weather 68
sonnet 373
sound terms 48
sources 353
speech, making a 374–9
  ending 377
  notes 378
  opening 376
  subject 377
  timing 376
  troubleshooting 379
  warm up 378
spelling
  doubled consonants 39
  irregular 35
split infinitive 168
spoken English 8, 10, 13–32
  grammar 10
statements. *See* sentences
structure. *See* writing
style. *See* writing

subject 113, 114, 114–116, 115, 123
subject-pronoun. *See* pronoun
subjunctive mood. *See* verb, mood
subordinate clause. *See* clause
subordinating conjunction. *See* conjunctions
superlative adjectives 154
syllable 37, 39, 49, 152–3, 194
  comparative adjective 152
symbolism 373
synonyms 33, 360, 368. *See also* thesaurus
tag question. *See* questions
telephone conversations. *See* conversations
telephone etiquette 16
tenses. *See* verb
texting 363
th 48
theme 369
thesaurus 32–3, 360, 362, 367
three-dot ellipsis 340
tone 354
tragedy 373
transcribe 49
triphthong 48, 49
turn-taking. *See* conversation
velar 49
verb 123, 163, 176–206
  agreement 17, 121, 198–99, 200, 226, 282, 315
  auxiliary verb 121, 125, 190–1
  base infinitive 177
  'being' words 177
  common errors involving irregular verbs 197
  common errors involving number agreement 199
  common errors involving regular verbs 195
  concord 198
  contracted forms 178
  'doing' words 176
  gerund 183
    possessive case 184
  infinitive 114, 120, 168, 177–8, 180, 182, 193–6, 201–6
  intransitive 189
  irregular verbs 196–7, 201–6
  main verb 178–9, 190, 191
  modal auxiliary verb 191
  modal verb 121, 125, 192
  mood 176, 185
    imperative mood 120, 185
    indicative mood 185
    subjunctive mood 185–6
  number 198
  participle 181

verb (ctd)
  participle (ctd)
    misrelated participle 183
    participial phrases 183
    past participle 181, 183
    present participle 181
  phrase 131
  regular verbs 193
  tenses 177–80
    continuous past tense 179
    continuous present tense 178, 190
    future tense 180
    past perfect tense 190
    past tense 179, 186, 193–8, 201–6, 269, 302
    perfect tense 179, 181
    pluperfect tense 182
    present continuous tense 182
    present perfect tense 179, 181
    present tense 178, 182
    progressive present tense 178
    simple past tense 179
    simple present tense 178, 181
  transitive verbs 186, 189, 209
  voice 186, 189
    active voice 186–8
    passive voice 30, 186–8, 190, 345–7
verbal noun. *See* gerund
vocabulary 32, 362
voice. *See* verb
voiced sound 49
voiceless sound 36, 39, 49
vowel 37–40, 44–5, 47, 49, 135, 152, 157–8, 194, 370
  long vowels 37–8
  short vowels 37–8
  vowel sounds 35–6
who 123
whom 123
wh-questions 123
will 180
winding down. *See* conversation
writing 341–365
  alternative words and phrases 343
  formal or informal 349–365
  organizing 353
  passive voice 345
  plain English 341
  planning 354
  structure 355, 356, 375
  style 354
Yes/No questions 121